Education

Education Studies:
An introduction

Lisa Murphy, Emmanuel Mufti and Derek Kassem

Open University Press
McGraw-Hill Education
McGraw-Hill House
Shoppenhangers Road
Maidenhead
Berkshire
England
SL6 2QL

email: enquiries@openup.co.uk
world wide web: www.openup.co.uk

and Two Penn Plaza, New York, NY 10121—2289, USA

First Published 2009

A catalogue record of this book is available from the British Library

ISBN-10: 0335223516 (pb) 0335223508 (hb)
ISBN-13: 9780335223510 (pb) 9780335223503 (hb)

Typeset by Kerrypress, Luton, Bedfordshire
Printed and bound in the UK by Bell and Bain Ltd, Glasgow

The *McGraw·Hill* Companies

Contents

Preface

This book provides the increasing number of students on Education Studies and related courses with a text that discusses key issues in education that they will encounter within the first year of their course. It is an introductory text, but one that encourages critical engagement from the reader. Unlike many introductory texts, the chapters of this book do not provide potted summaries of the issues, but rather adopt a critical stance that enables the reader to develop a detailed, critical understanding of the key issues within Education Studies.

The book acts as a precursor to the existing volume *Education Studies: Issues and Critical Perspectives*, allowing the reader access to the key debates within that text.

Acknowledgements

The authors would like to thank Wilf, Margaret, Sarah, Rashida, Samuel, Jackie and Clara for their ongoing support.

Derek Kassem would like to thank Frances Syres for her help and support throughout the last year.

The authors would also like to express their gratitude to Fiona Richman, our editor at Open University Press, for her continued support and understanding, without which this book would not have come to fruition.

This book was written with assitance from Andrew Kennedy (Chapter 10 Early Years Education), Diahann Gallard (Chapter 7 How People Learn) and Angie Garden (Chapter 11 Inclusion: A Case for Special Treatment).

All royalties from this book are being donated by the authors to the Louise Lambert memorial prize at Liverpool John Moores University.

Part 1

Theoretical Perspectives

1   What is Education?

I have never let my schooling interfere with my Education.

(Mark Twain (1835–1910))

What is the study of education?

Throughout your education, you will have studied a range of subjects at both primary and secondary level. Some of you will also have studied at FE colleges or in HE institutions. You may also have engaged in some studies away from schools, in youth clubs, summer schemes and at various other locations. Prior to any formal educational experiences in institutions, you will no doubt have learnt to walk, talk, interact with others in social situations, and perhaps even read and write. If you were educated in England, you will no doubt have attended a primary school and a secondary school where you will have studied a range of subjects; some you will have enjoyed while others less so. You will have had excellent inspiring teachers and others whose impact upon you was not so positive. You have no doubt jockeyed for position among those you attended school with, your peers. You no doubt received punishments, some fair, others not, and at times received rewards and praise. You may have received high levels of support from your family or carers or perhaps you were left to develop your own interest in education. In short, you have received an education and even in this short introductory text we can begin to see that education is not solely about the content of the subjects that you learnt but instead is multifaceted and complex and involves much more than those elements which may immediately spring to mind when discussing it.

The study of education, therefore, at first glance differs significantly from many of the subjects you will have studied before, in that it examines, in detail, a process as opposed to a subject area.

Throughout this book, you will find a range of issues relevant to the study of education. The list is not exhaustive, nor is designed to be so. This is not a book that will tell you how either to teach or how to learn. Instead, it will raise issues that will enable you to begin to understand the power and importance of education. It will open up ideas of why and how people succeed and fail within it. It will demonstrate the political nature of the education process and how education can be used to support, develop, change and challenge society. For those of you who plan to work in the education field, in whatever capacity, Education Studies can develop that deeper understanding of the process enabling you to be a more effective and a more knowledgeable practitioner.

This chapter sets the scene for the later chapters and will enable you to place them in context through its initial discussion of the key issues. It will also chart the development of Education Studies as a discrete degree programme independent of initial teacher training.

What is education?

When we consider that we all, regardless of whether we went to school or what type of school we attended, have been educated in some way, it seems inconceivable that the concept of 'what is education?' should still lend itself to a healthy debate. However, the concept of education is not merely contested, it is fluid and ever changing, which in itself is an indication of the difficulty faced in forming a definition. See 'The Struggle for Secondary Education' (Chapter 2 in this volume) for further details on the historical development of formal education. Furthermore, as the quote from Mark Twain above suggests, education is not solely the preserve of institutions such as school, college and university and, in fact, from many perspectives, those institutions are the very antithesis of education.

As previously mentioned, we can view education as the formal process which the majority of readers of this book will have engaged in. That is the process of nursery, primary and secondary school, and more frequently, some form of tertiary education. What this view of education fails to take into account is the role of others in the educative process. What role do parents have? What role do peers and the media have? Furthermore, do all of these elements support each other or at times do they appear to contradict each other?

For these and other reasons, seeking an acceptable definition of education could be considered a fruitless endeavour. There are no shortages of proposed definitions, from the most basic dictionary ones to more detailed discussions on moral education as outlined by Law (2006). Each of these definitions contains more problems than they provide answers for. If we suggest, as is common, that education is the teaching and learning of worthwhile information, we must further ask, how do you teach?, how do you learn? And, most importantly, what is worthwhile?

Task 1.1 Stop, think and do

- How would you define education?
- Prepare a list of the elements that make up education and consider what it is they try to transmit to you. Can you place your list in an order of importance? Why have you chosen these elements?
- Search the Internet for quotes on education such as that by Twain. What do they tell us about education and the issues in defining it?

The purpose of education

A more pertinent and useful discussion is concerned with the purpose of education, as it is only through this that any definition will begin to make sense. Throughout this volume the chapters examine the role of education as the development of morality, a meritocracy that separates individuals according to ability, and as a tool to ensure that the status quo of class, ethnicity and gender mixes in society is maintained. What all of these elements suggest is that education has a role to play in preparing individuals to form a useful part of society.

Many articles and chapters discussing education highlight the views of Peters (1966), who described education as being something that we intend to transmit, that we transmit it in a morally acceptable way, and that, furthermore, what we are transmitting should be worthwhile. This attempt at a definition is of course highly problematic. What information could be considered worthwhile bearing in mind that we are, in the case of primary school children, seeking to predict what will be worthwhile in 20 years time. With the rise of the internet and its accessibility on phones and other mobile technology, is it still useful to learn facts such as the names of kings and queens through the ages or capital cities when we can easily access that information at the touch of a few buttons? Of course, it would be easy to put together a compelling argument that suggests the learning of these facts was never useful but it does raise questions on what knowledge is necessary, worthwhile and useful.

Economic well-being

One aim of education is to maintain and develop the economic well-being of the individual and society generally. This is a key UK government consideration and is one of the five key areas in its policy for young children and the services that support them, 'Every Child Matters' which is an indication of the crucial role that politicians understand education to play in society. So what is the role that education can play in enabling individuals to play a full role in an economic society and what implications might that have for education?

One of the first implications of this can be seen in the development of strong central government control over the curriculum, teaching methods or pedagogy, and frequent testing in order to check standards. This idea that education is about preparing individuals to play an economic role in society has come much to the fore under the New Labour Government, who came to power in 1997. It is fundamentally linked to the idea of human capital in that, rather than traditional investment in machinery, modern companies needed to invest in people, their skills and their knowledge in order to compete with companies worldwide in what we describe as a global economy. In 1997, the Department for Education and Employment (DfEE), which was then responsible for overseeing education nationally, stated: 'Investment in learning in the 21st Century is the equivalent of investment in the machinery and technical innovation that was essential to the first industrial revolution. Then it was capital, now it is human capital. (DfEE 1996: 15 cited in Tomlinson 2005: 7).

Effectively, the suggestion was that ideas such as new mobile technologies would provide the foundation for a modern British economy and that our education system needed to respond to the needs of employers in this new global market. This view of the purpose of education has had a major impact on the entire system, including the expansion of the higher education system towards the involvement of 50 per cent of the population aged 18–30. In addition to that expansion, the role of primary and secondary education is not only to prepare pupils for future employment but also to ensure that global employers, from all across the world, view the United Kingdom as a nation with a highly skilled, highly educated workforce, which will encourage inward investment of companies throughout the land. A more detailed discussion of the implications can be found in Chapter 12. However, at this stage, it is worth noting that high levels of testing and public scrutiny of schools, together with the focus of skills for employment have led to what is seen by many commentators to be a narrow curriculum which will not meet the needs of many children within society.

There are other concerns linked to that issue of employment. If we are seeking to produce highly skilled, motivated and qualified individuals, it is clear that not all individuals will reach this level. What role will be open to those who do not in the next few decades is not always apparent, although the rise of unemployed, unengaged youths could be seen as a fair indication of this. This would be problematic even if the education system operated as a full meritocracy, that is, one purely based upon merit where only one's ability and dedication counted. However, as even a casual glance of statistics relating to educational achievement will tell us, chances of success in the education system depend on ethnicity, gender and, most importantly, social class. The evidence around educational achievement demonstrates that who you are, in terms of those categories above, exerts a major influence on your educational experiences and achievement at all levels of attendance. This issue is discussed in far more detail in Chapter 9. But at this stage it is worth emphasizing that the education system is not value-free and that we cannot attempt to examine it unless we appreciate it is complex and it is influenced by and also influences the society it reflects.

Influences upon education

> Ask me my three main priorities for government, and I tell you: education, education, education.

> (Tony Blair 1996)

The above quote from the then Opposition leader demonstrates two crucial elements concerning education. First, its value in interesting the population at large when you are seeking votes, and second, the importance placed on the role of education by those in positions of power. While the first issue once again highlights how all of us are influenced by education, the second is one we need to consider in detail. Previously we discussed how education is connected to the economy and prepares individuals for employment but in reality education can do much more than simply provide us with skills and knowledge. Education can be used as a powerful socializing tool, it can teach us to accept society as natural and unchangeable and we may question, to whose benefit. Therefore, perhaps one of the most important questions we will consider throughout this book is this: does education reflect society or does it shape it? This would then lead us naturally to a supplementary question; if education does shape society, is this done knowingly and, if so, does it have a particular agenda?

The role of government

Education is a highly regulated industry. Regulation covers the age at which you start school, the length of time you spend in the classroom, the number of days you spend in school in any given year and the core subjects you study. Additionally, the training teachers receive and the requirements of that training are centrally controlled. Teachers and schools are further controlled by a standardized assessment process that not only checks the progress of the child but also the teacher of their class and the school they attend.

At the heart of the political interference that education is subjected to is the idea of improvement in public services through competition. In many previously nationalized industries such as the utilities gas, telecommunications, water and electricity, this has resulted in de-regulation, allowing other providers to offer similar services with the aim of reducing prices and improving the service to the consumer. The premise of this is that those companies who set their prices too high or do not offer an acceptable level of service will lose out to the competition. How successful this approach has been to the consumer is certainly debatable but this neo-liberalist ideology of improvement through competition remains at the heart of New Labour's political strategy.

It is clear that it is not possible, at this current time, to fully deregulate the education industry and allow a range of providers to manage and control state schools and universities in a traditional competitive environment, so competition in education needs to take other forms. Each academic year a league table of schools is produced. These published league tables are based on the results of the Key Stage Standardized Assessment Tests (SATs) that children take at set times throughout their education. If we take the example of the Key Stage 2 SATs, which children take in their final year of primary school, we can begin to question both the purpose of the tests and the use that they are put to.

Theoretically, parents can choose the school that their child attends. However, in reality, their choice is determined by their location and ability to manipulate the system. This issue is discussed in more detail in Chapter 4, 'An Introduction to Contemporary Educational Policy'.

The development of Education Studies

As the UK population boomed in the 1950s it was clear that the education of the next generation was to play a major role in the economic and social success of the country. In 1963, the Robbins Report responded to this need by suggesting that teachers should be full graduates and subsequently the BEd (Bachelor of Education) degree was founded. This degree not only included school placements and issues directly related to classroom management and how children learn, but further included elements of the academic study of education. This later element primarily focused upon the history, sociology, philosophy and psychology of education. These elements were considered essential to teachers' understanding that children did not form a homogeneous group and that instead the needs of children could differ not only in terms of ability but through the range of social factors, such as class and gender, that influenced them.

However, this approach to the education of children was criticized on a number of levels. First, that it was too liberal and did not truly relate to the world of employment, and, second, that politicians, the media and parents were unable to assess the quality of the education that children received. Subsequently, the academic content of teacher education began to be reduced in favour of training focusing upon classroom and teaching techniques. While this process began during the 1980s, it is still ongoing today and prescribed pedagogic approaches and curricula have increasingly become a more integral part of the teacher training programme (Bartlett and Burton 2007). Leaving aside the debate as to the merits of such an approach, it is clear that this approach has allowed the development of the range of Education Studies degrees to emerge, focusing upon the academic study of education.

What is Education Studies?

As previously mentioned, Education Studies is the academic study of education and while the exact content will differ from institution to institution, certain elements will remain core to the degree programmes.

Education is not an uncontested environment and as you progress through this volume you will encounter a range of perspectives. One thing that you will immediately notice is that education is not limited to what takes place in schools, or indeed other formal institutions such as universities and colleges. The role of politics in education is of crucial understanding, as is the family background of an individual. The responsibility we put on education and the approaches we bring to it are all of importance. Finally, the ways in which we internalize information and how we learn as adults and children remain of crucial importance. Each of these issues is found within this volume and will no doubt form an integral part of your studies. It is further worth noting two issues: first, education is in a constant state of flux, it is essential to keep abreast of the changing nature of the subject, the impact of new policies, changing economic needs and the political pressure those responsible for the discipline find themselves under. All these issues mean that education will change rapidly and an awareness of both these changes and their implications is crucial to our understanding of the topic. Second, as each of us has been through at least one level of the education system, the implications of the debates you will find throughout this volume will not be completely new to you. What will differ, however, is your awareness of the issues as you reflect not only upon your personal experiences but combine that with the deeper understanding you gain through your studying and your readings.

The Quality Assurance Agency (QAA), in their benchmark statement, describe Education Studies thus:

> education studies is concerned with understanding how people develop and learn throughout their lives, and the nature of knowledge and critical engagement with ways of knowing and understanding. It offers intellectually rigorous analysis of educational processes, systems and approaches, and their cultural, societal, political, historical and economic contexts. Many courses include the study of broader perspectives such as international education, economic relationships, the effects of globalisation and the role of education in human rights and ecological issues. They all include critique of current policies and practice and challenge assumptions
>
> (QAA 2007: 1)

It is worth noting a number of issues in the above statement. First, that Education Studies is not just about school but concerns itself with education in all its formats, both informal and formal aspects of the discipline. Second, that any current system of education reflects wider issues within society, both nationally and increasingly globally. The changing nature of the economy, issues within society, such as obesity and anti-social behaviour, and the lack of political engagement all influence the nature of education, particularly within the school environment. Third, that Education Studies is about critique and developing a deeper understanding of the issues; this critique is crucial as education is an issue that impacts upon us all, either directly or in terms of societies development.

Task 1.2   Stop, think and do

- What issues within society, such as the ones discussed above, can you think of that have become the responsibility of schools?
- Should these issues be the responsibility of schools?
- What does it tell us about the purpose of education?

Education Studies: the issues explored

The rest of this volume seeks to reflect the nature of the discussion within this chapter. While it is not exhaustive, it will provide the reader with a detailed introduction to the issues they will encounter as they progress with their studies. Part 1, 'Theoretical Perspectives', demonstrates that education is not an absolute. That is our current system is neither natural nor unchangeable; indeed, it is only relatively recently that education for all in the UK has been available. The part also demonstrates that the current system is ideologically based and that various alternative approaches and philosophies could be considered.

Part 2, 'Policy', shows us that political intervention in education shapes the experiences of learners. We can examine issues of international approaches and also the impact that international competition has upon the British system. In this part, alternative educational provision is considered, which helps us examine our current system in relation to alternatives.

Part 3, 'Society and the Individual', demonstrates that the education that individuals experience is as much to do with their demographics as it is to do with their inherent ability. It also provides us with an understanding of the way in which individuals encounter and internalize information.

The final part, 'Inside the School', examines not only what occurs within the classroom but furthermore the implications of practice and the ideological and political processes that influence them. The way in which the curriculum has developed and the political and ideological issues that this involves are also explored.

Conclusion

Chapter 1 should be viewed as an introduction to the issues you will encounter, both in your studies and throughout this book. It seeks to highlight a number of main issues. First, that education does not stand alone, it is subject to political interference, based upon both economic and social needs of the society we live in and the international communities we are part of. Second, education should not be seen as unchallengeable and unchangeable, the current system within the UK is not the only approach that can be taken and an investigation of alternatives helps to develop our understanding. Third, our demographics influence our educational experiences, often in negative ways, and knowledge of this is crucial if we are to truly understand and critique the system.

The final and most important message is that the purpose of education is not solely to develop an individual's knowledge and love of learning. It is as much to do with the need to prepare students or pupils for their role in the world of work. The influence that this has upon the practice of education should not be underestimated and it is an issue that will be explored throughout this book and your course.

2 The Struggle for Secondary Education

Introduction

During the twentieth century the development of secondary schooling has been the most controversial phase of education. In fact, some of the earliest debates concerning secondary education such as the extent of provision, the school-leaving age, the nature of the curriculum, selection and assessment are still current today. For this reason, this chapter will focus on the struggle for secondary education for all.

Secondary education is historically a comparatively new term within the British education system (Banks 1955) and was, in effect, imported from France by the educationalist Mathew Arnold in the late 1800s. Following the Platonic notion of education being provided for individuals based on their future roles and status in society, up until the 1940s secondary education was aimed at the most affluent and powerful sectors of society and was deemed to be of little benefit to the lower social classes. Education of the lower social orders was catered for by elementary education with the inception of the 1870 Elementary Education Act which was, as Lowndes states, 'not an Act for common universal education, it was an Act to educate the lower classes for employment on lower class lines, and with specially trained, inferior teachers who had no university quality' (1969: 4).

As the above suggests, and as the discussion below will indicate, the overarching factor in the development of state secondary education was social class. This chapter will, therefore, in its examination of the development of the state-funded secondary education system in the United Kingdom use social class and its role in education to make sense of the changes that have taken place over time.

Starting with an account of the initial steps in the development of state education, the 1870 Elementary Education Act (commonly referred to as the Foster Act 1870), the chapter dates the subsequent legislation of 1902 as the beginning of the debate on secondary education. It was this legislation that effectively created the system that we know today with the same contentious issues and debates being played out. For example, just as the role of the Church and faith schools was a key issue in the debate around the 1902 Act, faith schools continue to be an issue today as the current New Labour Government promotes them.

The beginnings of a state education system

At the start of the twentieth century, there was no secondary education system for the mass of ordinary people. Ordinary people were confined to an elementary school system that focused primarily on reading, writing and arithmetic, otherwise known as the 3Rs. The secondary system that did exist was for either the upper echelons of society who were educated at the so-called Great Schools of the day, now known as public schools, such as Eton and Winchester, or for the middle classes who were mostly educated at the endowed grammar schools. The education provided by both types of school went beyond the 3Rs and was designed to meet the needs of either the universities or the career needs of the professional classes.

The endowed grammar schools had existed for some time, in fact, some can trace their origins back to the Middle Ages. The endowed grammar school was, for the most part, a school founded in or before the sixteenth century for teaching Latin. It would later become a secondary school teaching languages, history and science during the nineteenth century. Such schools were called endowed grammar schools, as they had usually been set up by an endowment for the poor from a local benefactor. However, in 1840, the Grammar School Act gave the Chancery Court power to alter the original statutes of grammar schools to meet new needs. Consequently, they became schools for the middle classes. Working people were effectively excluded from any sort of secondary education.

The passing of the 1870 Elementary Education Act is frequently presented in history of education texts as the beginning of universal, free state education. The reality is that it took another 25 years or more for a free, compulsory, universal system of elementary education to come into existence. The 1870 Act provided permission for the school boards who, along with the Church and various other religious bodies such as the Nonconformists, ran education to set up schools. However, the move to free, compulsory full-time state elementary education did not occur until 1893 after the passing of three further Acts of Parliament.

The first reform after the 1870 Act took place in 1876 with the passing of an Act which prohibited the employment of children under ten years of age who lived within 2 miles of a school (Lowndes 1969). This was followed by a further reform in 1891 which abolished the payment of school fees in those institutions that charged under ten shillings per year and took steps to alter the fees in schools that charged more. The final instalment in the move to a state-controlled elementary education occurred in 1893 with the passing of a further Act of Parliament that raised the age at which a child could get exemption from school, partial or total, to the age of 11. It is only from this point that it is possible to refer to a national education system.

Inspection and standards were key to the oversight by government of the elementary schools and a system of payment by results was introduced as one of the main methods of control. The number of passes in each subject were examined by inspectors annually and they determined the amount of monies each school would receive as a grant to manage the school. This led to an education system that was increasingly criticized for its limiting nature due to the rote learning and teaching to the tests that was employed.

There was great concern at the time over the quality of education provided and the level of achievement by pupils across England and Wales. Indeed, some of the comments made over a hundred years ago do not differ significantly to those that may be found in a DfES or Ofsted report today, for example, the failures in arithmetic are due mainly to the scarcity of good teachers of it (Devon 1876, cited in McIntosh 1981: 7).

It must be noted that from the beginning of free, state education it has not been possible to refer to a British education system. The development of education in Scotland followed a different route from that of England and Wales. Today Scotland and Northern Ireland along with the various Island states, for example, the Isle of Man, and, since devolution, Wales, all have independent separate education systems.

The demand for education

Prior to 1870, education for the poorest children was often provided by charitable organizations such as the Ragged School Movement. Various religious bodies such as the Anglican National Society, the British and Foreign School Society (representing Nonconformist interests) were partly state funded to provide education from the middle of the century. As the 1833 Factory Act obliged employers to provide education for their child workers, the workhouse schools and the factory schools, along with the religious organizations mentioned above formed a 'national school' system. Despite this system, it should be remembered, however, that many children did not have a school place for a variety of reasons. For example, the founder of the Labour Party, Keir Hardie, never attended school but was self-educated (Benn 1992) as he started work at 8 years of age in order to contribute to the family income.

Due to the existence of the national system, the history of education often represents the development of state-funded provision as being led by well-meaning Church and other liberal reformers for the benefit of the working class of the day. However, as Gardner (1984) points out, this is not the full story. The working class, or ordinary people of this country, have contributed to the growth in education in a number of different and divergent ways. This fact is often largely ignored, or at best poorly represented in the text books.

Gardner (1984) chronicles the growth and development of what is often referred to as the Dame Schools, though he prefers the term working-class private schooling. Although the education provided by the Dame Schools varied in quality and extent, they were extremely popular among working-class parents and can be viewed as an attempt by the working class to provide education for their children that was not available to them anywhere else.

The popularity of the Dame Schools rather than the church and charity schools was due to a number of factors. As parents paid for their children to attend these schools, there was a degree of 'equality' between the teachers and parents and lack of social stigma linked to charitable status of the national schools. In fact, Gardner argues that the Dame Schools belonged to the tradition of private enterprise and free market provision and were, in effect, a working-class self-help system that parents as pay-masters, had a direct influence on. West (1994) and other modern commentators suggest that the growth of this independent private provision was effectively closed down by the state with the introduction of the 1870 Education Act to the detriment of education today.

Johnson (1979) points to an alternative educational provision through the radical movements that existed throughout the nineteenth century. Movements such as the Chartists who were leading the fight for universal male suffrage (one man, one vote) (Foot 2005) were associated with education programmes aimed at spreading their ideas (Flett 2006). In fact, the labour movement as a whole has a long tradition of education both within the trade union movement and the various political groupings linked to the movement. Education has been seen as a key to political understanding and hence has played a pivotal role in the struggle for socialism. The work of Brian Simon from the 1960s onwards identified the full extent of the struggle for education and the proactive role that ordinary or working-class people took in the increased demand for education. The role of the organized labour movement is particularly important in the conflict over the 1902 Education Act in England, which is discussed below. The main point here is that ordinary people in various ways played a role in the development of educational provision; it was not just a series of reforms that were introduced by their so-called betters for their benefit.

Moreover, another factor which is often neglected in education textbooks is that response to educational reform is not just limited to parents. The children or pupils also played an active role, demanding reforms of the system at various times. Working-class pupils took part in strikes at various times (Humphries 1981; Adams 1991), for example, school strikes occurred in 1889 across the country with clearly identified grievances:

> Free education, one free meal a day, no home lessons and no caning. The boys further resolved that they – and girls – should meet at a later date in the same place, parade through the streets and extend the proposed strike to the whole of London.

> (Newell, cited in Adams 1991)

The strikes spread to towns and cities such as Swansea, Cardiff, Glasgow, Birkenhead, to name just a few. The pupil strikes often occurred at the same time as social and political upheaval in the wider society. For instance, school strikes occurred again in 1911, a period of industrial unrest. There were fewer strikes between the Great Wars, though there was a limited amount of unrest among pupils. By the 1960s, there were school-based movements among pupils such as the Schools Action Union and there have been strikes and demonstrations by pupils comparatively recently against the war in Iraq. The key issue is that, though the history is sparse in terms of the records, pupils at various times have made demands and responded to changes in schools and the wider society. In other words, they must be seen as active partners in the process of education.

Towards a state secondary education – 1902–1939

By the turn of the century, education for ordinary people was free and compulsory, at least at the elementary level. Elementary education, however, was not the same as primary education today, instead it was a very limited form of education that was identified as being suitable for working-class children.

Secondary education was, during the nineteenth century, essentially the education of the sons – later the daughters – of the middle classes. This is expressed quite clearly by the Schools Inquiry Commission, reporting in 1868. They distinguish three grades of secondary education, corresponding roughly to separate grades of society, described carefully in terms not only of occupations of the parents, but of the leaving age of the pupils. Schools of the first grade, for example, were used by men with considerable incomes independent of their own exertions and the great body of professional men, especially clergy, medical men and lawyers, who saw education as a means to keep their sons at a high social level. Schools of the second grade, on the other hand, were used by men whose sons had to leave school at the age of 16 either to enter immediately into employment or begin some special training, for example, the army, all but the highest branches of the medical and legal professions, civil engineering and so on (Banks 1955: 2).

Task 2.1   Stop, think and Do

The idea that different types of school should exist for different types of children was current in both the nineteenth and twentieth centuries, and still, to some extent, informs aspects of education policy today:

- Identify the underlying social and political reasons for such attitudes and policies.
- Explain how they might still impact on education today.
- Who do you think benefited from educational segregation in the past, and who might benefit today?

This perspective was reaffirmed in the Bryce Commission of 1895 that laid down the structure for secondary education at the turn of the century. The only saving grace of this system was the limited number of scholarships that were open to the very brightest of working-class children to gain access to secondary education. Small numbers of children from the elementary school progressed to secondary education.

The more progressive school boards of the day, under the influence of the Labour movement, introduced higher grade schools – as it turned out, illegally. The higher grade schools sought to provide education beyond the statutory leaving-age for elementary schools. They offered an extended form of schooling that almost equated to a secondary education.

The board schools, as higher elementary schools were commonly known, began to encounter opposition from a number of different vested interests. The Anglican Church, for instance, was opposed to the board schools because in part they were finding it increasingly difficult to financially maintain their own schools and they were concerned that the religion that was taught in board schools did not conform to their doctrine. However, the Nonconformist Churches were for the most part happy with the board schools as they felt that their beliefs were being represented.

Opposition to higher grade schools also came from the grammar schools who, because they charged more for their services, felt the higher grade schools to be in direct competition with them – not least because they were often seen by parents as providing an equally good education. Right-wing Conservative groups also opposed the development of the higher grade schools for two different reasons. First, they did not consider that secondary education was appropriate or suitable for working-class or ordinary children, whom they felt were effectively being educated beyond their station. Second, the cost of the schools added an extra demand to the local taxes that the middle classes were paying.

At the turn of the century, all these issues came to a head. The conflict was further inflamed by the Cockerton Judgment which was the result of a court case to restrict the ability of the school boards to provide education beyond the elementary level. The higher grade schools were effectively illegal under the current legislation and the London School Board was surcharged for the expenditure they had incurred in providing their higher grade schools. Education was in turmoil. There was much debate and disagreement over both the very existence of elementary education and the provision of secondary education for ordinary children. Despite the unrest, it is worth noting that by 1944 still only 10 per cent of children had secondary school places (Bartlett and Burton 2007).

There were basically three different approaches to education at the time: Radical-Tory, Liberal and what might be considered Collectivist (Simon 1965). The Radical-Tory view can be characterized as dismissing secondary education for ordinary children as it was seen as unsuitable for working-class children per se while it was believed that elementary education should be provided for, and made compulsory for, all of the lower social orders (Simon 1965). The Liberal view can be seen as a variation of the Radical-Tory view in that they also viewed secondary education as qualitatively different from elementary education and, therefore, only suitable for the brightest of working-class children who would be provided with a ladder of opportunity through competitive scholarships. The Collectivist view of education was represented by elements of the Labour Party, most notably Sidney Webb and the trade union movement, although views of individuals and groups within this collective differed in many ways. Webb in many respects differed only marginally from the Liberal perspective as he believed in a ladder of achievement for very able working-class children, while groupings to the left of Webb wanted an extension of educational provision and argued that the higher grade school should be open to all.

The passing of the 1902 Education Act, although controversial in many ways, created, to a large extent, the education system that was to endure for the rest of the twentieth century. The labour movement viewed it as an attack on the democratic accountability built into the education system through the direct elections to the School Boards (Manton 2001). In fact, it was described as 'a reactionary measure, and a serious setback to the progress of free, unsectarian, and democratic education in the country' (Children, Labour Annual Conference 1903, cited in Manton 2001: 169).

The opposition to the 1902 Act not only came from sections of the labour movement but also various religious bodies as the Act was to include all the schools previously administered by the Anglican Church.

The Act laid out the structure, for the first time, for a secondary education system. However, the system was not free, universal or open to the mass of ordinary pupils. Secondary education was still seen as appropriate only for the higher social orders of the day. The secondary system saved the grammar schools, abolished higher elementary schools and abolished all 2,500 of the school boards and replaced them with 318 local education authorities. The school boards had been viewed by the right-wing as far too radical and under the control of progressive and left-wing forces. The new local education authorities took over the running of some 14,000 voluntary-aided church schools and the grammar schools, as well as all the elementary schools run by the old school boards. Most history of education texts pass over the controversy surrounding the 1902 Act, neglecting to point out the debate and conflict over the passing of the Act. In many ways it was an attempt by the state to reassert control over education and restrict the provision that was available to the mass of children within Britain.

The 1902 Act was quickly followed by a further Education Act in 1904 that reinforced the approaches to education formalized in the 1902 Act. It laid out the rules and regulations on which the school system was to be based, providing, through the Elementary Code, a national curriculum along with regulations for the administration of the secondary schools under the control of the local education authorities. The form of education provided by these secondary schools mimicked the private schools in the education that they delivered. For grammar schools, this approach to the curriculum was to be their mainstay for the rest of the century. The Act advocated the creation of an ethos of nationalism, respect and notions of duty within the secondary schools. The socio-historical context of the time infused the education system as this was the period in which Britain had just been through the Boer War and was engaged in active competition with the Central European powers such as Imperial Germany.

As indicated above, the demand for education by ordinary people was an important element in the development of the education system. This now transferred to the demand for secondary education for all. The period from the beginning of the twentieth century was marked by increasing social upheaval and unrest, characterized by industrial strife and other social movements. This was mirrored in actions by school pupils of the day (see above) and by demands for greater social opportunities and equality, which were at the root cause of the conflict of the day.

The social unrest only came to an end with the outbreak of the Great War (1914–18). The war, however, showed up the inadequacies of the education system illustrated by the low levels of basic skills among the population and, of course, the poor health and fitness that existed (this was to reoccur during the Second World War). The problems identified during the war gave rise to reform movements after its conclusion. As Simon (1965: 252) points out, 'a war so destructive of the nation's youth, acts as a midwife of social reform', so that at the end of the war there was distinct pressure to speed up educational reform.

The first major piece of legislation after the war, in terms of education, was the 1918 Education Act also known as the Fisher Act. The legislation was a product of the post-war Liberal Government of Lloyd George. The Fisher Act represents the first move towards an extension of the secondary education, if only in words. The leaving age was raised to 13 or 14 for most children and some secondary schools that had existed outside the state system now applied for state funding. The consequence of the Fisher Act was to see a massive growth in the numbers in secondary education. In 1918, there were 81,056 entrants into secondary education as compared to the pre-war figure of 54,141 (Simon 1974), an increase of just under 50 per cent.

The Fisher Act not only attempted to reform the education system, but for the very first time also provided the finance to do so. Local Authorities were to be provided with a grant for education that accounted for 50 per cent of their expenditure. This was designed to encourage the more progressive education authorities to expand their provision (Simon 1974). The Act also rid the country of the system of half-time working, that is, a system where children aged 12 or 13, depending on the area, worked part-time and attended school on a similar basis. Now all children had to attend school to the age of 14. There was a further proposal to extend educational provision between the ages 14–16 on a part-time basis and eventually to extend provision to 18.

Just as every other progressive reform in education had met opposition, so too did this particular reform. In this case, opposition came mainly from industrialists, the same social group who had opposed the 1870 Act, claiming that it would make industry uncompetitive. Nevertheless, the proposed reform and introduction of what was called continuation schools passed into legislation, although it was granted that it would not be realized until some time in the future. The reality was that the reforms were never instituted, that is, most children still left school at 14 and the vast majority of children did not gain a secondary education.

The inter-war period was also a period of social upheaval with major conflicts and strikes throughout Britain. In 1926, there was the General Strike and a miners strike that lasted for a year and, in 1929, economic collapse with the Wall Street Crash. In response to these and other events, political movements such as Fascism started to grow in force and significance across Europe and in the United Kingdom, with the Fascists taking over a number of countries including Hungary, Romania, Italy, Portugal and Spain after the Civil War 1936–39. The Nazis took power in Germany in 1933. Against this background of major economic and political instability, around the world education was not at the forefront of government policy.

Nevertheless, in spite of all these political difficulties, there was further agitation for the provision of universal secondary education. R.H. Tawney, a leading social reformer of the day, published a short booklet called *Secondary Education for All* in 1922, which contributed to discussion of education policy in the Labour Party. Tawney stated, 'The main educational effort of the nation should be directed to building up a system of secondary education for all children from eleven to sixteen' (1922: 97).

However, due to economic policy and conditions of the time, the government was moving in the opposite direction and set up a committee to review public expenditure. The committee produced a report known as the Geddes Report that suggested, among many other cuts, that the education budget should be slashed by a third. To make possible such a budget cut, it was proposed that the school entry age should be raised from 5 to 6, that teachers' pay should be reduced and that teachers should be compelled to contribute to their pension fund, that the fees for secondary education should be increased while the number of free places should be reduced and eventually cut completely. Other measures included substantial cuts in school meal provision in a time of high unemployment, cut-backs in nursery provision and school health services, along with cuts in the meagre provision for children having a special or particular need.

The Geddes proposals ultimately represented a halt in the move to extend educational provision in the secondary age range. It advocated the undoing and removal of the most important aspects of the Fisher Act (Simon 1974) and many of the improvements to education which had been made since the inception of a state commitment to education for ordinary children.

Although some of the Gedddes proposals were implemented, with the effect that fairly quickly the number of pupils in secondary education began to fall from the high point reached in 1919, Geddes and his proposals did not eventually win the day. This was due partly to the opposition they faced from Fisher himself and the labour movement more generally, and partly because of the political realities of the day. The general mood in the country would not accept such drastic cut-backs in educational provision. This became apparent as by-election after by-election was lost by the government of the day.

Though education provision suffered set-backs throughout the inter-war period, there was a growing re-evaluation of the form of education that was provided for the mass of ordinary people and some progress was made. For example, the 1921 Education Act allowed local authorities to raise the school-leaving age to 15, if they wanted to and could afford it (Simon 1974).

Tawney (1922) argued that the fundamental flaw in the English education system was that it was provided on a social class basis (Carr and Hartnett 1996). The Scottish and Welsh systems did not differ to any great extent from the English system on this issue. The Hadow Report of 1926 began the re-thinking of educational provision for the masses and, to some extent, raised awareness of the issue of educational provision based on social class status. It advocated a move away from imitation of the academic public school ethos, widening of secondary provision to include all children between the ages of 11 years and hopefully 15 and the restructuring of the then current system through the introduction of two phases of education, primary and secondary, much as we have today (Carr and Hartnett 1996).

The suggested structure of secondary education was to provide selective academic schools and non-selective modern schools (Carr and Harnett 1996). The very discussion of secondary education for all at a government level added to the general demands and agitation for the creation of such a system. One of the leading organizations that argued for the reforms was the National Union of Teachers, along with other groups within the general labour movement. A further development was the publication of the Spens Report in 1938, which called for the abolition of the term elementary education and the introduction of a tripartite system for secondary schools, along with the raising of the school-leaving age to 15 by September 1939. The Spens Report also recognized for the first time that the so-called ladder of opportunity available to the brightest of poor children, backed by free places at secondary schools, did not work as the main determinant of success in gaining the free scholarships was social class.

Before the report could be implemented, the Second World War intervened. The key issue facing the country was winning the war against the Nazis. While most resources were spent on the war effort, the coalition government of the day also looked forward to preparing for the peace when the war was won. There was in many respects a national concordat that social ills would be addressed and the situation would not be the same as at the end of the previous world war.

A further report was published in 1943 under the leadership of Cyril Norwood, a public-school, Oxbridge-educated educationalist, who held very traditional views concerning the nature of education. His report identified three types of pupil, hence the need for three different types of school. The report argued that there existed the academic child who was interested in learning for its own sake and the more vocationally inclined child who was interested in science and technology and applied arts. The third category was the child who could only grasp concrete things rather than abstract ideas (Carr and Harnett 1996). The result of this typology of pupil abilities was the introduction in the 1944 Education Act (also known as the Butler Act) of the tripartite system of three types of school: the grammar, the secondary technical and what became known as the secondary modern school. Each type of school was supposedly designed to cater for the different type of child and hence provide them with the most appropriate form of education. Though the 1944 Education Act was not a Labour Party reform as such, the ideology contained in the Act was by and large the view held by the leadership of the Labour Party that went on to form the government at the end of the war in 1945.

The end of the war brought a social and political consensus that was to last until the election of 1979. The 1945 Labour Government introduced major reforms not only of the education system but also of health and social welfare. Workhouses were abolished and unemployment pay was reformed. These systems stayed in place largely as they had been introduced for the next 30 years or more. In terms of education, not only did the Act introduce for the first time secondary education for all, but it raised the leaving age to 15 for everyone. It also introduced primary education, increased provision for children with special needs and expanded the rather neglected area of early years education. This was all achieved against the backdrop of severe economic problems left over from the poverty of the 1930s and the costs of the war, including the costs of re-arming in the light of the Cold War with the new enemy, the Soviet Union.

1944–1979, the period of consensus?

The end of the war in 1945 brought with it an expectation, on the part of the mass of people, that there would be a general improvement in society. Issues of poverty, ill health, bad housing and poor education would be dealt with once and for all. The 1944 Education or Butler Act was to be the main mechanism by which the improvements in education would be achieved. For the first time, there was a Ministry of Education that could provide coherent national education policy. As indicated above, there was now a system of secondary education for all up to the age of 15. The Act did not actually lay down the structure of secondary education other than that the County Boroughs would be responsible for the provision of education in their areas. The two main political parties, Conservative and Labour, followed the arguments developed in the Spens and Norwood Committees' reports to introduce the tripartite system (Carr and Hartnett 1996).

The changes in education at the secondary level were not without birth pangs. There was a shortage of teachers, buildings and resources and there was a lack of clear direction within the Butler Act. Many local councillors still saw the grammar school as the real secondary school. The result of this view of secondary education was that the secondary modern school received less resources, had larger classes and the qualifications of the teachers were lower than the other two sectors of secondary provision. Although pupils had to attend the schools until they were 15, many secondary modern schools did not provide a well-structured curriculum which catered for their needs and many did not provide the opportunity for pupils to take external, public examinations. In many ways, whether one supports the idea of secondary modern schools or not, the secondary modern school did not get off to a very good start.

Further problems resulted from the fact that the so-called tripartite system was really a bipartite system. In many areas the secondary technical schools did not exist to any great extent, often due to the financial cost involved in establishing and maintaining this type of school.

After the eleven-plus examination, children usually went to either a grammar school or to secondary modern schools. In reality, as only 20–30 per cent of children each year secured a place at a grammar school, the vast majority of pupils were educated at secondary modern schools. In essence, the school system was to be based on the notion that it was possible at the age of 11 to identify the ability of a child that would in effect be fixed for all time (Rubinstein and Simon 1972). In other words, it was believed that through the use of various intelligence tests it was possible to identify different types of children and hence provide for their different educational needs. The reality was that these schools conformed to the class structure of English and British society (Taylor 1963) as the vast bulk of grammar school children came from a middle-class background and the majority of secondary modern school children came from a working-class background.

Scotland did have a reputation for a much wider access to education and inclusiveness; however, as both Paterson (2003) and Jones (2003) point out, this was largely a myth. Scottish education was and is as socially segregated as the education system in the rest of the UK.

It should be noted, however, that despite its weaknesses, the 1944 Education Act did represent progress. It was from this point on that ordinary children had access to some form of secondary education even if it was only up to the age of 15 years. This might be regarded this as a mini-social revolution.

On the other hand, as will be discussed below, certain aspects of the secondary modern school caused dissatisfaction among parents and led to their support of the comprehensive system. The perceived negative aspects of the changes were the differential funding for grammar and secondary modern schools. Secondary modern schools received less money and they frequently employed teachers with lower status qualifications; moreover, many of these schools did not provide for external examinations.

Task 2.2   Stop, think and do

- What type of school did you go to?
- Make a set of notes identifying how the type of school you went to has impacted on your level of educational achievement.
- Try and find an individual, maybe in your family, who went to either a secondary modern school or grammar school and interview them.
- Compare your educational experiences with the person you have interviewed, what issues can you identify?

The development of the comprehensive school

The 1950s was a period of tight economic controls and education suffered from the restrictions on spending, as did other parts of the social provision funded by the state (Simon 1991: 168). However, it was during this period that a new type of school began to develop – the common or comprehensive school. Initially these schools were set up in rural districts, in Anglesey and the Isle of Man (Simon 1991: 169). The big challenge to the existing school structure, however, was to come from London with the publication and acceptance of the London School Plan. The first proposal was to open the first purpose-built comprehensive school, an all girls school, Kidbrooke, South East London. However, the London County Council (LCC) wanted to get experience of running these types of schools before embarking on building the Kidbrooke school. For this reason, in 1948, the LCC set up a number of so-called interim schools which were created through the amalgamation of local secondary moderns and selective schools.

The birth of the comprehensive system in London was a rather difficult affair. As the introduction of comprehensive education was not a party issue, it was, therefore, resisted not only by the Conservatives on the LCC, but also by elements of the Labour Party. It is interesting that, contrary to prevailing attitudes to comprehensive schools today, support for the changes were widespread among parents – specifically in the Kidbrooke area, even though this meant the closure of five schools including the local girls' grammar school (Simon 1991: 172). It should be noted, however, that the ensuing political conflict that Kidbrooke generated resulted in grammar schools becoming a political issue for the Conservative Party even to this day. Support for selection and grammar schools have almost become a litmus test for Conservative ideologists.

There were two interesting developments in the early stages of the restructuring of secondary education. First, the move to comprehensive education was conducted in a piecemeal fashion and took 20–30 years to complete. Second, there was widespread support from middle-class parents for the changes towards comprehensive education. Indirect evidence for this is to be found in one of the few studies of secondary modern schools which states that:

> Parental attitudes towards the Modern School tend to vary according to the social group concerned, and, it may be presumed, to how realistically parents have assessed their child's ability during primary school years. In an inquiry into parents' preferences for secondary education, Marin found that the highest percentage of parents expressing preferences for a Secondary Modern education was among the unskilled group and the lowest among professionals.
>
> (Taylor 1963: 52)

In a discussion of external examination provision, Taylor goes on to state that:

> It seems likely – although there is no statistical evidence available to provide support for the suggestion – that pressure on schools to provide examination courses will be greater in those areas where there is a larger lower middle-class element in the Modern schools.
>
> (1963: 122)

This would suggest that middle-class parents who had no option but to send their child to a secondary modern school were putting pressure on the school system to meet what they perceived to be their needs. The comprehensive school, in contrast to the secondary modern, offered the possibility of examinations and the chance of movement across the various streams. This meant that middle-class children who had failed the eleven-plus, and thus had not achieved a place in a grammar school, would have access to an academic curriculum after the age of 11.

Eventually the comprehensive school movement became a reality in London, if in a somewhat distorted form (Simon 1991). Subsequently, education authorities in other parts of the country also began to introduce comprehensive schools, initially Staffordshire, then Manchester and Birmingham.

By the 1980s, the majority of children of secondary age were being educated in a comprehensive school. The key issue is that though the comprehensive system faced, and still faces, opposition, it was seen as a solution to an existing problem and was demanded by parents. As only 20 per cent of children went to grammar schools, large numbers of middle-class and able working-class children were sent to secondary modern schools and this often impacted on their life chances. In effect, it might be argued, the tripartite system was enforcing social and educational segregation on the majority of pupils in the UK.

The Labour Party has always been identified with the comprehensive system. When they gained power in 1964 after 13 years in opposition, the Labour Secretary of State for Education proclaimed that it was the government's policy to reorganize secondary education along comprehensive lines (Simon 1991: 276). However, it was not until 1965 under a new Secretary of State, Anthony Crossland, that Circular 10/65 was published. The circular called for all education authorities to submit plans for the restructuring of secondary education in accordance with the comprehensive system, but there was no compulsion to enforce the policy. The result was that some authorities resisted the changes and others, such as Kent, introduced what they called comprehensive schools while keeping grammar schools. This, in a sense, defeated the original intentions of the policy.

Of all the sectors of education, it can be argued that secondary provision has been the most political and controversial. Various Labour leaderships have failed to deal with the issue of providing parity in secondary education for all pupils due to electoral concerns. Politics and policy are clearly inter-linked and education reform does not happen for some vague altruistic reason on the part of the power blocks in society. The debate over secondary education continues today with the introduction of academies, foundation and trust schools, which all challenge the comprehensive school system. The result of this continuing debate is that the issue of social segregation is still a major concern.

Conclusion

It was not possible, even with the introduction of comprehensive education, to talk about secondary education for all until 1972. It was in that year that the school-leaving age was raised to 16. Prior to this, the social pressures on ordinary children, especially girls, to leave school as soon as possible in order to become economically active and to contribute to the family income were substantial.

The raising of the school-leaving age to 16 had been promised in the 1944 Education Act, but had been postponed a number of times due mainly to the economic cost. Labour had promised to raise the age in 1964 but delayed the implementation in 1968. It was the Conservative Heath Government of the early 1970s that actually carried it out. Thus, it was not until 1972 that it is possible to claim that the UK achieved secondary education for all.

Any history is only a partial history, and this chapter is no different. The key issue that the chapter has tried to identify is that the continuing debates over education provision (see Part 2 on policy) are highly political in nature. Education history is as much a battle for resources and privilege as any other historical struggle. Secondary education has been at the forefront of these battles because the act of achieving in secondary education has life-enhancing possibilities and the majority of children in this country were denied this for one reason or another until the later part of the twentieth century.

Summary

1 The development of state-funded secondary education for all has been the most controversial phase of education during the twentieth century. The fundamental factor in the struggle for secondary education has been social class.

2 Prior to the 1900s, secondary education existed only for the upper and middle classes and was provided by elite public schools and endowed grammar schools.

3 Children from the working classes received, at best, elementary education in the 3 Rs.

4 Despite the 1870 Education Act, compulsory state-funded elementary education did not become a reality until 1893.

5 Although it is often overlooked by textbooks, parents and children played a significant role in the demand for state-funded education for all.

6 The 1902 Education Act laid out the structure for secondary education, but it was not free or available to the mass of ordinary people.

7 The 1944 Education Act set up the tripartite system: selection by the eleven-plus examination and entry into a grammar, secondary technical or secondary modern school.

8 Secondary technical schools were never widely established. The system was effectively two-tier with only 20–30 per cent of 11-year-olds, mostly from the middle classes, gaining places at grammar schools.

9 Problems with secondary modern schools led to many, including middle-class parents whose children had not succeeded in the eleven-plus, calling for a reform of the system.

10 In the 1950s and 1960s, the comprehensive system was introduced, but, it was not nationally enforced by government policy, so some LEAs maintained the two-tier system.

11 It is only possible to talk of secondary education for all from 1972 when the school-leaving age was raised to 16.

12 The nature of secondary education is still a highly controversial issue. Many believe that New Labour's neo-liberal policy of encouraging market forces in education (see Chapter 5) is propagating a tiered and socially segregated education system.

3 Educational Ideologies

What is ideology?

In order to consider a range of educational ideologies, it is necessary in the first instance to attempt some definition of the term ideology itself. This is not a simple task. As McLaren (1989) points out, philosophers, political theorists and sociologists have long debated the concept of ideology – few concepts 'are as pervasive and durable, yet few continue to provoke such a cleavage of opinion' (1989: 174).

Most would agree on a definition of what ideology is: 'some sort of "system" of ideas, beliefs, fundamental commitments, or values about social reality, but here the agreement ends' (Apple 2004: 20). Indeed, the debate concerning the definition of ideology has centred around conflicting interpretations of what ideology *does*.

A further factor which complicates the argument about true or false, good or bad ideologies, is the insistence on a strict categorizing or pigeon-holing of ideologies as mutually conflicting or opposing. An individual, a social or political group, or a whole society may endorse an overall or total ideology which may itself contain apparent contradictory beliefs regarding different aspects of life such as education, religion, social justice. Even a particular ideology, for example, an educational ideology, held by an individual or group may contain these apparently contradictions.

The term ideology was coined in the eighteenth century by the French philosopher, Destutt de Tracey (1754–1836), to distinguish a science of ideas free from prejudice, religious or subjective interpretation. Destutt and his contemporaries sought to uncover true knowledge about human nature and a means of ordering society in line with this (Head 1985). However, this interpretation of ideology, mostly due to the politics of Napoleon Bonaparte, was seen as fanciful, impractical and revolutionary (Meighan and Siraj-Blatchford 2001). The idea of ideology as an illusion or myth was picked up by Marx and Engels ([1845–47] 1970) and became a tenet of traditional Marxist theory. Ideology in much orthodox Marxist theory is seen as a distortion of reality, a false consciousness used by the ruling class to control economic production and the distribution of wealth and power in their favour.

From a postmodern or relativist perspective (see Chapter 12 'Ideology and Curriculum'), both Destutt's and the Marxist approach are problematic as they appear to assume that there is true knowledge about human nature and about how human society should be organized which is always true despite socio-historic and cultural contexts. The postmodernist philosopher Michel Foucault (1980) suggests the whole truth can never be known. Knowledge does not reflect an objective reality; it does not exist 'without a knowing subject' (McLaren 1989: 176). If knowledge is a relative and subjective interpretation of reality based on a certain ordering and organization of the world in relation to individual and group experience, then an ideology *per se* cannot be right or wrong. It must be viewed as one interpretation of human nature and society or as an ideal for the better functioning of society.

Traditionally, there have been two schools of thought concerning the function of ideology. The so-called *strain theory* has defined ideology as a positive and useful concept for understanding the complexities of human nature and social organization and thus makes it possible for individuals and groups to act. Conversely, the *interest theory*, derived from the Marxist tradition, considers ideology to function negatively, as a means of asserting power and misguiding individuals or groups within society (Larrian 1979: 17–34).

Within any sphere of life, competition between ideologies, what Hall (1988: 42) terms a 'process of ideological struggle,' may result in: legitimation, domination or incorporation (Meighan and Siraj-Blachford 2001). An ideology is legitimized when it is accepted as an appropriate belief system. This can be achieved via direct enforcement using military, surveillance, police and punishment, or it can be achieved via social institutions such as the media or religion. When one particular ideology is legitimized above alternatives, it is considered by many within the society to be the norm, the most logical and appropriate set of beliefs and modes of behaviour. It becomes the consensus position (see Chapter 8 'Social Factors in Education') and achieves cultural dominance. This state of affairs was defined by the Italian social philosopher Antonio Gramsci as one of cultural hegemony (Gramsci [1929–1935] 1971). The dominant ideology may incorporate others by inclusion or absorption. In this situation, however, the extent to which non-dominant ideologies are given equal status and considered a viable alternative to the consensus view is often highly questionable.

It is as a result of this process of ideological struggle – of the legitimization and dominance of the ideology of one group in society over all alternatives – that an ideology may be said to deceive or mystify. If the total ideology of a given society truly incorporated and equally validated the particular ideologies of specific groups, recognizing that all ideologies are fluid and dependent on socio-historical and cultural contexts, it would constitute a properly conceived and effective system that connected to 'real problems and real people' and did not 'dupe people' (Apple 1989: 36).

This chapter will define ideology as a broad set of beliefs and opinions about human nature and society, and/or about how they ought to be, held by the individual and by groups of individuals. Adopting a relativist approach, it is suggested that ideologies cannot be inherently true or false because they are a set of beliefs and opinions constructed from and related to experience and knowledge of the world. However, the use to which an ideology is put, be it in the educational sphere or any other area of human society, may have positive or negative implications.

Components of educational ideologies

An educational ideology is a broad set of beliefs and opinions about the purpose and function of education and its formal arrangements, and/or about how they ought to be, held by the individual and by groups of individuals.

There are numerous ways of categorising diverse educational ideologies. Many approaches to categorizing educational ideologies have compared and contrasted dichotomous pairs such as: teacher-centred versus child-centred; product-based versus process-based; traditional versus progressive; authoritarian versus democratic; knowledge transmission versus freedom-based learning. This approach tends to suggest that ideologies on either side of the divide will share similar views and beliefs about education and educational systems. However, as mentioned above, there is much overlap between ideologies and such a dichotomous approach may actually obscure the fact that a particular ideology may contain aspects from seemingly contrasting schools of thought. Furthermore, the dichotomous approach does not account for the fact that some of the contrasting pairs work at different levels or layers within the education system: classroom, school, national/political, philosophical/theoretical.

Other attempts to provide a typology of educational ideologies have sought to avoid such strict dichotomies. Morrison and Ridley (1989) provide a typology which organizes ideologies into three broad groups: (1) focus on the individual, including approaches which are child-centred, process-based often progressive and concerned with developing freedom of learning; (2) focus on knowledge, often teacher-centred, traditional and transmission-based; and (3) focus on society which may be either authoritarian or democratic, product or process-based, transmission or freedom-based to varying degrees.

Raynor (1972) categorizes educational ideologies into four groups: aristocratic, bourgeois, democratic and proletarian. Three of these approaches are described as following the Platonic view of education (see Chapter 12 'Ideology and the Curriculum') in that they prepare the individual for a particular role in society which reinforces the social position into which s/he was born. The aristocratic approach prepares an individual for a role as a gentleman and/or as a leader. Bourgeois education, by means of educational achievement, specifically examination success, confirms the right of an individual to hold elite positions in work and society. The proletarian approach, by means of practical and vocational training, prepares workers for the subordinate positions in the workforce and in society. In contrast, democratic educational ideologies are concerned with developing an individual's full potential and see equality of educational opportunity as the right of all despite social background.

As will be apparent from this brief outline of varying attempts to provide typologies of educational ideologies, there is no clear-cut way to categorize the numerous educational models. An alternative way of categorizing educational ideologies is provided by Meighan and Siraj-Blatchford (2001). They suggest that classification based on a series of educational components is more useful. The 'components theories' they suggest are: knowledge, discipline, teaching, learning, teaching resources, location, organisation, distribution of power, parental role and assessment and aims (2003: 197–205). Although the benefits of such an approach to categorizing educational ideologies are recognised, it could be suggested that the volume of component theories described here do not necessarily clarify the issue. Many of the proposed component theories could indeed be subsumed into a much smaller number and provide a useful tool for categorizing educational models while still recognizing the fact that some of the models may work at differing levels or layers within the education system.

Furthermore, as education is concerned with knowledge, if knowledge is equated with power and politics, and is regarded as working within the realm of power distribution, it follows that education is 'political activity in the broad sense' (C. Matheson 2004: 22). It is necessary, therefore, to clearly signpost the correlations between political ideologies and educational ideologies.

For the purposes of this discussion we will employ a four-way typology to categorise diverse educational ideologies: elitist/conservative, revisionist/technocratic, romantic/psychological and democratic/egalitarian. These categories are a combination of those found in Davies (1969) and Cosin (1972). Furthermore, we will use four broad criteria to describe these categories: learning, teaching, organisation and politics. The first three criteria are a condensed form of the component theories proposed by Meighan and Siraj-Blatchford (2001: 197–205). Table 3.1 describes the four categories of educational ideologies in terms of these four criteria. Let us now consider each of the four criteria used for categorization in more detail.

Table 3.1 Comparison of major educational ideologies

Ideology	Component			
	Learning	*Teaching*	*Organization*	*Politics*
Elitist/ Conservative	Individual Structured Transmission-based Academic and physical Competitive Learner as scholar and sportsman	Teacher-centred Authoritarian End-product, formal assessment Teacher autonomy To produce leaders	Institutional Hierarchical Authoritarian discipline Religious Selective Grouped – sex; ability; age Valued extra-curricular	Conservative Private sector Limited state control
Revisionist/ Technocratic	Individual Structured Transmission-based Vocational and practical Competitive Learner as trainee	Teacher-centred Authoritarian End-product, formal assessment National Curriculum to develop workforce	Institutional Hierarchical Authoritarian discipline Religious Selective Grouped – ability; age	Neo-conservative Neo-liberal Public sector State control

Ideology	Component			
	Learning	Teaching	Organization	Politics
Romantic/ Psychological	Individual and group Self-selective Creative and practical Non-competitive Learners as explorer	Child-centred Non-authoritarian Process-based Informal/varied assessment Teacher autonomy To develop whole child	Non-traditional environment Non-hierarchical Democratic discipline Non-religious Non-selective Mixed groupings Valued extra-curricular	Social democratic Liberal Private sector Limited state control
Democratic/ Egalitarian	Individual and community Self-selected and/or structured Mixed curriculum Non-competitive Learners as explorer/ scholar/worker	Child-centred Non-authoritarian Process and/or product-based Varied assessment Teacher autonomy? To promote equal opportunity/to transform society	Varied locale Non-hierarchical Democratic discipline Non-religious Non-selective Mixed groupings Valued extra-curricular	Social democratic Public sector Limited state control?

The learning component specifies whether the model proposed focuses on child-centred learning and whether learning is based on individual activities and/or group activities. The level of independence or autonomy based on self-selection of learning content may also be considered in contrast to a curriculum involving transmission of knowledge which is selected and structured for learners. This component includes attitudes to knowledge in terms of the content and structure of the learning curricula. Differing educational ideologies value different types of knowledge. Traditionalist approaches, elitist or revisionist, tend to favour formal subjects such as English, mathematics and science which are delivered to learners in a regulated and timetabled curriculum. Conversely, more progressive models, romantic or democratic, may favour everyday practical knowledge or creative skills, such as domestic studies, social skills, musical skills.

The teaching component describes the role of the teacher as one or more of the following: a transmitter of knowledge, a facilitator of learning activities, a mentor or role model, an authoritarian or non-authoritarian figure. Teaching also encompasses assessment and aims. Assessment may be formal through examinations or course-work, whether spoken or written, or it may be informal via teacher observation or teacher–student conferencing or review. Assessment may be diagnostic or formative in order to promote and improve further learning or summative/end-based. One educational model may employ a variety of assessment types as well as assessment which is not teacher- or external examiner-based, such as peer-assessment and self-assessment. The aims and outcomes of educational ideologies are various. Some models, elitist or revisionist, focus on the end-product in the form of formal qualifications and awards while others, romantic or democratic, may be concerned with personal development. The aim of education may be to produce citizens who conform to society's total ideology and who have been trained to assume specific roles or those who will change and transform society.

Organisation comprises the location of learning, whether it is institution-based in a school, college, university or in out-of-classroom locales such as libraries, real-life situations or the home. The organisation of the learning locale may be hierarchical in terms of leadership or headship, senior management, and so on. On the other hand, it may be democratic and decisions may be taken by group meetings and voting which may include the students and non-teaching staff as well as the management and teachers. Some other issues which form part of the organisation component of an educational ideology are: discipline, be it authoritarian or democratic; the utilization of, and value attached to, extra-curricular activities; organisation of the student body into age-based, ability-based, gender-based or mixed groupings; and affiliation to religious groups.

Kassem et al. (2006: 69–70) suggest that there are three major political ideologies within Britain today. A social democratic ideology promotes equality and seeks to provide, through high taxation, a strong welfare state and well-funded public services. In terms of education, a social democratic ideology promotes equality through a comprehensive education system with little or no selection which focuses on the needs of the students and allows a high degree of teacher autonomy and a largely unprescribed curriculum. Widening of participation in education at all levels, including higher education, is encouraged as is elimination of the elitist system. Within this ideology there is a move towards limited state control of the education system.

Neo-conservatism supports a free market economy with privatized services and low taxation. As the focus is on the market in all areas of life, including education, choice and diversity of services via open competition are encouraged. Neo-conservative education policy involves high levels of state control with a prescribed curriculum and pedagogy which is teacher-centred and has a strong emphasis on moral education. Britishness and assimilation of minority groups are promoted.

Neo-liberalist ideology is grounded in the marketization of the state which encourages private funding within public services, such as schools, and promotes market forces such as choice, diversity and competition. To encourage competition in education, strict control over standards through inspection, league tables and diversity in range and type of school is required. In a similar vein to neo-conservatism, neo-liberal ideology promotes a high degree of state control in education.

> ## Task 3.1 Stop, think and do
>
> Having read this section, draw up a table which compares the typology of educational ideologies give by Raynor (1972) with the typology given in Table 3.1.

Philosophy and educational ideology

Before turning to a consideration of some of the major educational ideologies, this section will briefly outline the philosophies of rationalism, empiricism and romanticism. In very broad terms, these three philosophies have been a fundamental influence on Western thought and ideology and still impact upon educational philosophy and ideology today.

Rationalism considers reason the source of knowledge. It is a method or a theory founded on the belief that truth is not sensory, that is, is not gained through the five senses, but is intellectual and deduced through the employment of reason. Man is born with some innate knowledge and preprogrammed with the ability to reason, which allows this knowledge to be deduced. As with all philosophies, there is a continuum of standpoints. Some rationalists would take the view that reason has precedence over all other ways of arriving at knowledge and truth, suggesting that there are indeed other ways at arriving at knowledge, whereas extreme rationalists would argue that reason is the only route to knowledge.

The French philosopher, René Descartes (1596–1650), is often cited as one of the principal thinkers of the rationalist school. Descartes ([1637] 1960) asserted that man could only be certain of anything because he could be certain of himself as a thinking subject. Descartes based his theory of knowledge on the proposition *cogito ergo sum* which means 'I think, therefore, I am.' He believed that thinking or self-consciousness and the processes of deduction enable man to access truths which could then be broken down into components which the mind could grasp. Sensory experience, along with dreams and intuition, are dismissed as an unreliable source of knowledge. Rationalists set up a dualism between the mind and the body which is still debated by philosophers today.

Describing the rationalist approach in the light of the four components of education specified above is not straightforward. In a sense, this philosophy could be considered as child-centred learning as its aim is the development of the individual's intellect and powers of reasoning. However, as rationalism favours the pursuit of formal knowledge as the goal of learning, it would seem to promote a traditionalist approach to the curriculum with its focus on academic subjects such as science and mathematics. The teacher could be conceived as a transmitter of formal knowledge or as a facilitator providing the student with learning activities through which s/he could develop and train his/her deductive abilities. It could be argued that rationalism advocates formal, end-based assessment in order to ascertain whether knowledge has been acquired. The locale of learning could be a formal setting such as a classroom or the individual could arrive at knowledge through private study in out-of-the-classroom settings such as in a library or in the home. If it is given that there is a specific range of knowledge that an individual is to learn, for example, scientific and mathematical truths, then it would seem that this would entail state control over the curriculum and pedagogy in line with neo-conservative or neo-liberal educational politics.

Rationalism is often contrasted with empiricism, sometimes termed humanism, which holds that knowledge is arrived at via experience, usually through the senses. However, this contrast is somewhat of an oversimplification as most rationalists, including Descartes, also believed that some knowledge, such as knowledge of God and mathematical truths, is derived from empirical or experiential methods. Similarly, some empiricists, such as Locke, also believed that certain knowledge, again knowledge of God, could be arrived at via intuition and reasoning. In other words, both schools of thought suggest that there is some knowledge which is beyond both sensory and/or rational deduction.

The English philosopher, John Locke (1632–1704), was the first to formalize the theory of empiricism. Locke believed that at birth the human mind is a *tabula rasa*, or blank slate, in other words, that humans have no innate or inborn knowledge. He asserted that nothing is knowable without sense-based experience. Locke did believe, however, that there is something, character or an 'original temper' (Locke [1693], 1996: 41), innate in human beings. He suggested that 'God has stampt' ([1693] 1996: 41) this character on men's minds and that this character comprises one-tenth of the make up of a human; the other nine parts are acquired through experience and education.

As Locke wrote explicitly about education, specifically in *Some Thoughts on Education*, first published in 1693, describing his philosophy in terms of educational components is more straightforward than applying Descartes' rationalism to educational ideologies. Locke studied medicine, science and philosophy at Oxford University and later became Lord Shaftesbury's personal doctor and personal tutor to Lord Shaftesbury's son. His writings on education are, therefore, particularly concerned with the education of young gentlemen on a one-to-one basis and so could be described as elitist. As a practising doctor and as an empiricist, who believed that bodily and sensory experience is the source of knowledge, Locke was very much concerned with nurturing a healthy body. In fact, as Locke saw the goal of education as the development of virtue, what might be termed moral education, his approach to education could be considered more in line with ideas about upbringing rather than schooling (Smith 2006: 47). This focus on morality and virtue has some resonances with the neo-conservative approach to education.

He focused on development of the whole child, commenting on diet, clothing and health, and advocated the teaching of practical skills as well as academic disciplines. Learning is very much through doing and experience rather than via transmission of information. Locke did not believe that a child has a natural disposition to learn but that the child must be turned on to learning by the teacher. To enable the teacher to engage the child in the learning process, Locke advocated the use of toys and games in learning. The teacher's role is to inspire a student with a desire to learn through seeing the value of knowledge. In a sense, the teacher is a facilitator of learning and a mentor or role model.

The influence of Locke's ideology can be seen in education today in the UK in the move towards learning through play and games in the early years and literacy curriculum, in the concept of personalized learning and in the idea of the teacher as a facilitator and modeller of learning.

Locke's approach to education, while focusing on nurturing and the moral development of the pupil, cannot be classified as child-centred or psychological. He did not believe that a child is naturally inclined to learn and is less concerned with 'the happy and fulfilled child than with the civilized and accomplished adult the child will become' (Smith 2006: 48).

The empiricist approach to education advocated by Locke contrasts with the so-called romantic or naturalistic view proposed by the Swiss educationalist Jean-Jacques Rousseau (1712–1778). Rousseau's seminal text, *Emile or On Education*, published in 1762, is a semi-fictitious account of the education of a young boy of the title name under the tutorage of Rousseau himself. The text may have some basis in reality as Rousseau was indeed the private tutor to the two sons of a minor nobleman in France between 1740–41.

Rousseau believed that the child is born naturally good and with an inbuilt disposition to learning. The belief in innate goodness of humans led Rousseau to deny the Christian belief in the existence of original sin, for which he was banished and exiled from both Paris and Geneva for some time.

Learning, according to Rousseau, is acquired through the senses and should be based on practical activities and doing. He believed that man developed naturally through four stages which he roughly defined as: birth to 12, 12–15, 15–20 and 20–25. Rousseau asserted that learning and education should be carefully organized and structured by the teacher to fit with these stages.

Throughout infancy and childhood he felt that education should be negative in the sense that children should be taught to develop patience, tolerance and stability by teachers deliberately putting obstacles in their way. During this stage of development, children should learn through exercising their bodies and their senses. Gradually, as the child passes through puberty and adolescence, education becomes positive with direct teaching of reasoning skills, morality and religion. Rousseau stated that during childhood individuals are physical beings and ought to learn about themselves in relation to objects, but during adolescence individuals begin to learn about themselves through interaction with others. It is now the teacher's job to ensure that the student has suitable people to interact with.

Rousseau believed that education should be organized in natural settings away from classrooms and textbooks. The teacher's role is to organize a well-ordered learning environment and to regulate the topics, activities and experiences of the child, particularly in the early years. In this way, the natural goodness and natural inclination to learning of the child can be engaged and steps can be taken to ensure that the child does not become ruled by desires or impulses or corrupted by society.

According to Rousseau, the goal of education is self-discovery and freedom; freedom in the sense of knowing one's self, one's abilities and limits, and thus having choice and control over one's actions. Within this system the freedom of each individual is maintained by mutual respect for the rights and freedom of others. This philosophy of education is termed romantic/psychological as it is concerned with the development the individual. To some degree, however, Rousseau's ideology could be termed elitist and conservative as it is based on private, one-to-one tutoring and, although it is concerned with self-development and is, therefore, student-centred, the learning activities and organization are strictly controlled by the teacher.

Rousseau advocates learning in a natural environment away from a school or college and out of the city, as he saw both as corrupt and corrupting influences in his era. As he considered education as vital to the individual's and society's struggle against tyranny and corruption, he suggests that the system described in *Emile*, what he termed 'domestic education or the education of nature' ([1762] 1979: 41), was the only viable option in his corrupt society. As his approach to education was socio-historically based, it could be suggested that he would have argued that a different, more democratic system of education would be more suited to a more democratic social political order (O'Hagan 2006: 58).

Much of the early philosophical and ideological debate about education focused on the education of boys of the middle and upper classes due to social attitudes to the position and roles of the genders in society (see Hunt, 1987, for an overview of the education of women). Book V of Rousseau's *Emile* outlines the education programme advocated by Rousseau for girls and women through the fictitious character of Sophie, whom Rousseau creates as the appropriate partner for Emile ([1762] 1979: 357–480). Rousseau, claiming that there are essential cognitive and psychological differences between men and women which fit them for different and complementary roles in society, advocated different kinds of education for the two genders. In brief, he asserted that women should be educated to be dependent rather than independent and free, which is the end-goal of male education. Interestingly, although he believes that males should not be given religious or moral education until they are able to reason in adolescence, as girls are not able to formulate complex moral ideas, they should be given religious instruction much earlier 'for if one had to wait for girls to be in a position to discuss these profound questions methodically, one would run the risk of never speaking to them about it at all' ([1762] 1979: 377). Luckily, attitudes to the abilities of the female sex to understand complex and profound moral and philosophical matters have advanced somewhat from Rousseau's day.

Rationalism, empiricism and romanticism have had an obvious influence on philosophical and psychological debate concerning nurture or nature. The nurture/nature debate revolves around the issues of whether knowledge and morality are inherent, or inborn in humans, or whether they are acquired through upbringing and experience. Rationalists, such as Descartes, and romanticists, such as Rousseau, are generally considered to favour the nature side of the debate, believing that humans are born with some things inherent, be they cognitive structures and rational abilities or natural goodness, talent and intellect, as in the rational and romantic views respectively. Empiricists such as Locke are usually considered to follow the nurture line of thought believing that humans are blank slates when born and that all knowledge and morality is acquired through experience. However, as pointed out above, even Locke believed that one-tenth of the human – the 'original temper' was inherent.

Some major educational ideologies

Table 3.1 provides a simple overview of the main educational ideologies discussed here in terms of the four criteria outlined above. As each of the broad categories is comprised of many particular educational models the descriptions given are highly generalized. It will be noted that some of the defining criteria in Table 3.1 are followed by a question mark which is indicative of the fact that this criterion may be applicable to some but not all of the educational models within the broadly defined category.

Education and social control

The two educational ideologies which support social control through education are the elitist/conservative approach and the revisionist/technocratic approach. Both these ideologies seek to maintain the status quo by educating individuals who will assume particular roles within society and, consequently, the approaches to learning, teaching and organization which they favour have several similarities.

The elitist ideology is generally defined as promoting the public school ethos and seeks to develop in learners the qualities and values which have been associated with the ruling classes and those destined to hold superior positions within the superstructure as leaders, politicians, lawyers, and directors of influential businesses and financial corporations (Giddens and Stanworth 1974).

Learning is focused on the teacher-centred transmission of knowledge and skills in a structured and authoritarian formal institution. Curriculum and assessment are formal and are focused on the end-product of qualifications. Historically, the public school ethos promoted physicality and sportsmanship, equally, if not above, academic achievement, as it sought to prepare students to assume positions as leaders within the imperial world. This focus on competitiveness in academic success as well as physical prowess is still a major factor of this approach.

Learning institutions are typically traditional public or private, boarding or day schools, and long-established elite or red-brick universities. Public and private schools have traditionally been selective in terms of gender, ability, social class or economic status and often have a religious affiliation. These schools are not state funded, and, therefore, are subject to limited state control and intervention. For example, although they are required to provide students with a broad and balanced curriculum in line with the National Curriculum (DES 1988), they are not obliged to follow government strategies or to enter students for Standard Attainment Tests (SATs). Consequently, there is a certain degree of teacher autonomy concerning the curriculum and pedagogy. However, as such institutions tend to be strictly hierarchical and authoritarian in terms of management and organization, the teaching and learning usually takes place within a tightly defined and monitored system.

Public and private schools comprise roughly one-tenth of all schools in UK and by their very nature as fee-paying institutions, they are elite. However, as Hackett (2001) (cited in D. Matheson 2004: 25) points out, there are a number of state boarding schools in England where students can receive a public school education for a third or half of the cost of that of a fully independent school.

Revisionist or technocratic ideology, in line with the elitist approach, also seeks to prepare individuals for certain roles and positions in society. However, the positions for which the two ideologies prepare students are different and this is reflected in the overall aims of the two approaches. In rather simplistic terms, while the elitist/conservative ideology's aim is to produce leaders, the revisionist/ technocratic aims to develop a workforce which is suitable and relevant to the needs of society. Education within this ideology is related to the concept of relevancy. The concept of the relevancy of education in terms of providing the individual with the relevant ability and knowledge to make a living within society and in terms of providing a workforce able to promote the economy of the overall society, is a recurring issue in political debate.

As revisionist ideology seeks to produce workers, the emphasis is on vocational and practical training, skills and competencies, rather than on academic achievement. Thus, while the overall approach to teaching and learning is similar to that of the elitist approach as shown in Table 3.1, the content and pedagogy differ. In order to produce workers with skills and competencies relevant to the contemporary society and its economic success, education must be state-controlled. Revisionist ideology advocates state-funded, teacher-centred, transmission-based education within a variety of traditional institutions which are hierarchical and authoritarian. In its original conception this approach would advocate selection on the basis of ability, and competencies, as was seen on a large scale in the UK in the tripartite system of the 1940s and 1950s, so that workers could be trained for roles which accorded to their perceived natural or latent intelligence and skills (see Chapter 2 'The Struggle for Secondary Education'). While the comprehensive school has replaced the tripartite system in most of the UK, the current trend towards selection based on school specialism and the more vocationally based post-14 curriculum proposed for some of the school population could be seen as a return to selection for training.

Neo-conservative and neo-liberal ideologies both advocate the marketization of education in order to provide competition through choice and diversity. A total educational ideology which accommodates both elitist and revisionist/technocratic approaches, producing leaders and workers to maintain the social status quo, is compatible with both political systems.

Education and democracy

The basic principle of social democratic/egalitarian educational ideology is equality of opportunity for all, regardless of gender, ethnicity or social class, within the education system and, consequently, within the larger society and the workplace (Davies

1969). Furthermore, the social democratic tradition advocates the gradual elimination of the elitist system which is seen to stand in the way of open and fair access to educational opportunities and competition for economic and social advantage. In order to achieve this goal, state-funded, non-selective comprehensive education in which the teacher is non-authoritarian and discipline is democratic is advocated by social democratic/egalitarian ideology. Teacher autonomy over curriculum and pedagogy is dependent on the extent to which is it felt that it is the teacher's role to actively promote democratic political values and principles.

The term democratic implies that all involved have some agreed level of participation in the decision-making processes and so have some power within a given situation. In relation to an educational ideology, this would mean participation in decisions about learning, teaching and organization.

In democratic systems, there is a continuum of power-sharing. Shallow forms of democracy involve the sharing of a small amount of power. For example, teachers and school management may implement agreed rules governing the learning, teaching and organization; these rules can be appealed against by an individual or committee. Student bodies may elect a representative or a committee of representatives to appeal against rules or to be actively involved in decision-making. Forum-style democracy exists when all members of an establishment or institution are involved in discussion about decisions. The latter type of decision-making is a move towards a deeper form of democracy, but in all of these arrangements ultimate power over learning, teaching and organization may still lie within the remit of those in authoritative or hierarchical positions and may be withdrawn from the learners at any time (Meighan and Siraj-Blatchford 2001: 210–11).

Democratic educational models are generally considered to be child-centred, but as equality for all and reform of society in line with this principle are often the ultimate goals, development of the individual may be viewed as secondary to creation of an egalitarian community. This approach was advocated by the American educator John Dewey (1859–1952). Dewey believed that the learning experience and curriculum should involve academic and practical subjects and should be based on doing rather than on transmission of information so that a child could become an independent learner (Dewey [1916] 1997). The focus here is on process, and learning can take place in non-traditional locales, allowing learners some selection of subject matter and some input into organization of learning. This system is not, however, freedom-based as the teacher has a crucial role to play in linking the learner to sustained intellectual development and educative experiences which it is felt will allow development of both the individual and the community or society (Apple and Teitelbaum 2006).

Even within the Marxist tradition, where education may be viewed as a means of counteracting hegemony, child-centred, non-authoritarian, non-structured educational models are often rejected as it is felt that the only way to challenge the dominant hegemony is by learning what the hegemony learned in a structured, disciplined way.

As the American psychologist and educational commentator Carl Rogers points out, it is questionable whether a situation of deep democracy is attainable within mainstream state-funded education systems, particularly within the Western societies which are arguably ruled by the overriding neo-liberal policies of competition, choice and diversity (Rogers 1983). Students have no say over curriculum and pedagogy, choice of teachers or educational policy and teachers have no say over choice of colleagues, administration procedures and curriculum and pedagogy. In order to see true democratic principles at work within educational systems, it is necessary to consider alternative forms of education such as critical pedagogy and the freedom-based movement which will be discussed in Chapter 5.

Progressive education

Romantic/psychological ideologies are usually classified as progressive educational models. Generally, such models are considered to have been derived from the naturalistic approaches advocated by Rousseau. The curriculum, though carefully managed by the teacher in relation to the perceived stage of development of the learner, is to a certain degree selected by the learner in line with the principle of interest. In the UK, this model of education as favoured by the Plowden Report (DES 1967) has been termed Plowdenism and has much in common with the ideology of Maria Montessori's approach to education ([1909] 2005).

Montessori developed her educational model when working with children who were excluded from mainstream education due to supposed special educational needs or due to social deprivation. She believed that much perceived inability to engage with learning is a result of poor pedagogy and inappropriate learning environment. To engage learners, education should start by building self-respect through the ability to master the practicalities of life and should then progress to more creative and intellectual activities.

Montessori groups learning into three-year periods. She believes that teachers should base the curriculum on observation of the learner and on activities which engage the learner's interest and are appropriate to his/her stage of development. Learners have some choice of activities from those offered by the teacher. The teacher is facilitator and keeper of the carefully controlled environment. In one sense, this approach is both child-centred and teacher-centred.

Traditionally, in the UK, schools and nurseries employing the Montessori Method have been private and thus have stood outside of state control. However, some state primary schools have adopted this ideology, noting a marked improvement in academic achievement and behaviour (McCormack 2006).

Another progressive ideology is that of Steiner–Waldorf schools, founded by the Hungarian philosopher and spiritualist, Rudolf Steiner [1861–1925]. Steiner's ([1907] 1996) ideology is based on the development of the child, not in a natural sense as advocated by Rousseau and Montessori, but in a spiritual sense. Steiner believed that the spiritual development of the child fell into seven-year cycles and he based the curriculum on activities which would enhance development at each stage. For example, the first stage is marked by play, exploration of nature, modelling and imitation of the teacher who is seen as a behavioural and spiritual role model. Steiner schools are non-selective, teaching is process- not product-based, the curriculum is focused on creativity and self-expression through movement, music and art, assessment is informal with no grading and, while the development of spirituality is central to the system, there is no affiliation to traditional organized religion. On the other hand, as the school day and the role of the teacher are clearly defined and structured and, as the curriculum is focused on spirituality, the ideology cannot readily be described as child-centred or freedom-based (see Clouder and Rawson 2003, for a detailed account of the Steiner–Waldorf ideology).

Similar to Montessori schools, Steiner schools in the UK are private and stand outside of state control; however, success with this approach has not failed to attract the present government's attention and there is a proposal for the government to sponsor a Steiner academy (Wilce 2006).

Task 3.2   Stop, think and do

Research the idea of andragogy developed by Malcolm Knowles (2005) in *The Adult Learner*. 6th edn. London: Butterworth-Heinemann. Explain where you would place Knowles' ideology on Table 3.1 using the four components learning, teaching, organisation and politics.

Summary

1   Ideology is a strongly contested issue and much of the debate revolves around what ideology does rather than what it is.
2   An education ideology is a broad set of beliefs and opinions about the purpose and function of education and its formal arrangements and/or about how they ought to be, held by the individual and by groups of individuals.
3   There are many ways of categorizing educational ideologies and categories often overlap and are not mutually exclusive.
4   A simple typology of educational ideologies is provided by four criteria or components: learning, teaching, organization and politics.
5   The rationalist, empiricist and Romantic philosophies have had a lasting effect on educational ideology.
6   There are many similarities in the elitist and revisionist educational ideologies and both involve state control of education.
7   It is difficult to find true democratic ideology within state education.
8   Romantic/psychological education ideology often stands outside of state provision due to its focus on non-traditional curriculum.

Part 2

Policy

4 An Introduction to Contemporary Educational Policy

Introduction

Education has played a key role in the politics and policy of the United Kingdom for the past 30 or more years. It is possible to date the growing significance of education in the political life of the nation to 1976, when the then Prime Minister, James Callaghan, made his, now famous, speech at Ruskin College, Oxford (Callaghan 1976). This speech has set, in very broad terms, the direction of education policy since then. The issues that Callaghan identified in the speech that were impacting on education would not sound out of date if spoken by a politician today. For instance, consider Callaghan's comments on the level of competence displayed by school leavers: 'complaints from industry that new recruits from schools sometimes do not have the basic tools to do the job required', 'there is the concern about the standards of numeracy of school-leavers'. These issues and more were taken up by the Conservative Government that took office on 3rd May 1979 and again by the New Labour Government that subsequently took office on 1st May 1997.

This chapter is an introduction to the main ideological forces that have driven education policy over the past 30 years. In effect, the chapter looks at how the problems that the education system faced were understood and interpreted by politicians of all parties, and the solutions they have posed. In order to address these concerns, the chapter will define and explain the policy changes that have occurred in education over the past 20 years or so, and the educational implications of these policies.

What is policy?

Policy is frequently perceived by many people as one of those areas that is far removed from their lives and not interesting in any way. The term 'policy-geek' is often used to describe someone who is keenly interested in the development of policy as if it was some form of esoteric area of knowledge that was not for the ordinary person. This is very far from the truth. Policy impacts on the lives of everyone in society. Policy affects our lives, our futures, and the lives and futures of our families and friends. Therefore, a good understanding of the policy process is extremely important. Furthermore, an understanding of educational policy is important for those who have an interest in the development of education in our society. What should be noted from the very beginning is that every author who writes on policy does so from his or her own socio-political perspective. The very words that are used carry a message and identify an ideological commitment on the part of the writer. The discussion below will seek to explore for the reader the nature and form of the policy discussion that currently dominates the education world within the UK. For one of the tricks, so to speak, of policy initiatives is to convince the public that the proposed policy is the only alternative that is available. What the reader should understand is that there are always policy alternatives.

The nature of policy

So, what is policy? On a very simple level, it is how we run our lives. The important point is that by adhering to a mode of behaviour, a policy, there has been a decision made on how you intend to govern your affairs in the conduct of your social relationships within your family and the wider society. In the same way, policy by government is the intended set of rules, governance, and resources that are provided by the state. Education policy will determine the structure of education. For example, when do children leave school? We can see from Chapter 2 on the history of education in this volume that the school-leaving age was a contentious issue for many years. It continues to be a divisive issue today, as the current government are discussing changing it again to 18 years, or for at least there to be some form of compulsory training for those not in full-time education between the ages of 16 and 18. Clearly, from this example we can see that the school-leaving age policy will impact on a number of individuals' lives and, of course, on organisations. If the issue of the school-leaving age is explored a little, we will gain a better picture of the way policy impacts on society.

Task 4.1 Stop, think and do

The chapter suggests that when a policy change takes place the impact of the policy is not always immediately recognized by those who will be affected. The example used in the chapter is the raising of the school-leaving age to 18.

- Choose a policy or government initiative of your choice and:
  a   identify all those who might be impacted upon by the policy;
  b   identify those who will benefit from the policy change;
  c   identify those who might be disadvantaged by the policy change.

- Write a short justification or criticism of the policy based on the analysis you have undertaken.

A policy problem

If the school-leaving age is raised to 18, what would be the impact? If those who argue for the policy are to be believed, the policy will solve many social ills that currently affect society. At a stroke of the pen, youth unemployment, at least for those between the ages of 16 and 18, will be eliminated. This is not an unusual driver for education policy as many governments in the past have considered raising the school-leaving age as a mechanism to address youth unemployment. The other arguments used by the proponents of the policy attempt to address issues relating to the skill level in society. The need to have a workforce that is able to compete in the global economy is dependent, so the argument goes, on a highly skilled workforce. The policy also seeks to address the other social ills that afflict society, such as anti-social behaviour. The argument in this case is that those individuals who leave school with little or no qualifications or skills or, in the worst case, a lack of basic skills, are effectively confined to the social scrapheap of society. That is, they will remain jobless, in poverty and prone to all the problems that people in such circumstances are affected by, for example, poor housing, ill health, low-income levels and possible growing anti-social behaviour, and in the worst circumstances, drug addiction. The policy is, therefore, presented as a panacea for multiple social problems and economic imperatives. It is asserted that it is the clear and only solution to the problems it attempts to address. However, the impact of the policy will go beyond the individuals who are its target, for employers will no longer have access to a labour force between the ages of 16 and 18. This has always been a cheap form of labour and has provided employers with the possibility of training their workers. It will impact on the families of those individuals, as they will not bring in any income to a family that might really need the extra money.

The importance of policy

The point of the above example is that policy is not an abstract idea but is, in fact, about people's lives, hopes, and aspirations. Policy determines who gets what in society and who has easy access to resources. Policy also determines the nature and form of education, from what is taught to how it is taught. In the medium term, it is a major factor in an individual's life chances.

While the above indicates the importance of policy and the role it plays, we also need to understand how policy develops. Policy is the product of a range of ideological theories about society that a range of individuals and organisations hold including: politicians, members of think tanks, civil servants, business and trade union leaders, pressure groups, ad hoc organisations that arise out of a particular issue, for example, the anti-academic alliance, local government politicians and, of course, political parties. What actually becomes a policy and, therefore, is implemented is a product of the contending forces identified above along with the constraints imposed by the economic and social conditions of the time. An important aspect of policy that is often neglected is that while there may be differences between the various individuals and organisations, they may, in actuality, be mere variations on a theme. In other words, disputes over policy may be at the margins rather than about the overriding ideas. There is often a general acceptance or consensus over the main issues that have to be dealt with, but not the underlying approach that has to be taken. In terms of education, this becomes very clear when politicians of all parties discuss education, for they all use phrases such as: choice, standards, levels of achievement, and parent power. When politicians use these words, they will mean slightly different things to each politician and to their party; nevertheless, they do indicate the overall consensus between the parties.

The development of education policy in the post-war period

The period from 1944 until 1979 is often described as being one of governmental consensus. The major parties held similar views of the needs of society and differed only at the margins of policy. For example, if services other than education are considered, once the National Health Service had been set up by the Labour Government of 1945–51, the subsequent Conservative Governments of 1951–1964 did not abolish the NHS and go back to the private-based provision that existed before the Second World War. In much the same way, once the Butler Education Act of 1944 had reformed secondary education provision, the tripartite system was largely accepted until the 1950s and then a gradual acceptance of comprehensive schools began to emerge in all parties, at least in most areas of the country and by most local politicians. The result of the general consensus was that at secondary level education did not change much over this period of time (Trowler 2003).

It is argued by many commentators that the period from 1979 onwards witnesses the then consensus towards education policy break down. However, when the policy developments in education are examined, what is remarkable is not that policy consensus has broken down, but rather a new one has taken the place of the previously held views. This is especially true from the period 1997 until today. All of the major political parties now talk of parental choice being one of the key flagstones of their education policy. It is almost a battle to see who can offer the most choice to parents along with other incentives linked to achieving higher standards.

The social democratic way

To really appreciate the importance of policy in education, it is necessary to understand the ideology and the principles that inform policy both today and in the recent past; for a fuller discussion on ideology, see Chapter 3 in this volume. From the end of the Second World War until the Conservative election victory in 1979, it can be argued that there existed a social democratic consensus between the two major parties that alternately held power over the period. The main principles that can be characterized as social democratic are: a commitment to full employment; the introduction of the welfare state; a policy of redistributive taxation as a form of social justice – that is, income going from the rich to the poor; an economic policy that is based on a mixed economy – that is, both state involvement and private enterprise working alongside each other (Kassem et al. 2006).

This model is largely based on the economic ideas of Maynard Keynes who, it was argued, had solved the problems of 'boom and bust' economics that had dominated the economic landscape before the war. The key idea was a significant and important role for government in the economic life of the nation. Thus, when there was an economic downturn in the economy, the government would be expected to spend their way out of the problems.

The above are, of course, general principles and as such do not directly link to education. However, the notion of social justice, redistribution of wealth and the support for the poorest of society, can be translated into educational terms. From 1944 onwards, both the major political parties adopted roughly the same educational policies, although it appeared that, just as today, they had different policies. The approaches that the parties took can be broadly described as a move to comprehensive schooling. It might be noted that one of the historical ironies in education policy is that under the Thatcher Government of 1979–90 more grammar schools were closed down in that time compared to any other. There was a general expansion of educational opportunities – through grants for higher education students, introduction of nursery schools and general early years provision and grand initiatives such as the Open University. There was a degree of positive discrimination in favour of the poorest schools and economically deprived areas and a growing commitment to a policy of equal opportunities. This can be most clearly seen in the area of ethnic minority achievement. Over the years, various strategies have been attempted to address underachievement by a range of ethnic minority pupils, for example, the Swan Report, called *Education For All*, was published under the Thatcher Government. Policies also championed in various forms over the period 1944–79, local community accountability through local councils and their education committees along with the introduction of school governors. Control over the curriculum, to a large extent, was in the hands of the professional judgement of the teacher and schools, though they were also supported through various organisations such as the Schools Council (abolished in the first years of the Thatcher Government). Finally, all supported the independence of, and freedom from, control or oversight by outside bodies of teacher training. The education departments of universities and teacher training colleges decided what should constitute teacher education (adapted from Hill and Cole 2004).

The major political parties implemented all these policies to a greater or lesser extent. Even if, on a national level, there was some opposition to comprehensive schools, at local level, councils still implemented the policy. It might be argued that there were financial imperatives working through the economies of scale as large comprehensive schools benefited financially compared to the small, elite grammar school. By the 1980s, only a few local authorities had resisted the process of moving all secondary schools into the comprehensive model. Kent is an example of this as they have maintained their grammar schools along with the entrance exam, the eleven-plus. By 1993, 90 per cent of children were receiving their secondary education in comprehensive schools (Benn and Chitty 1997). This consensus does not mean there was no debate over the form education should take or the importance of selection. However, the debate was framed by a general agreement on the nature of the education system and how it should perform to improve the lives of the ordinary child and future citizens of the nation.

Conservative debate

There were, of course, dissenters within the Conservative Party. Some argued against some of the reforms that were being implemented, for example, child-centred education and what was identified as progressive teaching. The right wing of the Conservative Party argued for a return to what they considered to be traditional teaching and standards (Knight 1990). Rhodes Boyson, a leading Conservative educationalist and a headmaster of a north london comprehensive school, along with others published what were known as the Black Papers (Cox and Dyson 1969). They sought to challenge the then current educational orthodoxy and re-align education policy within the Conservative Party during the 1970s. While the ideas contained in the Black Papers were not accepted by the then Conservative Heath Government, when Margaret Thatcher took over the leadership of the party, the ideas they espoused began to be integrated into the party's educational thinking and policy. This was especially true as the Conservative Party began to move further to the right under Thatcher and Keith Joseph (a Minster of Education under Thatcher).

Changing perspectives

The end of the 1970s saw the breakdown of the consensus as the Tories moved to the right. The Tories had adopted a policy perspective that is known as neo-liberalism, associated with what is called the radical right (Hill and Cole 2004). Initially, the Labour Party did not follow this move, as they still held to the social democratic model of society. This is clearly evidenced in their pamphlet on private schools published in 1980, in which they state:

> Policies for combating privilege in education are part of a democratic socialist assault on privilege, wealth, power and influence in our society. We are confident that these policies, together with our determination to improve standards of opportunity and provision throughout the maintained sector, will have the effect of bringing major and irreversible change to the structure of our society and the continuing advancement of the interests of working people and their families.

(Labour Party 1980: 50)

Just as the Labour Government, in rhetoric at least, had been informed by a set of social democratic principles, the Thatcher Government adopted a set of policy principles based on the economic ideas of such theoreticians as the right-wing economist Hayek, who was based at the London School of Economics. The key idea in this approach to policy is a commitment to individualism with a reduced role for the state, especially in the ownership of economic assets. This involved a policy of privatization and the reliance on the private sector to provide services that had previously been provided by state-owned concerns. There is a commitment to the use of the market with a stress on consumer choice as the mechanism for the distribution of resources. Social need was not the driving force for policy as it had been under the social democratic model. In terms of public services such as education, there is an increased notion of accountability through the use of targets and the measurement of performance both of individuals and institutions. The use of competition should also, theoretically at least, result in the reduction in the cost of public services. The marketization of public services is also linked to a revised notion of the individual who uses the service. They are no longer considered students, pupils or patients, rather they become consumers, customers or clients. This stress on the consumer as opposed to the producer of public services, the teachers and doctors, also allows a distrust of professional judgements to develop as the consumer asserts their rights (adapted from Hill and Cole 2004).

Changing direction

The reform of a service as large and complex as education is, to say the least, very difficult in part due to the nature of policy itself. Policies may be misunderstood, obstructed, re-interpreted and, as Ball (2008: 7) argues, just simply unworkable given the context in which they are being enacted. Therefore, the Conservative Party did not embark on the changes to education in one go but made them over a sustained period of time. What cannot be assumed either is that the Conservative Party was of one mind in terms of education policy at the beginning of their 18-year rule. There were significant differences between different sections of the Party. However, at the beginning of the 1980s, the Conservative Government pursued a policy of Excellence in Education, which was presented as more than just a Conservative idea (Knight 1990). The policy approach led by Joseph attempted to provide a clearer vision of what education should be and was formulated in a context of a fundamental rethink of the role to be played by education in a general strategy for social and cultural change (Knight 1990: 151). The re-appraisal of education:

> was based on a technical/vocational conception of education ... [and] the importance of young people having access to *good education* (author's emphasis) in order that they might be given the mental resources to enjoy their freedom ... Joseph ... drew attention not only to the concern about academic standards but also to pupil behaviour, discipline and work habits ... policy had to be orientated to meet the needs of the non-academic pupil, for whom key basic subjects would mean more if they were associated with greater prevocational content in parts of the curriculum.
>
> (Knight 1990: 151)

What Knight is suggesting is that there was a major change in government thinking regarding education. 'The winners' of the debates that took place within the Conservative Party are a group commonly known as the New Right.

In order to change the system of the day, the New Right needed to challenge a range of powerful sections of government that controlled education provision, what might be called the local state.

Challenging centres of power

Local education authorities (LEAs) were part of local government and were responsible for a wide range of education services, not just schools. For instance, in 1979, they were responsible for further education colleges, polytechnics (now the post-92 universities such as Liverpool John Moores, then Liverpool Polytechnic), special schools, school meals, education welfare services and, in fact, all aspects of education other than the then universities. The Conservatives challenged the power and monopoly of the LEAs by taking responsibility for further education and the polytechnics away and, in schools, introducing local management of schools (LMS).

Local management of schools

Up until the introduction of LMS in 1988, as part of the Education Reform Act, LEAs controlled the budgets and finance of schools under their control; LMS took this power away and gave it to head teachers. This policy initiative did two things: first, it took away the economic power of the LEA, therefore challenging its ability to use financial power to control what took place in schools, and, second, it gave power to head teachers and their management committees. The allocation any one school received was based on the number of pupils on the roll, therefore, the more pupils a school could gain, the more income it would receive. This effectively set school against school, in other words, competition was introduced into the education system. Parents were now consumers who could effectively, so the argument went, shop for the best school for their children and good schools would grow. Conversely, poor schools would decline as the number of pupils they could attract fell, thus becoming economically unviable and eventually closing. Thus the market would act as a regulator of quality within the education system through the mechanism of competition.

Parental choice

For LMS to work, the system of how pupils were allocated to schools had to be changed. No longer would the LEA be able to offer parents one or two schools to choose from, rather it had to be a system based on parental choice. This was known as open enrolment, in other words, a parent could opt for any school they wanted to send their child to. While the rhetoric of the day suggested this was the case, the reality was somewhat different. For instance, the problems of the physical capacity of the school to accept pupils and travelling costs for parents impacted on the real extent to which parents had a choice of schools. Moreover, the issue of informed choice must be considered here – how would parents know which is the better school in their locality? The solution was further reforms to the education system, all contained in the 1988 Education Reform Act (ERA), such as the introduction of a National Curriculum and an assessment structure for all schools.

Task 4.2   Stop, think and do

Choose a political party and examine their latest election manifesto showing how they claim to implement choice in education:

- Identify who you think will benefit from this choice.
- Identify any factors that might in real terms hinder an individual's ability to exercise choice in educational provision.

Explain how the notion of choice is related to the introduction of the market in education and which theoretical perspective on social policy supports these ideas.

The National Curriculum

To ensure that schools could be properly compared with one another, the government introduced the National Curriculum. This was controversial both within the Conservative Party and with those of differing political views. Resistance within the Conservative Party came from those who wished to completely privatize the schools system, who believed that all schools should become small businesses and that survival would be based on their ability to attract pupils. However, even the more extreme free-marketers eventually accepted the National Curriculum which placed central government in control. The National Curriculum is a traditional view of what children should learn (White 1988) and is highly structured with sets of attainment targets that children would be expected to achieve. This ensured that all schools were effectively producing the same product and, therefore, allowed easy comparison through a testing system that was also introduced at the same time. It is important to note that although the curriculum introduced to schools was called a National Curriculum, it was not national in the sense that it did not cover all parts of Britain. It did not apply to private schools. Thus it really was an English and Welsh state school curriculum. It is also worth noting that teachers, generally, were opposed to the introduction of the National Curriculum not least because it effectively challenged their control of the curriculum. Professional judgement was now under the control of the state. This reform is in sharp contrast to the ideas underlying LMS that was supposed to be about freeing schools from the control of LEAs. At the same time as decentralizing the school funding system, the government was effectively nation-alizing the curriculum that was to be taught, at least in state schools.

Standard Assessment Tasks

The introduction of a national testing regime (Scotland did not follow this system and Wales since devolution has changed their approach to testing) was the standard by which the effectiveness of a school could be measured. The form of testing to be known as the SATs (Standard Assessment Tasks) were introduced. All children in state schools in England and Wales at the ages of 7, 11, and 14 were to undertake these assessments. The arguments in favour of the tests were couched around ideas of teacher accountability and the parents' right to know how their children were progressing with their education. Another way of looking at the SATs would be to see them as part of the structures that the government was putting in place to enforce a market mechanism within the school system. There is a product, the National Curriculum, and the SATs are a measure of how effective the product has been delivered.

League tables

As mentioned above, the key element of being able to exercise choice in any market is information; this is informed choice. The government realized that while the market existed and the pressure of competition was being structurally built into the system, parents needed further information on which to base their choice of school. Thus the government introduced league tables based on the pupil performance in the SATs of every state school in the country. This is the last building block in the educational market that now exists within the state education system. It should be noted that league tables have been very controversial; not least because when they were first introduced, they were based purely on the raw exam results that schools generated. They did not take into account issues such as the impact of poverty on children (usually taken as the percentage of free school meals provided by a school), number on school rolls of children with English as an additional language (EAL) or from single parent families, or any other measure of deprivation and social exclusion. Therefore, it was not surprising that the initial league tables resulted in schools in the more affluent areas being seen as the more effective schools. The tables did not measure the extent to which a school had successfully helped children to overcome the difficulties they faced.

Quality assurance

To ensure that quality was maintained in schools, the government set about restructuring the school inspection system. There had been an inspection system before the 1988 Act, but most schools were rarely inspected. The government, effectively, was implementing a quality control system of regular inspections of schools, once every four years. The teacher was at the centre of this inspection regime, with each teacher receiving a grade as to their competence to teach. Schools that were deemed to be failing would enter what is known as 'special measures' and were ultimately forced to close down. The inspection was an added measure by which the government intended to drive up what they considered the low standards of education.

All is not well

The Conservative Government had reformed and restructured the education system but there were a number of problems not least with the Natoinal Curriculum itself. There was serious disquiet in a number of quarters, including the professional subject associations and advisors to the government on the National Curriculum. The speed at which the National Curriculum was introduced had led to concerns over the high level of prescription built into the system and arguments over the organisation of the content of the curriculum. In response to these concerns the then Conservative Government set up the Dearing Committee to re-examine the National Curriculum with the aim of slimming it down and making it less prescriptive. The actual tests used in the SATs have also undergone a number of reviews. The biggest issue was the still perceived poor levels of achievement of pupils in the UK compared to its near economic competitors. The weaknesses were identified as the poor quality of the teaching force and the lack of a systematic approach to teaching key subjects such as mathematics and English, especially in the primary phase. These concerns were to inform the continued changes introduced by the Labour Government in the previous ten years.

1997 and all that

The New Labour Party came into power after 18 years of opposition a very changed party from when it left office. There had been a name change to flag that it was not the party of the past. The changes that had taken place were based on a new approach to what, they would claim, was a more just society through the effective delivery of public services (Barber 2007). The theoretical approach was labelled the Third Way. The Third Way was a response by leading left of centre intellectuals and Labour politicians to the perceived failure of traditional social democracy and the increased challenge of globalization. Thus New Labour politicians were to engage with the market and the private sector in a way that social democracy had never done before. This fundamental rethinking on the nature of the state and its role has a major impact on education policy under New Labour. An example of the rethinking of education and the individual's relationship to the education system is the introduction of fees for university students. The introduction of fees not only makes the individual student or their family responsible for making a financial contribution to their education, a process of what might be called deferred gratification, but also changes the relationship between the student and the university. There is a clear move towards the student ceasing to be a student and instead becoming a customer or client. This process reinforces the market in education by making the student/ customer more aware of what they might expect from their institution. This demonstrates the Third Way commitment to the market and notions of individual responsibility that is also to be found in Conservative education policy.

Setting the tone

New Labour's approach to education policy was established almost from the moment they entered office. One of the first acts by the new Secretary of State for Education, David Blunkett, was to confirm the Conservative appointment of Chris Woodhead as the ongoing head of the Office for Standards in Education (Ofsted), and to set targets for schools to achieve in the SATs for their pupils.

These policy initiatives clearly signalled the way that the new government was going to proceed in terms of education policy. It would be a stress on delivery and achievement, and failure was not to be an option. The new government laid out their policy perspectives in the White Paper *Excellence in Schools* (DfEE 1997a). They claimed that there would be a hands-off approach; if a school were successful, it would be allowed to carry on with limited intervention by government (DfEE 1997a). However, intervention has been the character of New Labour education policy. New Labour were not content to leave everything to the market mechanism that had been developed in education over the previous 18 years.

Intervention

The interventionist approach can be seen in the major policy initiatives regarding the school curriculum. Though the Conservative Government had originally set up the National Literacy Project, it was New Labour that went on to implement it as a national teaching strategy in all schools. The National Numeracy Strategy and, eventually, the Key Stage 3 Strategy quickly followed this. The common element in all these strategies is that for the first time the state was defining what was considered to be an appropriate pedagogy (see Chapter 5). There had been a national curriculum before the 1944 Butler Education Act, but a state-defined pedagogy had never existed before. The enforcement of this pedagogy was the inspection system; no teacher could afford not to be seen to follow the prescribed structure for lessons if they wanted to survive an inspection. The level of the intervention has moved on over the years to such an extent that now schools are required to teach reading through synthetic phonics (Rose 2006). The close management of what went on in schools was at the same time linked to choice and freedom for parents to select a high achieving school. Moreover, the choice in school system was to be achieved by increasing the range and diversity of the types of schools available to parents, especially in the secondary phase of education (see Chapter 5).

Academies

In pursuit of the policy of choice, the government has introduced a number of different types of schools into the system; all these schools are outside the control of local authorities. The new types of school have been Foundation schools, Trust schools and the current initiative is to set up two hundred Academies. The Academies are not dissimilar to the Conservative Government's City Technology Colleges, in that they are linked to business investment (F. Beckett 2007) and are independent in terms of their financial control, admissions and curriculum. The policy for Academies suggests that they will replace failing schools in difficult social areas; however, the reality would suggest the schools are developing in a different direction with private schools bidding for Academy status, for example, Belvedere School in Liverpool. Successful state schools have also been earmarked to become Academies in opposition to the feelings of both teachers and parents (F. Beckett. 2007).

Academies are allowed to opt out of national agreements on wages and working conditions of teachers as well as the National Curriculum. This effectively is not only attempting to diversify the nature of educational provision across the country but also seeks to further erode the power of previously influential groups in education such as the teacher unions. The Academies have proved to be a very controversial initiative not least because of the nature of some of the business sponsors they have attracted (F. Beckett 2007), but also because some of the schools have been heavily influenced by various religious groups and some are teaching creationist science.

Faith schools

The New Labour Government has also sought to increase the number of faith schools available to parents. Faith schools have proved to be popular to parents as they seem to obtain good examination results for their pupils but some researchers argue that faith has just become another label for a middle-class school that excludes the poor (Ball 2008). The faith school debate also raised issues relating to the extent to which they would impact on the social cohesion of society. Those opposed to the increase in numbers of faith schools often point to the religious divide in Northern Ireland as an example of the possible consequences of faith schools. Be they faith schools, Academies or Trust schools, the policy initiative that this represents is both a greater diversity of provision, stronger links with private industry and a challenge to the ideas of social democracy as previously conceived.

The whole child

What has been unique about the New Labour education agenda is the extent of the intervention in a wider context other than schooling. The New Labour agenda has seen the introduction of initiatives such as Sure Start and Every Child Matters (ECM). Sure Start grew out of the commitment to overcome social exclusion by the government. Poverty in early childhood was identified as being one of the single most important causes of future social exclusion. If factors that impact on young children and their families could be overcome then, so the argument went, social exclusion would be prevented in the later years. Sure Start was designed to be a one stop shop for education and the social needs of young children with all the relevant services working together. Centres were placed in areas identified as having a low socio-economic standing compared to the wider community. However, there has been debate over the degree of success they have had in solving the problems they set out to address (Ward 2005).

Every Child Matters similarly is an initiative that is attempting to bring together a range of services that work with children and young people who are most at risk. The strategy grew out of the concern over the failure of a range of services to prevent the death of Victoria Climbié and the subsequent report by Lord Laming (2003). ECM seeks to bring together all agencies working with young children who are at risk in any way. It does not just mean children who are at risk of injury or harm. For instance, one group that has been identified of concern are looked-after children as they notoriously fail in terms of education; typically only 1 per cent obtain university places (Kassem 2006). The approach of ECM extends to schools, social services, universities and the police, in fact, to any body that deals with or works with children. Sure Start and ECM indicate the commitment by the government to address issues of poverty and underachievement of children though the market mechanism is still viewed as key to addressing the problems faced by these groups (see Kassem 2006 regarding looked-after children). The important point here is that the policy goes beyond what had ever been attempted before, the child's needs are looked at in the whole, at least at the level of rhetoric.

Conclusion

When discussing policy, the reader must always remember that no one writes about policy from a neutral perspective. How the information is presented and the evaluation of policy will always be influenced by the writer's political and ideological perspectives: this chapter is no different. What the readers must do is think for themselves and read around the issues that have been identified before coming to their own conclusion.

Summary

1 Policy is important – it affects and informs everyone's life.
2 Policy does not exist in a vacuum – it is shaped by the socio-economic and political context in which it is formulated and implemented.
3 There are always policy alternatives, though those who favour a particular policy do their best to convince others that this is not so.
4 Frequently there exists a consensus among political parties regarding policy in its widest sense – differences appear at the margins and in relation to how policy is to be implemented.
5 Education policy in the UK today is driven by market forces – students and parents have become consumers, competition is seen as a way to improve standards and private enterprise is encouraged.
6 The current New Labour party in England have taken on board and developed the marketization of education set in motion by the previous Conservative Government.
7 New Labour do not, however, trust the market to the same extent as the Conservatives and for this reason have sought to control and manage education through the National Curriculum and a state-defined pedagogy.
8 New Labour education policy since 1997 has heralded intervention-ism in all areas of education, from birth to higher education, as has never been seen before.

5   A Different Schooling?

The concept of choice

While it is unnecessary here to define choice in its broad, common-sense meaning, it is useful to consider the role that the concept of choice plays in political debate. Social choice theory has its origins in the writings of the eighteenth-century French philosopher and political theorist, Condorcet (1743–1794). Condorcet advocated liberal politics, free and equal education and equal rights for women and people of all races. He believed in a constitutional society in which government, whose power is limited by law, is elected by voting and in which power is shared by the public and the government. Condorcet (1976) recognized that within such a system, even when all adults have equal voting rights, the choices of all could not be satisfied. This has been termed Condorcet's paradox by modern social theorists such as the American economist Kenneth Arrow. Arrow (1953) defines the problem of social choice theory, termed Arrow's improbability theorem, as that of satisfying the choice of the individual while ordering society along a set of rules and systems which meet the needs and the preferences of the majority.

Arrow's improbability theorem, like Condorcet's paradox, suggests that no social choice theory can meet the needs and choices of all within an electorate. As will be discussed below, the current Labour government in the UK claim that its neo-liberal education policy will provide real choice which will satisfy the requirements of all parents and break the link between poverty and low achievement and aspiration (DfES 2005b). In a sense, such policy claims to have solved Condorcet's paradox.

The 1988 Education Reform Act which introduced the National Curriculum (DES 1988) and the 1992 White Paper, *Choice and Diversity: A New Framework for Schools* (DfE 1992), represent the introduction of neo-liberal policies into education in the UK by the then Tory Government (Whitty 1989). As pointed out in Chapter 3 and Chapter 4, neo-liberal politics and policy are based on the open market and on competition in all social institutions. The individual in such a society is seen as a consumer and, in order for the market to function, the consumer must be given choice and diversity of products which create the competition. As Harvey (2005) points out, in such a political framework it is the role of the government to create and maintain the markets.

The Tories introduced a market-based approach within the education system in 1988 with all the accoutrements of a regulated market: school league tables, Standard Attainment Tests (SATs), a rigorous inspection regime by the Office for Standards in Education (Ofsted) and open enrolment. The intention was to create inter-school competition (Adnett and Davies 2003) or localized markets in which the consumers, the parents, were supposedly provided with a choice of provision that would meet the needs of their children. The market force of parental choice and open enrolments was predicted to increase the quality of education in schools as a result of this competition for pupils.

The concept of choice was then on the agenda of all subsequent education policies of any of the major political parties. New Labour identified choice as a key policy aim in 1997. Their manifesto stated, 'all parents should be offered real choice through good quality schools, each with its own strengths and individual ethos' (Dale 2000: 350).

Included in this menu of choice is the provision of a diversity of educational settings: specialist schools, Foundation schools, Academies, faith schools and Trust schools, and a commitment to personal learning to meet the needs of individual learners (DfES 2005b). Furthermore, the idea of choice is linked to a notion of social justice and of unfairness in the previous system. By encouraging private investment in state education, creating ' independent non-fee paying state schools' (DfES 2005b: 33), the government proposed to offer the choice of good schools to all parents and pupils, not just to those who can afford private education or who can move house into the catchment area of schools considered to be good.

When discussing the nature of choice in any area of life, three key factors must be considered: the range and nature of the options from which the choice is to be made; the knowledge basis of the choice, and for whom the choice is available. In simple terms, what is there to choose between, how well informed the choosers are and who gets to choose. In each of these areas, neo-liberal education policies in the UK and elsewhere are problematic.

The choice

As Meighan and Siraj-Blatchford (2001: 393–4) point out, in much of the debate about choice in state-funded education, historically and in contemporary society, the term 'choice' has been a misnomer. Debate has focused around a narrow interpretation of formal, traditional, authoritarian education. On one side a stricter form of authoritarian education has been advocated which incorporates both the elitist/ conservative and the revisionist/technocratic ideologies. The opposing school of thought has favoured a more romantic and democratic approach which purports to be child-centred. However, in the UK since the 1970s and 1980s, the backlash against the more progressive and democratic type of education advocated by Plowdenism (see Chapter 3) and the introduction of the National Curriculum (DES 1988) and the national strategies for teaching literacy and mathematics (see Chapter 4), have resulted in state education at best paying no more than lip service to child-centred education. Concern with falling standards and poor discipline in schools and with overall lack of national economic growth has resulted in a state-defined pedagogy and curriculum in which there is little room for consideration of the child (Murphy et al. 2006).

MacDonald (2006: 93) identified at least 13 different school types being sponsored by state funding in the UK. Table 5.1 outlines the comparative structure and organisation of some of the principal school types, both state and private, currently available in the UK. It is useful to note any type of state-funded school can apply to be a Trust or Foundation school. In fact, New Labour would like all schools to be partly privately funded, that is, sponsored by a foundation or charitable trust (DfES 2005b).

New Labour claimed that the focus of their education policy is standards not structures (DfES 2005b). However, the words of Tony Blair in justifying the move towards specialist schools and academies 'to escape the straitjacket of the traditional comprehensive' and 'to break down the barriers to new providers' (Blair 2005) seemed to belie such a claim. Indeed, the House of Commons Education and Skills Committee (HCESC 2003), in a report on diversity in secondary education, with specific attention to specialist schools, expressed concerns about the apparent mismatch between the government's insistence on choice and diversity and the reality. The report stated that where 'one might expect to see much that is distinct in terms of pedagogy and curriculum', in reality, 'diversity has been defined largely in structural terms, with focus on increasing the number of school types and thereby the superficial differences between schools' (HCESC 2003: 26).

The choice offered by neo-liberal education policy in the UK is a pseudo-choice. Whether a parent opts for a foundation or faith-based primary school, a specialist secondary school or a city academy, the same curriculum will be delivered by the same state-controlled pedagogy. In short, it is a choice between different school structures and not between different educational ideologies. This does not constitute choice in any meaningful sense of the word. It is the choice between McDonald's, Burger King or Wendy's – you get a burger in each case. Or to draw an analogy from film, it is similar to the discussion in Tarantino's *Pulp Fiction*, in the US you get a quarter pounder but in France it is a le Royale. Different name, same product.

The justification for the structural reforms and the so-called choice offered in education is the supposed improvement in educational standards that has taken place since the election of the New Labour Government in 1997. The evidence offered in the Government White Paper (DfES 2005b) is that at the end of Key Stage 2, in 1997, 62 per cent of children obtained level four in the English SATs, while in 2004 this had increased to 79 per cent. Equally, in mathematics there has been, on paper, an improvement from 63 per cent achieving level four in 1997 to 75 per cent in 2004. At secondary level in 1997, 45 per cent of children achieved 5 or more GCSEs at grade A*–C. However, by 2004, this had risen to 54 per cent (DfES 2005b).

Table 5.1 School provision in the UK – main school types

School type	Funding	Curriculum	Ownership of land and buildings	Selection procedure	Religious affiliation	Employment of staff
Academy	Private sector/charitable trust & government	National Curriculum (NC)	Government &/or private sector	Local Authority (LA); non-selective	May have affiliation	LA
Specialist	Private sector/charitable trust & government	NC with emphasis on specialist subject	Government &/or private sector	LA – 10% selected in specialist aptitude	May have affiliation	LA
Voluntary aided	Charitable trust & government	NC	Often the charitable foundation	Governing body &/or LA; % religious affiliation	Often church or other faith; may be humanitarian organization	Governing body
Voluntary controlled	Charitable trust & government	NC	Often charitable foundation	LA; % religious affiliation	Usually church schools	LA
Foundation/Trust	Charitable foundation/trust & government	NC	Governing body or charitable trust	Governing body	May have affiliation	Governing body
Comprehensive	Government	NC	LA	LA	May have affiliation	LA
Community	Government	NC	LA	LA	Often no affiliation	LA
Grammar	Government &/or charitable trust	NC or institution-based	LA or charitable trust or governing body	Governing body; 11+ or other test	Usually have affiliation	LA or governing body
Private/independent/public	Private – fees &/or sponsorship/investment	Institution-based; state exams; some follow NC	Governing body or charitable trust	Governing body; often common entrance exam	Usually have affiliation	Governing body

The evidence for the justification of the reforms in terms of the superior performance is questionable in a number of ways. The extent of the improvement in results in primary schools is not as clear as it might seem. Research evidence questions the extent of the improvement in performance by children in the SATs (Massey et al. 2002). While all the studies recognize there has been an improvement, it is a far more modest improvement than was claimed by the government. It might be possible that some of the improvement that has actually taken place is due to the Hawthorne effect which suggests that people's behaviour and performance change following any new initiative, simply by the fact that time, attention and usually money, are being focused on behaviour and/or performance. In other words, the national focus on literacy and mathematics could in itself have produced an increased level of attainment. A further explanation of improvement in test scores could simply be the old adage 'practice makes perfect': teachers may have become better at teaching to the tests. Tymms et al. state that 'it is possible that children's familiarity with the testing procedure and test formats could explain all or some of the rise' (2005: 21).

The choosers – knowledge basis and who gets to choose

In neo-liberal education policy, the choosers, or customers, are clearly identified – parents and pupils. A key element in any meaningful notion of choice is that the chooser is fully informed and is aware of the consequences of their decisions. Social choice theory focuses on the costs, incentives and opportunities of a decision, but it takes little account of the knowledge basis of choice which influences the capacity and access to decision-making (Hindess 1988). In other words, the mechanism by which the market economy suggests that parents choose a school, the basis of competition in terms of results, does not take social context and the social position of the parent/pupil chooser into account (MacDonald 2006).

Bourdieu (1986) suggests that in order to be an effective 'player' in the market-based economy, an individual must possess the appropriate economic, cultural and social capital to make effective choices. In a sense, the ability to choose is closely tied to the social context and position of the chooser. Capital is defined as a means of exchange or currency within the market. Economic capital is the availability of resources such as money, and social capital involves belonging to groups and networks which provide influence and support. Cultural capital, which parents pass on to their children, is knowledge, skill and education which provide a person with advantage, higher status and high expectations. Having the appropriate cultural capital within a society means that parents and children will possess knowledge and skills which make the education system familiar to them and enable them to succeed within it.

To help parents and pupils choose a good or appropriate school in the UK, they are provided with a mass of data from individual school policies and documentation, Oftsed school inspections and league tables. In order to process and use this information to their advantage, they require the appropriate capital. However, this is not always the case.

Ball et al. (1996) identify three types of parent chooser within the education system: privileged or skilled, semi-skilled, and disconnected. Skilled choosers, usually from middle-class or professional backgrounds, tend to have the appropriate capital to compete effectively within the school system. Brown (1997) has labelled the choice-based system in education a 'parentocracy' in which skilled choosers, due to their economic advantage, experience and capability, are able to access data and use the system to their advantage. The choice-based system in the UK enables specialist schools and trust schools to select their intake of pupils, in some cases up to 20 per cent. Skilled choosers may have the economic, social and cultural capital to provide their children with the skills and knowledge to pass the selection procedure. For example, they may be able to pay for music lessons or sports coaching which may provide the child with an advantage in selection procedures when applying for a place at a music or sports specialist school with a good reputation. Furthermore, such parents may have advantage in what could be termed the selection-by-postcode factor. Economic status may enable them to live in or move to areas of greater social privilege which may have sought after schools. These skilled choosers are more likely than any other group to secure places for their children at schools of their choice (Brown 1997).

Gewirtz et al. (1995) found that while semi-skilled choosers, from a variety of social and cultural backgrounds, possess some of the appropriate capital to engage in the selection process, they often do not have the economic means to benefit from the selection-by-post-code situation. Moreover, as their competency at using data to understand the difference between schools is often insecure, they frequently fail to secure school places of their choice.

Disconnected choosers, usually from the working class, often lack the appropriate capital to manipulate the choice-based school system. Reay and Ball (1997) point out that such parents often approach education and school selection with anxiety and a sense of failure. This may lead to disconnection when exercising their right of choice.

Denessen et al. (2005) identified four general domains of choices: (1) ideological, often religious and/or pedagogical; (2) geographical, as in distance from home or work; (3) quality of education; and (4) non-educational, such as composition of school population in terms of ethnicity and social class and role of extra-curricular activities. While skilled choosers may use educational success as a criteria when choosing a school (Ball et al. 1996), they will often also select schools based on identifying which school's learning environment, approach to social education and extra-curricular activities best fits the character of their child. Semi-skilled choosers often choose a school based on its reputation within the community and disconnected choosers often select schools based on practical convenience such as closeness to home (Ball et al 1996). In other words, not all parents are conforming to the notion of behaviour for the market to operate. Many parents are not well-informed participants and do not make decisions purely on self-interest but, in fact, their choices show that other factors come in to play. The effect of this is to subvert the market.

At present, there is evidence of segregation within UK state schools and of the fact that schools with higher proportions of pupils from underprivileged social backgrounds and schools with more ethnic minority pupils are not achieving as well in terms of results as schools in more socio-economically advantaged areas (Benn and Millar 2006). Given the differing ability to choose of the categories of choosers outlined above, the fact that many parents are not choosing schools in line with academic success, and given the government's policy of increasing different school types and school ability to select pupils, it appears that choice has strengthened social advantage for some but has failed to offer equal access to all.

It seems that in the current UK state-funded education system, there is quasi-choice – a choice between different school structure and organisation perhaps, but not between educational ideology. Even within this narrowly defined arena of choice the government have not solved Condorcet's paradox. The choice offered within the UK education system is not satisfying the needs of individual choosers, but at best is meeting the needs of the majority within society, the skilled, middle-class choosers. Moreover, the ability of the current choice-based education system to fully satisfy the needs of this group of choosers is also highly questionable. Even when choosers are well informed, high levels of competition for places in sought-after schools often result in parents not attaining places for their children in the school of their choice. A *Times Education Supplement* survey in 2005 found that 50 per cent of 11-year olds in some parts of the country did not get their first choice of secondary school. Interestingly, this percentage was highest in the Greater London area where, given the number and diversity of schools on offer, the opposite result might have been expected (Paton 2005).

Here we have focused on the concept of choice in terms of parent and pupil choosers; when other sectors of the education system in the UK are considered, such as teachers and schools, it becomes apparent that they also have a highly restricted choice. As teachers are restricted by the stranglehold of the National Curriculum and policies, testing and league tables, though individuals and individual institutions may seek to implement a more child-centred and democratic ethos and approach, there is little real choice in ideology. Moreover, choice is further limited for schools. The government stated that while all schools 'have freedom to shape their own destiny' (DfES 2005b: 24), all new or replacement schools, secondary and primary, will be foundation, trusts, voluntary aided or Academies. The extent to which the choice is limited is obvious from the fact that the government intend to renew or rebuild all secondary and half of all primary schools in the next 15 years (DfES 2005b: 16).

Having considered the concept of choice in education, with specific focus on the UK, it could be suggested that in the UK, as in many other countries in the world, it is only those who are able to opt out of state-funded education and pay for schooling who have any real choice, that is, the choice between different education ideologies rather then different school structures. Alternatives to traditional education have recorded success both in England and elsewhere which will be illustrated below.

Deficit models of education

The traditional transmission-based form of teacher-centred education which suggests that the teacher has some information that the learner does not, can be defined as a deficit model of education. The teacher's job here is to provide the learner with the knowledge and skills which s/he lacks and so remedy the deficiencies (D. Matheson 2004: 4–5). As state education within the UK and elsewhere is controlled in terms of curriculum and pedagogy (see Chapter 12) and is specifically geared towards testing and standards, it can be defined as a deficit model of education. This form of education is at odds with the ideology of some critical educational thinkers, such as Paulo Freire and A.S. Neill.

The work of critical thinkers in education

Paulo Freire and critical pedagogy

The work of the Brazilian educator, Paulo Freire (1921–1997), stands in direct opposition to the transmission-based, deficit model of education which Freire termed *banking* in the sense that the student is an empty account to be filled by the educator (Freire [1970] 1996). After the publication of his famous work *Pedagogy of the Oppressed* was published in 1970, the term critical pedagogy was used to define educational ideology such as his which sees education as a means of addressing social problems and of transforming society along democratic lines. Freire believed that education is not deficit-filling, but based on dialogue which draws out and develops the learner's prior knowledge of the world.

Freire worked with poor, illiterate and oppressed adults in Brazil. He saw education as 'the practice of freedom' (1973: 149) and as a means of helping people to help themselves by placing them 'in consciously critical confrontation with their problems' and making them 'the agents of their own recuperation' (1973: 16). Freire termed his approach to education *conscientização* or conscientization which he defines as 'the awakening of critical awareness' (1973: 19). Through awakening in the learner the ability to critically evaluate his/her society and his/her place within society, Freire believed that education could be a means of integrating people into the democratic process and a means of bringing about true democracy. Freire believed that this was not possible with a traditional curriculum which is disconnected from the real lives of the students, with the traditional school which he saw as passive rather than dynamic, nor with traditional teaching methods in which the teacher is seen as the possessor of knowledge and the learner is considered to be ignorant. Such an approach to education he believed 'anaesthetizes the educatee and leaves them a-critical and naïve in the face of the world' (1973: 152).

In his education programme which was implemented by the Workers Party Government in the state of Rio Grande do Sul in Brazil, Freire advocated a form of participatory democracy. In a sense, Freire believed that if education is to bring about true democracy, the process of education itself must be fully democratic. In the process of conscientization, the notion of school was redefined as a cultural circle, teachers were called co-ordinators, pupils were group participants, lessons were based on dialogue between co-ordinator and student, and the curriculum, which grew from this dialogue, was based on a set of words which were relevant to the lives of the students. The process was initiated through dialogue about culture and society between co-ordinators and groups of illiterate adults. The purpose of this dialogue was to encourage the participants to recognize their value within society, their place within the culture and to see how the acquisition of literacy could help them transform their place in society and society itself.

It is useful here to give a brief summary of the actual Freirean programme for teaching illiterate adults to read and write (1973: 47–58). Once a group of adults had elected themselves for the literacy programme, the first phase of the process involved the co-ordinator, through informal dialogue with group participants, researching the vocabulary of the group and beginning to select a set of between 15 and 18 'generative words' which had direct relevance to the group's lives, for example, words to do with work or farming. Once the generative words, usually trisyllabic words, had been selected and agreed upon by the group, each word was codified in the form of a picture, filmstrip or poster of a situation involving the word. The co-ordinator and the group discussed and explored the codification of the word and then the co-ordinator drew attention to the word. The participants were asked to visualize the word which was then shown to the group without the codification/illustration. Next the participants were shown 'discovery cards' on which the initial consonant of each syllable of the word was shown with each of the five vowels, for example, as the Portuguese word for brick is *tijolo* – the discovery card for this word would show the phonemic strings *ta-te-ti-to-tu*, *ja-je-ji-jo-ju* and *la-le-li-lo-lu*. At this point participants were asked verbally to identify and to make up words using the phonemic strings. Freire records that at this stage of the process, without being given direct instruction, many of the participants began to write and read (1973: 55).

Freire, as co-ordinator of the National Literacy Programme in Brazil, had planned to extend this programme with a post-literacy stage developing texts within the cultural circles which would have dealt with major themes and issues within Brazilian life. He also intended to extend the programme of participatory democratic learning into schools and colleges. Unfortunately, his work was halted by a military coup in 1964. Nevertheless, Freire's method of conscientization was a success in Brazil and has had a lasting impact in the field of critical and radical education globally. It is an illustration of the possibility that an alternative is available to traditional transmission-based, teacher-centred education.

Though Freire worked mostly with adults, there is no reason why this approach could not be employed with children using a set of generative words relative to their experience and lives. This would, however, involve a radical upheaval in terms of attitudes towards the role of teacher and learner within governmental education policy and in the consciousness of the general public. Freire himself noted that one of the major problems in setting up his programme was instructing the co-ordinators, not in the technique, but in the creation of a new attitude, that of seeing education as dialogue, not transmission (1973: 52).

Freedom-based learning

Advocates of freedom-based learning, while sharing an opposition to the transmission, teacher-centred model with proponents of critical pedagogy, insist that the learner's freedom and autonomy should be limited as little as possible. Learning begins with the individual's needs and goals and not with the demands of society. The essence of free schools is that learners set limits to their own freedom and decide themselves when they will learn and what they will learn. The teachers in a sense get out of their way. Here freedom-based learning stands at odds with critical pedagogy. Critical pedagogy, which seeks to educate learners to transform society by questioning inequality and unfairness, would assert that being neutral or indifferent to political questions and to the moral condition of the world is to some extent an endorsement of transmission-based learning. In other words, it can simply result in the objective transmission of knowledge. For such thinkers the learner's personal interest and needs cannot be the only measure of educational value, working towards a democratic society must come first (Miller 2004).

Free schools originated in the modern school movement in Europe some years before the First World War. By the 1960s and 1970s, there were a number of free schools in the UK, the USA and other parts of the world. The most famous free school in the UK is Summerhill School which was founded by A.S. Neill in 1924 in Lyme Regis, Dorset, and is still operating under the supervision of his daughter in Leiston, Suffolk, despite continual governmental criticism and inspection which cumulated in a court case in March 2000.

A.S. Neill had been a teacher in Scottish state schools before the First World War and, after fighting in the war, had the opportunity to work in a progressive school in Germany. His own experiences of a government-controlled school, both as student and as teacher, and his experience in Germany, led him to develop his own ideology of education and to open Summerhill based on his views. Summerhill is a fee-paying co-educational boarding school with no selection procedure.

Between 1915 and 1972, Neill wrote 20 books on education, the most influential being *Summerhill* (1968). In this book, which became a best seller and had a profound effect on the global free school movement, Neill clearly sets out his ideology of education: 'We set out to make a school in which we should allow children to be themselves. In order to do this we had to renounce all discipline, all direction, all suggestion, all moral training, all religious instruction' (1968: 20).

Similar to Rousseau (see Chapter 3, in this volume) , Neill had a strong belief in the innate goodness of children and believed that if a child is allowed to develop freely and naturally, this natural goodness will manifest. He saw no need for moral promptings and sanctions to be externally imposed upon children by adults in authoritarian positions. For this reason he rejected moral and religious instruction which he believed represses natural goodness and could actually make a child bad: 'The child is innately wise and realistic. If left to himself without adult suggestion of any kind, he will develop as far as he is capable of developing' (Neill 1968: 221). Neill emphasized emotional well-being, happiness and personal fulfilment over the intellect. He asserted that happiness and inner contentment can only be achieved through freedom and self-direction and advocated a Freudian explanation for anti-social behaviour: external repression leads to inner hostility; inner hostility which cannot be expressed towards outward authority leads to self-hate; self-hate results in anti-social behaviour (Hobson 2006: 2).

Freedom and self-direction are fundamental to the learning experience at Summerhill and are provided for the child through the ability to choose whether to attend lessons or not and through having an equal voice and vote at the weekly whole school group meetings which decide all rules, all structures and all punishments. While Neill did not advocate rules governing behaviour which would affect the individual alone, such as attendance at lessons, he did believe that democratic authority could be exercised when the behaviour of one individual, for example, bullying, did affect other members of the community. As Neill did not believe in authority-based punishment, all instances of anti-social behaviour at Summerhill are brought before the group meeting and an appropriate punishment, such as payment of a fine or missing a social activity, are decided upon by the group. As pointed out by Gribble (1998), the benefit of such a system is that as the adults at the school do not impose the punishments, the relationship between the adult/teacher and the child is not damaged. Moreover, as attendance at lessons is voluntary, conflicts between teachers and students are extremely rare at Summerhill.

In terms of the curriculum at Summerhill, creative subjects such art, craft, dancing, drama and music are given more weight than academic subjects. It is believed creative subjects promoted creativity, imagination and emotional well-being; are therapeutic for psychological problems and allow less academic children to excel at something (Hobson 2006: 2). The curriculum for early years is dominated by play and focus on creativity, while children over 12 have a personalized timetable based on their interests, which is drawn up for them at beginning of term by consultation between the child and an adult/teacher. Of course, the child does not have to follow the timetable and it can be reviewed or revoked at the child's discretion. Pupils can choose whether to take formal exams such as GSCEs.

Neill's educational ideology and its practical application at Summerhill have been constantly debated and criticized. In the first place, it has been suggested that Neill's writings and philosophy, based mostly on his own experience, are unsystematic and simplistic. His work consists of many unsupported assertions and anecdotes and he tends to generalize from individual cases to universal educational principles. Moreover, educators have questioned the anti-intellectual basis of his theory which rates learning as unimportant and seems to suggest that children can fully utilize their freedom and make meaningful choices without a solid core of knowledge and understanding upon which to base their choices (Hobson 2006: 3–4).

Nevertheless, despite criticism and close government scrutiny, Summerhill continues to flourish and actually managed to win an appeal held before an educational tribunal in 2000 against a governmental call to close the school down. Summerhill is the most inspected school in the UK, having undergone nine Ofsted inspections between 1989 and 1999. In 1999, Summerhill failed an Ofsted inspection largely due to the fact that, as attendance at lessons is voluntary, this factor was seen to contravene the government's requirement for a school to provide a broad and balanced curriculum in line with the National Curriculum (DES 1988). The school was told to revoke its policy of voluntary attendance at lessons or to ensure that if pupils chose not to attend lessons, they were pursuing supervised private study. The school refused to comply with this demand and appealed to the Independent Schools Tribunal.

As pointed out by Newman (2006), in a review of the 1999 inspection and the subsequent tribunal hearing, Summerhill won the appeal when the government's case collapsed four days into the hearing. To some degree the case against the school collapsed as the inspection team were deemed not to have followed their remit. When inspecting a private school, Ofsted has to assess the school in the light of its own aims and policies as well to ensure that the school is fulfilling the minimum requirements laid down by the government for the school to remain registered as a school. One of those requirements is to provide a broad and a balanced curriculum. The policy at Summerhill is that much of the learning is done by the pupils in out-of-classroom situations and in extra-curricular activities; however, the inspectors did not visit these activities or take account of the out-of-classroom learning.

Newman, calling Summerhill's success in the hearing 'a victory for ... genuine choice in education' (2006: 62), points out the irony implicit in the fact that while New Labour professed a strong commitment to choice and diversity in education (see above), they were trying to close down a school which represents these very qualities. Newman concludes that the choice offered to parents and learners in the UK 'is a prescribed and illusory choice' and is, in fact, no more than 'the opportunity to choose what is acceptable to the paternalistic State' (2006: 68).

Summerhill does indeed offer a real alternative to state-governed, authoritarian education, but as it is a private school and beyond the reach of many, it is not a viable choice for a large proportion of those who would opt for a more progressive educational ideology.

Task 5.1   Stop, think and do

Research the Free School Movement of the 1960s and 1970s. Prepare a case study of any free school besides Summerhill School, for example, the White Lion School in England or Sudbury Valley School in the USA. Consider the history of the school, the approaches to teaching, learning and organisation at the school and critical comment on the school.

Illich and deschooling

In 1971, Ivan Illich (1926–2002) published the influential and prophetic book *Deschooling Society* ([1971] 2004). Illich saw education, not as a deficit model, but as a lifelong and community-based process: a process based on the sharing of knowledge and skills in which all have equal access to learning and teaching. He called for the disestablishment of schools as they existed and functioned then in society, believing that traditional, institutional transmission-based learning was no longer valid in the modern, technological age:

> Universal education through schooling is not feasible. It would be no more feasible if it were attempted by means of alternative institutions built on the style of present schools. Neither new attitudes of teachers toward their pupils nor the proliferation of educational hardware or software (in classroom or bedroom), nor finally the attempt to expand the pedagogue's responsibility until it engulfs his pupils' lifetimes will deliver universal education.
>
> (2004: vii)

He believed that in all countries education was the same, despite the ideology professed by any government. This was due to a global similarity in the hidden curriculum (see Chapters 8 and 12) in all education institutions. He felt this hidden curriculum instilled in all learners the capitalist, neo-liberal belief that increased production and consumption of things and services will lead to a better life and that it encouraged institutional dependence and acceptance of the social hierarchy.

In contrast to institutionalized learning, Illich advocated self-directed education for child and adult alike, in informal, community-based setting and with flexible and informal arrangements. Illich believed that if education was disestablished, it should not be state funded and should not be compulsory. Proposing a complete separation between state and education, he asserted that individuals should pay for learning themselves. If education was non-compulsory and privately paid for, he felt that it would be more authentic, there would be an improvement in its quality and there would be a reduction in discrimination against people for a perceived lack of education.

Illich stated that a good education system should have three goals: (1) to provide all who want to learn with access to resources at all times in their lives; (2) to allow those who want to share their knowledge and skills with a means of locating those who want to learn from them; and (3) to provide an arena where this exchange of learning could take place (2004: 75).

The alternative to institutionalized education which Illich suggested was in the form of four learning webs or networks. Resource services would store educational objects, such as books, tools or processes, in a variety of places. For example, libraries, museums or workshops, and allow learners to access them when required or arranged. He proposed a referencing service and a skills exchange of those wishing to provide learning which would give their contact details, expertise offered and availability for teaching purposes. Finally, he suggested a peer-matching communication network which would allow those wanting to learn to describe the learning activity they wished to undertake in order to hopefully find a partner who could provide the learning experience (2004: 77–104).

Illich's work can be seen as prophetic. Despite the fact that some of the technology to which he referred, for example, tape-recordings, may seen dated today, in the computer-based, website and internet age, the networks he proposed could be a real possibility and are in fact already being utilized to a certain degree in some areas of life, though these may not be educational.

A true alternative?

As illustrated above, there is limited choice offered by state-funded education in terms of ideology rather than school structures in the UK and in many other countries today. Furthermore, the type of education provided by the state in many societies, which is little more than a rehashing of a nineteenth-century model of transmission-based, teacher-centred learning, does not seem appropriate in the contemporary information-rich world and, as technology is advancing at such a rapid rate, it is hard to see how it will still be a viable option in the future.

An alternative which increasing numbers of parents in the UK, the USA and elsewhere are opting for is that of home-schooling. In home-schooling, families use the home as base for learning, utilizing a variety of information sources such as the media, the internet, and computer software. However, most home-schoolers also integrate community-based activities as contexts for learning, such as trips to libraries, to museums, to art galleries and into nature. Studies have shown that children who are home educated are often more stable and mature and more socially aware than those who experience only the restricted and limited learning context of the school (Meighan 1995).

Once again, however, as with choice available through private education, home schooling may not be an option for many parents who have to work themselves or feel they lack the skills to devise a home learning curriculum and programme.

Meighan and Siraj-Blatchford (2001: 409–15) describe the idea of flexischooling: 'a new blueprint for education derived from the notion that the conventional rigid model of schooling is no longer an adequate vehicle for the development of young people' (2003: 409). Flexischooling offers self-direction and choice to learners and parents by offering a variety of learning contexts: school, home and community; by utilizing traditional and cyber learning tools and through a catalogue curriculum which is based on natural learning. Meighan (2000) explains the concept of the curriculum in the proposed system of flexischooling. The curriculum is a printed or electronic catalogue of set courses, ideas for creating courses, self-instruction packages, instructions on how to set up learning co-operatives and lists of available learning resources and opportunities within the community. A natural curriculum is one based on learning activities and programmes which seek to answer a set of existential questions such as: Who am I? Who gets what? Where are we going? How am I doing? Who decides what? The natural curriculum and flexible learning methods would replace a state-imposed curriculum which is based on the questions, required answers and required assessment set by the government-controlled education system.

Task 5.2   Stop, think and do

Read Meighan and Siraj-Blatchford's (2001: 409–15) account of flexischooling. Consider whether you think it is a viable option for modern education – give reasons why or why not. How might this system combine with Illich's (1976: 80–98) learning networks to produce an education system for the present and the future?

Summary

1   Real choice in education involves choice between educational ideologies and not just between types of school structure.

2   In neo-liberal education policy based on market competition, there is little real choice in education.

3   In the UK and elsewhere, the concept of choice in education is an illusion. Many parents and pupils lack the appropriate capital to use the system to their advantage and cannot get a place at the school of their choice.

4   Only those who can afford to opt out of state education can really have a choice between different educational ideologies.

5   Traditional, transmission-based education is a deficit model as the educator is seen as possessing knowledge and skills and has to fill the deficit in these areas in the learner.

6   Paulo Freire's system of conscientization was an alternative education ideology which drew on the natural knowledge of learners and employed democratic principles to empower poor, illiterate, oppressed people.

7   The free school movement in the UK and elsewhere provides an alternative education ideology based on self-direction, but as in many cases it is fee-paying, it is not available to all within a society,

8   Ivan Illich offered an alternative to traditional education based on knowledge and skill sharing which could utilize modern cyber technology.

9   Many parents today are seeing home-schooling as a flexible and non-traditional, student-centred alternative to institutionalized schooling.

10   Flexischooling is an alternative educational ideology fitting modern society and future technology based on a catalogue curriculum and natural learning.

6 England Nul Points?

Introduction

In 2003, England finished in last place by failing to score any points in the Eurovision Song contest. It may seem rather perplexing to the reader for a chapter in a book on education to start with such a trivial fact. However, the impression that the independent bystander might gain regarding the standard and level of achievements in school education in the UK might fairly assume it is not only in the Eurovision Song context that this country is failing to score any points but also in education as well.

International comparisons in educational performance have become a key element in the driving of education policy-making. There is an increasing availability of data from the education systems of many nations, both in terms of the publication of national statistics and international testing programmes. This has intensified the atmosphere of international competition and borrowing between national education systems (Wiseman and Baker 2005). There is also a great deal of emphasis placed on each nation's relative position in contrast to their near economic rivals. Education policy is, in effect, increasingly being driven by international comparisons of national school outcomes as identified by a number of international league tables.

It must be pointed out that schools are not the only sector of education that are impacted on by international league tables, the reader has to only consult the *Times Higher Education Supplement* (THES) to see league tables for universities around the world in almost every aspect of their endeavours and, of course, there are also national league tables.

Various commentators, educational pundits, and politicians of every hue eagerly await the results of surveys almost in the same way that football fans watch the results coming in at the end of the football season. However, the commentators, to carry the analogy a bit further, are all Crystal Palace fans, like the author, and are doomed often to disappointment of one sort or another. Headlines such as 'UK pupils fall behind in science survey' (*Financial Times*, 30 November 2007), 'Another League Table Shock for British Education' (*PA Business*, 29 November 2007), 'Secondary school pupils slide down world table in reading and maths' (*Morning Star*, 4 December 2007) are just indicative of the responses to the release of the data. The response is not unique to England: 'Wales poor in global school league tables' (*The Western Mail*, 6 December 2007). Alongside the leagues tables there has developed a little industry within the media that contrasts the achievement of pupils today, for example, the

Times Education Supplement (TES) asked the question: could children of today pass the Victorian equivalent of a GCSE? (Brettingham 2008). Equally the UK television channel, Channel Four, has broadcast programmes that essentially compare the level of achievement of children today with an idealized version of grammar school pupils in the 1950s.

The surprise is that none of this is new; the comparison by politicians and commentators of education systems has been going on for a hundred years or more:

> When we look abroad at neighbour nations we find that though the French and Germans do not possess such a system of infant schools as our own, yet these and other continental nations vie with us and each other in drilling, training and influencing the young, that they multiply schools, and spend ever increasing amount of thought and treasure in building up national systems of education. Thus at home and abroad Government, Churches, Sects and Powers that Be, are determined to lay hands on the young and change them for better or worse!
>
> (McMillan 1904: 2)

The justification for this continuous comparison and league tables is the economic necessity of education excellence for both the individual and the national economy. The common-sense view current in government is that there is a direct link between education and the economy. This linkage between economic growth and education is portrayed as a key issue for today's educationalists and teachers and it all too frequently ends up as the ultimate justification for changes ranging from school organisation to the refocusing of the curriculum. Wolf (2002) argues that the truth of the issue is that, while education is a billion dollar industry and to be educated is extremely important for the individual, the links 'between education and growth are far less direct than politicians suppose' (2002: 15).

This chapter attempts to answer the question: why do politicians and other commentators on education policy often use the, supposedly superior, achievements of education systems of countries outside the UK to justify the need for reform and change within the English education system? The chapter will introduce the student to comparative education by an examination of the education systems of the UK's main industrial competitors. It will describe some aspects of the education systems of the USA, Japan and a number of European countries. The account of the various education systems will briefly examine a range of key issues, such as participation rates, educational selection, assessment and examination policies, and teaching strategies. At the same time the chapter will outline some of the evidence provided by the major studies used to compare international educational performance, for example, TIMSS, PISA, PIRLS, including reports from the OCED and UNICEF.

Factors and issues that impact on educational achievement such as poverty, gender inequality, ethnicity, and social class will also be explored, as much in terms of their impact on individuals as on the education system. In other words, the chapter will examine, 'who gets what within each education system' (see Chapter 9). The chapter will conclude with a discussion and summation that argues the real differences in educational performance are not to be found between educational systems, but within these systems.

What are international comparisons?

The simplest answer to the question above is that they are surveys that measure the achievement by children in a range of countries, which are then ranked according to the results. The logic is that the ranking will indicate the effectiveness of the various education systems that have taken part in the survey. Not all countries are included within the different surveys, as clearly the educational performance of industrialized Western nations should, as a matter of course, be superior to those nations characterized as developing nations. The simple reason for this is that the education systems of Western countries are more extensive and the vast amount of investment ploughed into them could not even be dreamt about in developing countries. What politicians who drive education policy in their respective countries are concerned with are the comparisons with their direct economic competitors. This is due to the fact that politicians, as suggested above, see education as a key factor in economic growth. It should be noted that education is important in the development of human capital resources within any given society as well as for the individual. However, the link between economic growth and education is not a simple casual relationship. Thus, the key surveys that are taken into account are usually clustered around the 30 or so industrialized nations within the Organisation of Economic Cooperation and Development (OECD). The OECD is an organisation that proclaims a commitment to democracy and the market – that is, to capitalism. The focus of the OECD is the collection of data on all aspects of society, for instance, education, the economy and social development across its members and up to one hundred other countries.

The most significant education surveys are directed at the 30 current members of the OECD. These surveys include Programme for International Student Assessment (PISA) – this is a survey of 15-year-olds in the principal industrialized nations. Other surveys include Trends in Mathematics and Science Study (TIMSS) and Progress in International Reading Literacy Study (PIRLS). The aim of all of these surveys, and hence the league tables, is that they provide a comparison for governments of their education system in terms of measurable levels of pupil attainment (Johnson 1999). There is, of course, other data generated as a result of the process undertaken during TIMMS and PIRLS that also provides important information. For example, relative pupil attainment to level of financial input, curriculum content, and subject provision (Johnson 1999). One possible interpretation of this mass of data is that it provides governments with a clear picture of the general effectiveness of their educational provision and, more specifically, the cost-effectiveness of their provision.

Some results – where do we stand?

If the pun in the title of this chapter was taken at face value, it would seem to suggest that the UK does very badly in terms of the various surveys. However, the reality is slightly different as, although the UK is not the best performing country in the international educational league, it is not about to be relegated to the second division. In many respects the UK performs just above average for both OECD and EU countries. Thus the UK is neither the best performer in terms of education nor, by any measure, the worst compared to other industrialized states.

It is these surveys among others that are used by the government and the media to describe the effectiveness of education within the UK. For the casual reader it would seem that if this is the case and the methodology employed is appropriate, then indeed schools are not doing well by the children of this country compared to our economic rivals. However, the reader needs to take care when rushing to such judgements, for as Baker and LeTendre ask: 'why is it that in all the TIMSS nations the educational background of parents has a large impact on school achievement even though school quality has been on the increase over the past three decades?' (2005: 8).

Before considering the relative position of the UK educational system compared to other states, it is worth examining the level of achievement in the UK's own terms. For while politicians use international data to frequently condemn or criticize the education provided by schools and colleges in the UK, they are also frequently extolling its virtues when the year-on-year exam results are published.

For the past 20 or more years, there has been a steady improvement in the formal levels of achievement by pupils at all levels within the UK. This means that the number of children achieving exam passes in assessments such as the General Certificate of Secondary Education (GCSE) and other formal tests have continued to improve year-on-year. For instance, in 2006/07, 62 per cent of 16-year-olds achieved five or more A*–C grades at GCSE or equivalent, this includes both mathematics and English (DCSF 2008). The same source indicates that 91.7 per cent of children at the end of Key Stage 4 achieved five or more passes at GCSE at A*–G grade or equivalent including mathematics and English. Equally, if the primary school results are examined, there has been a general improvement in the number of children reaching the government's declared targets. It is not being suggested here that everything is perfect within the education system within the UK; far from it, it is just that the issues are not as clear-cut and simple as many would have the reader believe. In fact, it should be noted that some researchers question the extent of the claimed improvement (Tymms 2004). Tymms (2004) recognizes that standards have risen, but suggests not as much as the official statistics would suggest.

In the most recent PISA survey of educational standards published in 2007, England came out just above the OECD average in science, for instance:

> The mean score for England was higher than the OECD average. This difference was statistically significant. ... England had the third highest proportion of students at the highest level of science attainment. Only New Zealand and Finland had a higher proportion at this level. (Bradshaw et al. 2007: vii)

Task 6.1   Stop, think and do

- How do you think commentators in the press respond to the publication of GCSE and A-level results each year?
- Use the internet or your library to research a range of different newspapers for their response to exam results at all levels of education in the UK over a number of years.
- Write a commentary giving an account of the way the results are portrayed by the media depending on the politics of the various media you have researched. What does this tell you about the way the exam results are used by politicians and educational commentators? Do you feel they fairly represent the GCSE and A-level results?

The main focus in 2006 for the PISA study was science, but the survey also examined mathematics and reading. Here again, England were performing just above the OECD average with 18 countries performing better than England and 26 with a lower outcome. What is also important in mathematics for England is that the spread of attainment was not as great in mathematics as it was in science (Bradshaw et al. 2007). In other words, the range of marks were closer together for mathematics as compared to science.

PISA also looks at reading, again as a minor focus compared to science for the year 2006. Again the mean score indicating reading ability was just above the OECD average with seven countries scoring significantly higher, 18 countries around the same level, and 30 countries below England's reading attainment (Bradshaw et al. 2007). What is also interesting in terms of the current concern over the boys' achievement is that the PISA survey of 2006 found 'females scored significantly higher than males in reading. This was the case in every participating country, but the gender gap was smaller in England than in most other countries' (Bradshaw et al. 2007: ix).

The results for the Scotland, Wales and Northern Ireland were also similar in science to England's. There was no statistical significance in the various part of the UK's performance from the PISA survey (Bradshaw et al. 2007). There were differences in mathematics:

> The mean score of students in England and Scotland was significantly higher that in Wales, and the mean score in Scotland was also significantly higher than the score in Northern Ireland. Males outperformed females in England, Wales and Scotland ... In Northern Ireland the mean score of males was higher than that of females but the difference was not statistically significant.

(2007: x).

What this suggests is that there is variation across the home countries in science, mathematics and reading, but the UK as a whole is neither the worst performer internationally nor the best. The UK has both strengths and weakness as compared with the other main industrial nations of the world. If one were to think of England as an individual student, one could suggest that it was of average ability, neither failing nor being spectacularly successful. This is clearly not the disaster that is portrayed by many commentators and England is actually scoring some points. Nul points it is not.

Task 6.2   Stop, think and do

- How do you think the UK education system compares to other industrial nations?
- Research a range of media including websites for the World Bank, OECD (Organisation for Economic Cooperation and Development) and other such international agencies.
- Write a short account of the relative strengths and weaknesses of the UK education system. Compare your analysis with that of leading educational commentators in the press and identify and any differences. Can you explain why you may have a different analysis from that of the media experts?

International comparisons – the difficulties

There is not the space here to engage in a detailed discussion on the methodology adopted by the various international studies on educational attainment. But the reader should be aware that there are a number of difficulties in any comparative study of educational systems. On the simplest level it is not always possible to compare like with like, the systems are different: there are different structures, curriculums, pedagogies, traditions and cultures. However, the various studies that compare the performance of students across countries are presented as if there are no difficulties in such comparisons. After all, with subjects such as mathematics there is a common-sense view that mathematics is the same the world over. Therefore, the argument would go that testing what children can do in the subject at various ages is not problematic.

Let us consider just two issues: age and curriculum content. First, if we examine age, we can see that the age profiles of different phases of education are not necessarily the same in each country taking part in any international comparison of standards. The age range of the children to be tested is often influenced by the mechanisms that each nation chooses to adopt for progression through the education system. In the UK, it is quite simply an issue of age, that is, as we grow older we automatically progress through the system. However, in other countries students have to demonstrate a certain level of academic proficiency before moving on to a new level of education. For instance, in the USA this results in some individuals never progressing beyond what is called junior high school, that is, they fail to graduate from high school. This notion or concept does not make any sense in the UK context, as Brown (1999) states:

In the United Kingdom (UK) or the Pacific Rim it hardly matters, since pupils are allocated to grade level (grade group) strictly by age, but in other European countries more than 25% of pupils are outside the grade-level as a result of being held back for examination failure.

The profile of the age group is, therefore, different in those countries where significant numbers of pupils are held back due to their inability to achieve the necessary level of academic proficiency. The keeping back of pupils from the next tier of education effectively reduces the spread of ability as one goes through the various age groups. Thus, countries that allow progression purely on age seem to have a greater spread of attainment than those countries that do not. If the mechanism for progression is not taken into account, it would seem that there is a greater degree of underperformance in some countries than others. Though the various surveys are aware of this, and do attempt to overcome such problems, the reader should be aware that it is necessary to look beyond the claims and investigate the methods adopted by any study that seeks to demonstrate winners and losers in the international league table of educational winners and losers.

A second issue that needs to be considered is the differences in curriculum content. In mathematics, for example, each country has a different emphasis on which aspects of mathematics is taught. The introduction of the National Numeracy Strategy (subsequently the Primary Strategy) and the Key Stage 3 Strategy has placed a high emphasis on numerical calculation in England. One would, therefore, assume that pupils in England may be able to perform better in numerical calculations than countries that did not place such an emphasis on calculation but instead stressed logic and algebra. To put it quite simply, the pupils taking part in the survey might not have been taught the same topics at the same time. The scheduling and structure of what is taught in any one nation-state will vary and hence pupil knowledge will vary from country to country. Again the supporters of such surveys will claim all this is taken into account, but it is necessary to consider that national differences do play a role in any attempt to compare the education systems of different nation-states.

In any discussion in the media regarding international comparisons of educational performance, there is rarely any cautionary remark made regarding the difficulties that these studies face in their attempts to capture the relative levels of achievement. Rather, the results of the surveys are unquestionably accepted both by the media and policy-makers as effective accounts of the status of national educational systems. This ready acceptance might suggest that there are other factors at play in educational policy that draw on the evidence provided by the ever growing number of international studies of educational performance. The various international league tables might be better thought of as a partial story just as the domestic league tables only give a limited picture as to the state of the education system or any one particular school. Any ranking in a league table that a school receives does not provide the background information or the context in which the school is operating. International league tables are in a very similar position. As indicated above, there are a number of factors that impact on performance which vary from nation to nation.

The question then arises – why have league tables? In short, just as the domestic leagues are part and parcel of a wider set of education policies, the same can be said of the international league tables. The context in which the increased international scrutiny of education systems is taking place is one of globalization which is informed by a set of ideas that require a restructuring of social policy and economic structures world-wide.

The globalization of education policy

There is a great deal of talk about globalization, but it is necessary to consider what it actually means both in terms of what it is and what processes it represents.

Ball indicates the impact that globalization has on education policy:

> [T]alk about globalisation – what it means, how it impacts on the nation-state – produces a set of imperatives for policy at the national level and a particular way of thinking about education and its contemporary problems and purposes. ... as a result of particular aspects of the process of globalisation, the nation-state is no longer adequate, on its own, as a space within which to think about policy. Policies are 'made' in response to globalisation and those responses are variously driven or influenced by their take-up of supranational agencies.

> (2008: 25).

Globalization is often characterized in the media as being about technology, better communications, the internet and cheap clothes. Globalization is in fact more of a process, a reshaping of the world in which we live and it is a contested process. Globalization is often presented as inevitable and unstoppable, and as taking only one particular form. The idea that underlies this version of globalization is neo-liberalism, which is, at heart, a set of theoretical ideas and socio-economic policies that has become the new orthodoxy in the Western industrialized world. For instance, none of the major political parties in the UK would disagree with the key ideas to be found in neo-liberal economic and social policy. Harvey defines neo-liberalism:

> Neo-liberalism is in the first instance a theory of political economic practices that proposes that human well-being can best be advanced by liberating individual entrepreneurial freedoms and skills within an institutional framework characterized by strong property rights, free markets, and free trade. The role of the state is to create and preserve an institutional framework appropriate to such practices.

> (2005: 2)

This translates into a range of key strategies or policies that most governments across the globe now adhere to, for instance, free trade, that is removing barriers to international trade and capitalist enterprise. Second, the belief that there should be a level playing field for companies of any nationality within national economies. This might sound rather irrelevant to education but it means companies such as Edison, an American corporation, are attempting to move into the education market in a range of activities. Trade rules and regulations are necessary to underpin free trade with a system of penalizing unfair trade practices (Rikowski 2001). This represents a major change within education and the control of education policy.

The process of opening up educational markets or rather education systems to international free trade is implemented on a number of levels. Though national governments decide their own education policies, they are also influenced by supranational agencies such as the EU (European Union), the OECD, UNESCO (United Nations Educational, Scientific and Cultural Organization) and the World Bank. However, all of these organizations operate on the basis of persuasion (Robertson et al. 2006). Jones et al. (2008) argue it is the process of attempting to harmonize the education policies and structures within the EU. The other major supranational agency that is an active player within education is the World Trade Organization (WTO) and, as Robertson et al. (2006) point out, it is an important organization as it: 'Works through binding rules, rather than persuasion or leverage; and it has the potential to affect education systems and practices across a greater range of activities than have any other supranational organisations'. The reason why the WTO has such power in terms of education is quite simple. This is because the WTO was set up to promote trade and economic liberalization through a set of multilateral agreements between the governments of the world. This agreement is called GATS (General Agreement on Trade in Services) and education is now considered to be a service industry. The decisions made by the WTO are legally binding on all member nations. A combination of leverage for agencies such as the EU (Jones et al. 2008) and the rules and regulations as laid down by the WTO (Rikowski 2001) have led to a change in the nature of the educational provision within the nation-states of the industrialized world.

What is remarkable is that when one looks at the policies developments of any number of nation-states, there are huge similarities between them, especially in the language used by governments to describe their policies, that is in their rhetoric and discourse. The next section of this chapter will examine a number of policy initiatives that have international significance.

No Child Left Behind

The policy of the Bush administration in the USA known as No Child Left Behind (NCLB) is the largest federal educational initiative in the history of the USA (Hursh in press). The NCLB policy has been designed to impact on every aspect of what we in the UK call primary education, known as elementary in the USA, along with the American secondary system. NCLB affects assessment procedures, curriculum and the requirement that secondary schools provide military recruiters with the names of pupils. The last item has a familiar ring to the New Labour Government's declared aim to create Army Cadet units in state secondary schools.

The important aspect of NCLB is that the testing requirements and outcomes have a direct impact on school funding. This link between school funding and test outcomes is part of what is referred to as teacher accountability. One might draw parallels with our own system of SATS and league tables that have an indirect impact on school funding. Moreover, as with the SATS in the UK, there are targets for the schools to meet, there are set minimum requirements for schools under the NCBL to achieve for their pupils (Hursh in press).

The remarkable aspect of this process of testing, targets and results is that the sort of school that is failing in the United States is not dissimilar to the schools that are having difficulties in the UK. It is those schools in the poor and working-class areas that are failing to meet the minimum test requirements. Even the strategy of dealing with the problem of failing schools has a familiar ring to it. In the UK, the strategy is one of special measures and if this does not work, then a process called Fresh Start is adopted. In reality, the school is closed and then opened up again under new management. An example from the USA is to be found in the Rochester, New Jersey, school system, where all middle schools failed to meet the necessary testing standards for their pupils. This led the superintendent (local manager of the school system) to reorganize the school system through amalgamation into a new structure thus creating a new school and avoiding the associated funding penalties for failure (Hursh in press). This may, in fact, just be a case of postponing the inevitable.

What is interesting is that the NCLB policy is presented as attempting to raise standards for all children and, more importantly, as a response to global competition.

The key element to NCLB is the assessment procedures and with that the high-stakes element – that is there is a great deal at stake both for individuals and schools for failure. The justification for this approach to education is the need for competition in response to globalization:

> NCLB is an important way to make sure America remains competitive in the 21 century. We're living in a global world. See, the education system must compete with education systems in China and India. If we fail to give our students the skills necessary to compete in the world in the 21 century, the jobs will go elsewhere.

> (U.S. Department of Education 2006)

While there is a much discussion about the challenges of the twenty-first century and competition from around the world, the biggest issue facing the American education system is the educational divide between the rich and the poor (Sacks 2007). NCLB is not addressing this issue other than by high-stakes testing that schools, as in the Rochester example, attempt to circumvent in one way or another because they simply cannot address the social and economic issues that their communities face.

This process of high-stakes testing and a stress on competition is key to the attempt by those policy-makers who are committed to the development of educational markets (Johnson and Salle 2004). This process cannot only be seen in the UK (see Chapter 4), but also in many other countries. An example of this is to be found in New Zealand. Thrupp (1998) highlights the comparison between New Zealand and the UK, pointing out that:

> both countries have gone further and faster than most to introduce neo-liberal approaches to the marketisation of education ... there are few places where reform has preceded with such similarity of pace, rhetoric and policy

patterns ... One area where considerable parallels can be seen between the two settings is their approaches to school accountability.

Accountability is only part of the process of changing the nature of education provision. Another element is the involvement of the private sector on a far greater scale than previously existed. In the UK, this has seen private companies move into areas such as running local education authorities, providing the backbone of the school inspection system and playing a key role in the New Labour Government's Academy programme. In the United States there is a similar type of school – the Charter school.

Charter schools and other form of school privatization

As with the Academy and Trust schools in the UK, the justification for the Charter school in the USA is to challenge the supposed uniformity of the state system (Sarason 1998), that is, to provide diversity and parental choice. The notions of choice and diversity are key to a market approach to education. Rhetorical flourishes concerning such notions are used to justify a change in policy direction in terms of the nature of school provision.

There are a great many similarities in educational discourse between the UK and the USA regarding Academies and the Charter school movement. A Charter school: 'would be one created by some combination of educators, parents and others in the community, a school for which the founding group would have full responsibility for its governance, organization and purposes' (Sarason 1998: 51).

However attractive this idea may be, the reality is frequently very different. A number of different issues, such as the lack of diversity in the school body, come to the fore (Sarason 1998). This effectively means that schools are based on various forms of segregation. Another issue that the Charter schools have raised is the change in pay and conditions for teachers. This is not dissimilar to changes that have taken place in the UK Academies. Furthermore, there is concern regarding control over the curriculum by different interest groups who run the schools. This is especially important in terms of faith schools and the teaching of creation-based approach to evolution (Sarason 1998). Moreover, the Charter school movement is draining resources from the main school provision in a number of American states. All this is done in the name of choice and diversity, but in reality it is an attempt to create a market system in education with the state playing the role of facilitator rather than provider.

Another example of the marketization of the American education system is the development of the Edison schools. The Edison schools were state schools which were run and managed by the Edison Corporation on behalf of American state authorities. Edison was the largest private company that ran schools for the public education system in the USA. The extent and size of the company were truly impressive: 'claimed to be running schools for 132,000 US public school students in 20 states and as of 2001–2002 school year, it ran 136 public schools in 23 states' (Saltman 2005: 2). The aims of the Edison schools were to offer quality educational services, to operate schools for less money and to provide more services than traditional public, that is state, schools (Saltman 2005: 13). The justification for these schools has been value for money and, of course, the poor performance of American schools in the international league tables such as PISA. However, the evidence of American students' poor performance is limited:

> Despite being regularly maligned in the press, US public schools, when compared with public schools in other industrialized nations, fare well. Comparisons between US public schools and the schools of other industrialized nations reveal US students to be comparably educated to students of other industrialized nations. In 2000, no difference was detected between the mean scores of US 15-year-olds on the PISA reading literacy scale and the mean scores of 15-year-olds in France, Italy, Japan, and the United Kingdom.
>
> (Saltman 2005: 8)

There are some commonalities with this description and the situation within the UK. The media and educational pundits regularly malign state schools, and this is used to justify major structural changes to the system that brings private capital into the system. Despite the global justification of the quasi-privatization of the state school sector, the issue of the underachievement of the poorest in society is not really being dealt with. The Sutton Trust, a right-wing educational body that promotes private education for the poor, has found that still only 3 per cent of children who received free school dinners achieve three good A-levels – the benchmark for getting into one of the elite universities in the UK.

At face value, one may question the nature of such quasi-privatized educational provision and the extent to which it reduces democratic accountability in a system in which everyone becomes a customer. However, fundamentally there are two issues to be explored here: the justification for the privatization of the school system and whether such a system can, in real terms, meet the needs of the students. As Saltman (2005) points out, the Edison system collapsed. It could be suggested that they did not meet the grounds on which they were justified and that the privatization of the school system in terms of the international league tables is not based on the evidence of the various surveys. This not to say there are not problems in the American or British education system, but the idea that the grass is always greener elsewhere is not true. In terms of success, the mere privatization of the state school system does not address the issues of poverty and all the associated problems that children and families face.

Conclusion

The chapter has attempted to show that a form of globalization that advocates neo-liberal social and economic policies is increasingly dominating national education policy. The adoption of these neo-liberal education policies is the reality in the

UK as well as other countries across the industrialized world. Though most of the examples have been taken from the USA, similar examples can be found in many other countries.

Task 6.3 Stop, think and do

- What are the education policies of countries such as Japan, Australia and Germany? Do these countries really have policies that are in line with those outlined in this chapter?
- Go to the various government websites and download as many useful policy documents as you can.
- Carry out an analysis of the documents and identify both similarities and differences. What conclusions do you come to? Write a short account of your analysis.

The key issues that face all the education systems in the industrial world include notions of accountability through high-stake testing regimes justified on the grounds that parents need to know the progress their children are making and the idea that testing provides a system that will meet the needs of an increasingly competitive world.

Other issues include the restructuring of education systems to allow greater participation of private enterprise and this includes mainstream school provision rather than the servicing of schools and colleges. This is coupled internationally with an increased notion of competition within the systems and with associated inspection regimes and league tables of results to enforce the feeling of competition.

All these policy developments are being generated by the neo-liberal orthodoxy that holds sway in national governments as well as the supranational agencies such as the OECD and the EU with the big stick of enforcement of competition rules being wielded by the WTO. The significance of this is that there is a slow transformation of education away from public provision to a free market capitalist-driven system. This of course does not necessarily meet the needs of all pupils, although this is often cited as the reason for these reforms. As indicated by Sack (2007), the divide between the rich and the poor is just as great, if not greater, than before the reforms were introduced.

This chapter has provided one interpretation of the changes to the education systems of the Western world; however, it is for the reader to research and think about the issues before coming to their own conclusions. It is suggested that exploring the policy initiatives and documents, freely available on government websites, would give the reader an insight into the processes taking place and the similarities both in rhetoric and practice. It should be noted that these changes are not being accepted by everyone; one only needs to consider the demonstrations by teachers and students in France against the proposed reforms by the right-wing Sarkozy government and the opposition to changes in the university system by Greek students to see that it is a contested process.

Summary

1. In the Western world, education systems are compared according to international league tables.
2. The UK media frequently reports the fact that the education system is failing compared to that of other industrialized states.
3. Global statistics and league tables do not compare like with like and are often misinterpreted.
4. In real terms, the UK is not necessarily failing, though increases in achievement may be exaggerated by the government.
5. Governments justify global comparisons and international league tables on the grounds of economic competition.
6. International competition may be a means for governments to introduce neo-liberal educational policies through the quasi-privatization of the system and thus reduce their own accountability.
7. Scrutiny of education policies across the industrialized world reveals similar rhetoric and discourse to justify privatization of education under the guise of diversity and choice.
8. The American Charter school movement is strikingly similar to Trust schools and Academies in the UK.
9. Case studies have shown that these schools have repeatedly failed to meet the needs of many students, particularly in disadvantaged socio-economic areas.

Part 3

Society and the Individual

7   How People Learn

This chapter is presented as a challenge to the segmented paradigm that often occurs with a consideration of how people learn. Unlike the majority of textbooks which present a consideration of learning theories with a narrow focus on childhood development, this chapter aims to look at learning across the lifespan. In addition, it is argued that any consideration of how people learn needs a systemic approach to focus on individual differences effectively. To do this, the chapter will provide an overview of a selection of relevant learning theories presented as a broadening conceptual sphere, from the individual learner to the world context for all learners.

Task 7.1 Stop, think and do

- How do you view learning? – An increasing collection of facts? The development of understanding? Do you have a different definition?
- Is learning about the construction of knowledge for the individual, or does learning occur because we interact with others?
- Are some of us genetically predetermined to learn better than others, or does high quality learning depend on the school you attend, your economic status, or your culture?
- Do some people have greater motivation to learn than others? Can your desire to learn be stalled?
- Does learning stop when you leave school?

These are all valid questions you should ask yourself before focusing on the associated field of study. Your view of how people learn is the bedrock for evaluating the theories of others. The aim of the chapter is to consider not only *your* view on how *you* learn, but the factors impacting on how other people may learn, and the wider context of learning for all people.

Introduction

Learning theories are often limited to a consideration of childhood in isolation, without an effective link to how learning continues throughout the lifespan. This is no longer feasible as there is now a changing emphasis within Education Studies. It is important to note that the recent context shift of societal needs due to economic changes and pressures, how we live, how we work, and how society deals with these, has had a momentous effect on society's expectation of the role of education. Following key debates and papers in the 1990s, including the European Commission published White Paper in 1994, education is no longer seen as just an early preparation for life. Schools, universities and workplaces now take account of lifelong learning, that is skill development, ongoing qualification attainment and renewal, and are endeavouring to amend their positions to accommodate this. As lifespan consideration is now a guiding principle, our consideration of how we learn should also encompass this.

With lifespan cohesion in mind, we will first consider learning as an individual position.

Learning in the individual

One assumption of learning is that it is a cognitive or brain-based process. Functional magnetic resonance imaging (fMRI) studies can be conducted to explore neuropsychological processes relating to the structure and function of the brain to further our understanding of the mechanisms of learning. By mapping and matching which brain areas are being utilized for different cognitive functions, we can develop our understanding of things such as working memory, reading and arithmetic (Dowker 2006). This is a useful modern insight into how we learn, but care should be taken over the credence of brain mapping. What is being measured is brain signals or neurones firing when we perform an action or cognition which only indicate a correlation between the brain area implicated with the action or cognition. Our use of this type of information should be considered cautiously without assuming there is certain causation.

Prior to advanced scanning technology, theorists hypothesized about cognition based on the observations made of individuals. From these observations, the predominant theories associated with learning that emerged were 'cognitivist' (personal and internal) and 'behavioural' (a response to external stimulus). These two approaches contrast mainly at the level of control that the individual is attributed in the learning process. With the cognitive position, the individual is seen as active in their learning, being the engine driver of knowledge construction, whereas with the behaviourist position, the individual has a passive role, being manipulated by the factors external to the self.

The most influential cognitivist theorist was Jean Piaget (1896–1980), whose ideas have been a major influence on educational practice around the world. The premise of his view is that our learning is 'maturational', in that we have innate characteristics that unfurl over time and in 'linear' or ordered sequence in one direction. His hierarchical theory outlined four stages: sensorimotor, pre-operational, concrete operational and formal operational, for the development of thinking from birth to maturity. These are described by Child as:

> the gradual unfolding of thinking skills, starting with simple sensory and
> motor activities in babyhood and gradually being superseded by internal

representations of actions carried out by the child; then, through the agency of language, reaching the highest form of logical thinking, at first in the presence of objective evidence and finally by mental reasoning.

(2007: 90)

Piaget believed that by approximately 11 years of age there is achievement of abstract and systematic thought. This final stage was characterized by being able to take learning beyond the acquisition of facts to a new level, where the learner can use the higher skills of seeing the perspectives of others and intuitive feeling to construct real understanding. Piaget implied that by the last stage we are provided with 'tools' for adult understanding. However, alongside this is the assumption that as we reach adulthood, our learning journey stabilizes; that there are no new skills to be learned and that our adulthood experiences simply 'puts meat on the bones'. Piaget, perhaps, did not fully recognize that on reaching maturity we may undertake higher education study or other activities requiring prolonged or sustained learning whereby we reach deeper levels of cognition and understanding beyond his formal operational stage. In practice, as mature adults, we recognize that we are able to look at the world with changing and potentially improving insight, with ongoing cognitive development occurring as the post-childhood decades of our life pass. It could be argued that Piaget is typical of other developmental theorists, in that too narrow a focus is presented. Childhood is just the preliminary phase of learning development.

Conversely, another of Piaget's basic beliefs has better application to lifelong learning. This is his view that learning is an active process whereby we develop our concepts by 'doing'. This process of seeking to find answers has been termed discovery learning in education. To gain an understanding of discovery learning, you only need to observe children in free play or generally self-motivated activity. Everyday examples of this may be the child who is given an activity toy without instructions or guidance, or the toddler who wants a toy that is out of reach and explores ways to reach it. Children's play in the early years is characterized by first-hand exploration, and it is by physically interacting with the world that they gain knowledge and understanding that is meaningful (Bruce 2001). Discovery learning continues when the child begins school, in particular within the area of science teaching and learning in schools (Klahr 2000). It should also be noted that discovery learning was a main feature of the Plowden Report (DES 1967) regarding primary education.

Discovery learning does not stop at adulthood. Although the experiences we have and store over time provide a framework for our daily activities, the process of discovery needs to be ongoing throughout life as novel situations still do require us to plan, do and then review our actions. The difference over time is that the process of discovery can be superseded by a second form of learning as we get older. This second form of understanding is usually termed consolidation in that the learning role will change from apprenticeship to mastering what we discover (Gopnik 2005).

Aligned to discovery learning is problem-based learning which is in contrast to the idea that learning is all about being systematically exposed to facts and information. This approach to learning suggests that we learn better if we have a question to answer and we are challenged to solve a mystery. This process is at its most effective when the question posed is relevant to our personal construct (Kelly 1955) and tagged to our own experience. Thus, meaning connections are made and from this we develop a deeper understanding of concepts rather than collecting facts at a surface level of understanding (Marton and Saljo 1976). However, there is the possibility that experiential learning can also turn into mis-educative experiences (Dewey 1938), for example, consider a young boy's fascination with matches and fire!

Jerome Bruner (1915–) suggested that people learn better if they make their own sense of things and that this occurs when people continally build on previous experiences and concepts over time. Bruner (1960) illustrated this idea by using the term spiral curriculum. The spiral curriculum was a visual image to represent his idea that learners actively construct their own knowledge based upon experiences in the past being joined by new experiences. This constructing of knowledge by adapting and building on past experience in the light of new learning ultimately leads to broader, deeper, richer understanding. Bruner recognized that you can be fully engaged in a current learning experience but you can only take from it your measure, that is, what your existing level of expertise and experience allows you to appreciate. You may return to the *same* ideas later, when you will *understand it more fully*. In other words, Bruner (1960) asserted that effective learning can only occur by revisiting and merging prior understanding with new understanding.

Bruner also believed that thought is language-based and that to learn we need to attach the new information to something which is already part of our personal narrative. Our personal narrative is conscious thought that runs parallel to our learning and is part of a personal construct. Learning occurs when new knowledge is accepted as linking to what we know already. It is this constructive element in learning, the building onto our personal narratives, the linking of new information to conscious thought and personal representations that can focus our attention for longer and, therefore, make learning effective.

An important part of being an individual is that we have the ability to be introspective with our learning, that we have conscious *within-self* thoughts. The ability to reflect allows us to continually pin new knowledge to our personal constructs. It would follow that the older we are, the greater our personal construct is, and thus our learning could be said to be more effective. This is one argument in support of an emergent learning development focus right through the lifespan rather than a model that hits a plateau at maturity and is followed by a later life cognitive decline – in other words, the old dog not only can learn new tricks but also have an intensified understanding of them too!

Other theorists, for example, Skinner, Pavlov, Watson, have taken a behaviourist approach, suggesting that our learning expands from the self and is actually in response to the environment. As discussed earlier, behaviourism is a passive outlook on learning. In general terms, behaviourism is the hypothesis that it is a stimulus occurring outside of the individual, plus a response by an individual that leads to learning. For example, there is a huge puddle following heavy rainfall (stimulus) and the individual steps in it (response by an individual), the consequence would be an unpleasant sensation of soaking wet shoes and socks (negative reinforcer) and the learning would be not to step in puddles in future, but rather to step over or walk around them. In this approach our learning is reduced to the basic component idea that we avoid negative or unpleasant experiences, but repeat positive, pleasurable experiences. The criticism often presented for viewing learning in this way is that this is too simplistic and mechanistic a view of humanity (Pinker 2002). Behaviourism does not recognize the cognitions we have or the conscious or creative choices that we make based on our feelings, personal priorities, attachments and social influences. It perceives learning as extrinsically or externally motivated rewards and punishments without due consideration of the intrinsic or internal drive to learn. Intrinsic motivation is linked to the idea of self-efficacy, or the value placed on one's own view of one's ability (Bandura 1977). The individual with higher self-efficacy will tend to put in more effort to their learning and persist longer in learning activities, than those with lower self-efficacy (Schunk 1990). As such, self-efficacy must be a factor that is given due attention for learning across the lifespan.

Another individualized aspect of learning is the belief that humans have an innate cognitive ability or intelligence. It was Galton (1874) who first argued that individuals have a cognitive aptitude for learning that can be measured as an intelligence quotient (IQ), a single score assigned to individuals. The dispute over IQ centres around the idea that intelligence could be a fixed entity that is passed down though genetic bloodlines and thus would remain stable across an individual's lifespan. However, in contrast, it has been argued that IQ is dependent on life chances and choices, and that it is possible that IQ can improve or decline over time. The evidence for this is presented by case study investigations of enrichment or deprivation where observable changes to IQ have been reported. Enrichment involves the provision of a deliberately enhanced cognitively simulating environment whereas deprivation involves reduced cognitively stimulating environments.

An argument against the use of IQ tests is that they were constructed by a small number of people of similar backgrounds and cultural identities implying that the generalizability, or the potential for application to all individuals, is highly questionable. In addition, performance on IQ tests has been linked to socio-economic status and other family circumstances such as family size and cultural background/race and thus has courted controversy that there was a judgemental and discriminatory agenda attached to them (Murdoch 2007). Moreover, the tests, in spite of being termed general intelligence tests, actually focus on discrete abilities for memory-based spatial/linguistic abilities only. IQ measurements do not include other important individual characteristics valued by society, such as emotional intelligence (Goleman 1995), that is, being socially aware and responsive to your emotional needs and the needs of others, or multiple intelligences, such as musical, body-kinesthetic, intrapersonal, interpersonal as suggested by Gardner (1983).

Despite these objections, IQ scores are still being measured and compared, for example, by the MENSA organization which is a 'higher intelligence' community and by educational psychologists. An individual can be ranked and evaluated in society by placing their score in an IQ test alongside the population mean or average score. From the population mean there is a normal range calculated which includes a margin above and below the mean score. Those above or below the cut-off point are identified as having abnormal intelligence. Those people with abnormally low IQ scores may have their life choices limited, for example, by being offered a limited choice of schools or careers, yet those people with abnormally high IQ scores may have their life choices enhanced through elitism. Thus an IQ measurement can dictate future learning experiences and a self-perpetuating cycle may begin. It could be argued that the issue of intelligence is a clear example of how learning needs to be considered across the lifespan.

Further controversy relating to learning centres around the suggestion that there is a gender effect to learning. Gurian and Ballew (2003) described inherent differences between male and female brains and Glazer (2005) reported intrinsic aptitude differences due to gender for maths and science. The idea of a difference in learning approaches between males and females was explored by Baron-Cohen (2003) from which two cognitive styles were suggested: empathizing and systemizing. Males and females both took part in self-report measures and from the data gathered it was proposed that males were more focused on problem-solving whereas females prioritised social understanding, and that it was this that led to a variation in learning. This indicates that gender differences for learning are not to do with more or less efficient cognitive function and capacity, but are due to different priorities and motivations for learning which are gender-specific. It should be noted that reported gender differences for learning may not be due to innate factors, but are due to socio-cultural attitudes and resultant discrimination and barriers to learning experienced by the different genders.

Another mechanism has been proposed as being vital to effective individual learning. This is referred to as metacognition and is defined by Bartlett and Burton (2007: 128) as 'the process of coming to know more about one's own learning strategies'. Metacognitive awareness is a deeper form of reflection where there is not only an engagement in learning but a secondary perspective of one's own learning process. This self-awareness not only considers the individual's own learning, but places it in the context of the learning of others. For example, the individual considers, 'If I can do this, I could do this … but maybe I should do that.' Metacognition can be thought of as the use of an internalized mentor who analyses and appreciates how the self is approaching learner tasks, asks the self 'Why' questions and directs the self to more effective strategies observed in others. It has been suggested that those people who are able to employ such an internal mentor learn better than those with a more passive approach to learning.

Task 7.2 Stop, think and do

- Do you feel that your learning has reached a plateau as you have reached adulthood? Piaget's stage model for cognitive development ends at the Formal Operational stage and the end of childhood – do you feel that your learning will get better or worse from this point?
- Would you say that your learning development thus far has been linear, or do you revisit concepts, as suggested by Bruner?
- Do you feel that your aptitude for learning is innate, as suggested by 'measured intelligence', or do you see your capacity to learn as influenced by either the environment or your motivation for a specific task?

This section has presented an overview of some of the issues associated with learning for the individual. However, it is the specific aim of this chapter to broaden consideration of learning from the individual viewpoint, to consider learning that occurs as a result of humans existing in a social world. This is because our learning, although individual and often feeling like a private journey, does not take place in a vacuum. We learn in interaction with one another. We may be 'little scientists', as proponents of Piaget suggest, but the *context* of learning does, in most cases, involve others. For this reason, the next conceptual layer discussed is the learning that occurs with another person.

Learning with another

The premise of the work of Lev Vygotsky (1896–1934) was that learning is socially constructed and that it is the experiences that we have with others that provide an intellectual scaffold. Within this socio-cultural and social constructivist theory of learning, the term teacher is used in the context of a person supporting another in their learning rather than a professional role as an experienced other. The role of the teacher is to recognize where the learner's zone of proximal development (ZPD) lies. The ZPD is the gap between the learner's current understanding/ability and where targeted support should be. The teacher poses questions and provides activities within the hypothetical zone, which are neither oversimplified, and, therefore, having no cognitive challenge, nor so taxing that the learner is unable to make appropriate cognitive connections. It should be noted that the teacher can be a peer with a better understanding of the concept, a slightly older child at the ZPD level or even a computer-assisted learning programme. However, there is some debate about whether a computer can be included in the definition of an expert other which centres on comparisons of computer versus a conscious entity (Turing 1950; Penrose 1989).

A further advantage of the scaffolding of learning is that motivation is enhanced by inspiration from someone acting at the learner's potential level. In other words, there could be an assimilation of enthusiasm and focus for learning plus recognition of the possible outcome of the learning observed in another person. However, it could also be argued that there are potential negatives of learning with another. There is the possibility of poor or inconsistent support that is not targeted to the person's ZPD, or, even with effective pitching within the ZPD, the learner could become reliant on another person and unable to maintain or generalize learning when the intellectual scaffold is removed.

A common misconception associated with the notion of learning occurring with another is that learning is a simple process of transferring knowledge from one person to another. This is a simplistic and limiting view of learning that has one person as advisor and one as a recipient, and it does not take into account the two-way flow of interaction characterized by the dialogue that accompanies the interaction. This transmission view of learning suggests that the learner is engaged in the uptake of knowledge and, although there may be a conversation and an appreciation of the information provided by the learner through feedback, it fails to acknowledge the extra ingredient of effective learning.

The notion of mentoring recognizes this extra ingredient of learning with another. Mentoring is derived from the theoretical underpinnings of Vygotsky's ZPD where there is an element of knowledge transfer, but the value of mentoring is that both people involved take positive features from the interaction for themselves. It could be argued that the effectiveness of this type of learning is due to the fact that the interaction is satisfying some emotional need as well as supporting a cognitive process, which makes the learning both rewarding and meaningful with a positive impact on self-efficacy.

Task 7.3 Stop, think and do

If a computer programme is able to pitch questions, instructions and activities within the ZPD of a learner based on the ongoing responses from that person, would you accept computers as an alternative of Vygotsky's 'expert other'?

Think of a time when you had an interesting conversation where you learned something new.

- Was this a one-way flow of information, or did you respond to the other person?
- Do you think the other person modified what they were saying based on your responses?
- How did you feel during the conversation – a passive recipient of information or as an equal member of a conversation that happened to reveal new information?

Learning in relation to a group

Learning within a group has many dynamics that individual learning does not. Group dynamics take into account not only the individual attributes, personality and level of sociability, but the relationships between each group member in interaction with each other as well as the group relationship of everyone combined. As discussed earlier, we rarely learn in isolation. More often we are part of a group when we are learning.

Some of the benefits of group learning are sharing ideas and the capacity to solve problems that may elude the individual. However, effective learning may be stalled in a group situation where the relationship within the group is operating negatively or working against a common goal. Group interaction in such circumstances is often characterized by irrelevant discussions or disengagement. In such cases what tends to be missing is a contract of respect that underpins collaborative learning and acknowledges that personal value is equal, regardless of individual variation in current skill, knowledge or even contribution. Personal issues need to be segregated from the real focus or goal of the learning activity and put aside for the mutual benefit of all group members. The contract, whether written or spoken, formal or informal, should allocate roles prior to the group working together. Moreover, it should outline the unified focus for the group in achieving a learning goal so that all group members having a reasonable level of intrinsic motivation is necessary. The value of the learning goal should be recognized by all group members through communication.

The fundamental difference between individual learning and group learning is agreed learning outcomes (Dörnyei and Murphey 2003). Being made aware of and agreeing to the learning outcomes through negotiation within a group can also develop metacognitive skills in the individual. From this, it can be seen that the process of working within a group can be as valuable as the content of the learning activities with regard to effective learning. This is akin to Vygotsky's perspective that learning actually depends on an interaction with people in addition to the tools, such as language, experience, that social contexts provide.

A DfES publication called the *Primary Strategy Learning Networks* published in 2004 (DfES 2004d) recognised the potential for extending learning for groups of learners by encouraging groups to join together to form a learning alliance. For example, similar schools in the local environment or higher education institutions delivering similar courses may form a learning alliance. The practical application in education was clustering or learning networks developed between similar learning contexts to share current understanding and good practice. The aim was then to extend the learning and attainment of the group by working within the ZPD/mentoring for the group rather than the individual. Although the coming together of the groups may be a one-off collaborative experience, it was envisaged that sustained relationships would develop partnerships and permanent learning networks. However, despite the potential benefits of group clustering in terms of effective learning, the practical difficulty that goes with partnership formation must be noted. Learning networks or clusters can be time-consuming to form and take time, knowledge, interpersonal skills and resources to sustain (Bailis 2004).

Task 7.4   Stop, think and do

You should have some experience of group work from your previous or current studies.

- Do you believe that you were a productive member of that group on the task set?
- Do you learn better as part of a team?
- Did you relate equally well to each member of the team?
- Was there a group contract prior to beginning the group task – written, spoken or an informal 'non-verbal agreement' (an understanding)?

Learning in a society

Being social beings, people tend to cluster together as a collective with shared values, exchange of viewpoints and interpretation of a common situation among a learning community. This is where a larger group will work together as a society, not only sharing knowledge and understanding, but operating with the same set of judgements and values. Thus, within each society, there will be requirements based on the sole purpose of keeping the societal cohesion which can dictate what the people in that society are expected to learn or conform to.

Learning occurs from being part of a community through observation. People learn through observing others' behaviour and attitudes and the outcomes of those behaviours. Social learning theory regarded learning as occurring in a social context through imitation and modelling (Bandura 1963). Being part of a large community will provide more learning opportunities, but on the downside there is a wide variety of models to observe, both positive and negative. To account for this, continual reference should be made to the wider agreed code to refocus individuals on the most appropriate models so that their learning and behaviour are constructive and productive for the needs of the community.

It is the nature of culture that people who live within a society are judged by how they perform and achieve on the standards set for that particular society. Over time, there is a subtle evolution of expectations as the culture evolves. As a result, each subsequent generation born have the content of their learning modified in light of the shift in demand. This is termed modified cognition. Therefore, the knowledge, skills and attributes become prioritized and valued as a circumstantial factor, and will depend on the cultural context. In other words, learning is not just an individualized set of cognitive factors but highly embedded within the culture that the person lives in (Edwards and Harrison 2002).

Part of being an individual who is included within a society is an acknowledgement that there are roles for everyone. This requires a consideration of individual characteristics and a self-evaluation of how we might meet the needs of society at our individual level. Consequently, our learning is mediated not only by our intrinsic interest but by the expectations placed upon us by our parents, peers, teachers, and community. Our learning experiences are subsequently tailored to meet societal expectations. An illustration of this is the concept of work-based learning being recommended and incorporated into educational settings within the UK (Dearing 1997) as part of a national agenda. As well as learning being individualized, we must also incorporate society's needs in order for our place as a valued member of society to be assured.

Task 7.5 Stop, think and do

Think about the content of your current studies. Is it based on what is pertinent to your individual learner needs, or can you identify some elements that are included for your future role as an effective member of society?

World learning

World learning can be interpreted as the hands-on experience in real settings that is associated with the term work-based learning. However, this does not give support to a more valuable learning context, that is, the recognition of and the concentration on the wider world issues such as the global needs and economy. It is suggested that our consideration of learning should not be about the learning needs of the individual within their world (Mezirow 1997), where there is an egocentric viewpoint of self in the world. This idea needs to be set aside and, instead, world learning beyond the self to the higher tiers should be considered (Boyd and Myers 1988) as a transformative process for a collective consciousness (Bernstein 1992). This means that all people should be invited to unite their learning for the common need at a global level in order to provide the basics such as food, water, shelter, access to education, health and social services, as well as to work against the threats to these basics, such as extreme weather and climate, maladaptive large group behaviour and aggression.

In order for world learning to be possible, a medium is needed. The internet (World Wide Web) is our connectivity but, again, there are positive and negative factors associated with this. The wealth of information can aid world learning significantly but we also need to recognize that the internet, at times, lacks authenticity and accuracy of information for learning. Misinformation and deception in particular will hinder world learning and cause great damage to learning constructs. Trust is a key human attribute, and it is unfortunate when we are not able to place it in others; however, there is a need to exercise caution as effective world learning will always be accompanied by a shadow of ossification which can block or distort information and trust.

Task 7.6 Stop, think and do

Consider a recent issue where the world has come together, for example, a news bulletin for a missing child, a summit for climate change, a documentary about an individual country struggling with war or environmental disaster.

- What is the effect on you, the individual?
- How much input is possible from those individuals or cultures not directly linked to the context of the issue?
- Is there an impact across the globe when one issue emerges?
- Do you agree that there may be a 'collective consciousness' and that it can lead to transformative learning across the world?

Some of the most pertinent learning comes from studying the past. World lessons may reverberate down through the tiers to the individual to teach us how to avoid or address similar issues that have previously occurred in history.

Conclusion

This chapter has presented a consideration of how people learn that integrates the tiers of the learning in the broader context of the learner's life, with other people and for the wider global issues. It has provided an overview of some of the more pertinent ideas concerning how we learn, presented in a tiered progression from individual through to world learning factors. Each section of the chapter has looked at how people sometimes do not learn effectively, and unpicked some of the factors and influences that contribute to this.

The chapter has looked beyond the reduction of learning to a consideration of individual developmental factors. As indicated at the start of the chapter, this is not just a text about child development. People do learn, not just in childhood, but throughout the lifespan and are being actively encouraged to do so due to the current social and global context, predominantly the need for people to change the content of their work more often than in the past. Within the current global working and learning climate, it is the transferable knowledge and skills that people need to learn are required, and more educational settings are looking at developing this. However, perhaps, the biggest gains for the advancement of human knowledge and learning could be achieved by encouraging the individual to start looking beyond the self to the combined learning need across the globe.

Summary

1   The European Commission published a White Paper in 1994 that asked those involved in education to now consider how learning continues throughout the lifespan. Any consideration of how we learn should try to encompass this.

2   Jean Piaget has been a major influence on our understanding of how people learn, but his theory assumed we reach a level of maturity by the end of childhood.

3   Jerome Bruner suggested we revisit learning experiences, building our understanding over time which is linked to our own personal construct.

4   Although discovery learning is a key feature of childhood, we continue to engage in it in adulthood. We simply tag new knowledge to our ongoing personal construct to achieve deeper levels of understanding as we get older.

5   Lev Vygotsky's idea of a zone of proximal development (ZPD) has provided us with a framework for learning with another person. The other person can be a 'teacher' who encourages effective learning with targeted support, or a mentor where there is a mutual beneficial effect for both the learner and mentor when learning experiences occur within the ZPD.

6   *Primary Strategy Learning Networks* (DfES 2004d) called for groups to collaborate within education to further their understanding.

7   Group working can help solve problems that elude the individual, and learning networks share the learning benefits within a wider context.

8   The dynamics within a group is fundamental to the process of group learning, requiring respect, focus and values to be shared for learning to be effective.

9   Being part of a community provides learning opportunities via observation, but there is also mediation due to societal needs such as prioritized social knowledge, skills and attributes.

10 Learning can also be transcendental or beyond the self, where there is a union of learning focus for our collective global needs.

8 Social Factors in Education

All of us, regardless of our job, level of qualifications, attitudes, ideologies, ethnicity, gender or age, form part of the complex structure known as society. Due to the complex nature of society, it requires rules, some supported by legislation and protected by law, such as it being illegal to murder and steal. Other rules or norms are governed by manners and good grace, such as saying thank you and please, queuing and holding open doors for strangers. In order for such a range of individuals to co-exist peacefully, each of us has to observe the majority of those rules to avoid societal breakdown and anarchy. However, while these general rules or norms can be debated and their relevance at times questioned, the basic idea of civility to each other is one which is necessary for the smooth running of society. The main area of contention within society is not the day-to-day interactions and individuals' observance of norms and values, rather, it is the system of society that they maintain and whether that system is fair and equitable.

In a modern, post-industrial society, a range of different individual roles is called for, so we need doctors, engineers, teachers, solicitors, refuse collectors, electricians, entertainers, and so forth. However, whilst each of these jobs is important in maintaining society, the value we attach to them, both in terms of monetary value and perhaps more importantly social status, differs immensely. So, for example, a doctor will generally earn more and be considered to belong to a higher social class than a refuse collector. You may consider this to be logical; whilst it is clear that both jobs are crucial, the job of the doctor requires more training, more education and more knowledge than that of the refuse collector. In addition, more people are able to take on the latter role than the former so in classical economic terms of supply and demand, the doctor deserves their higher status and income. This book, however, is concerned with education and the main issue we need to consider is whether the opportunity to gain a higher status occupation, following a successful educational experience, is equally available to all groups within society.

In the UK, our class system is primarily based on occupation and academic qualifications rather than actual income. Additionally, the social class of a child will largely depend on the occupation and qualification levels of primarily their father. Individuals are placed in certain social class groups using the National Statistics Socio-Economic Classification (NS-SEC). Generally, there are eight categories into which individuals are placed although there are variations on issues such as those who are self-employed and the size of the company you work for. However, broadly speaking, the breakdown of social economic groups is as shown in Table 8.1.

Table 8.1 The National Statistics Socio-economic Classification Analytic Classes

Group	Definition
1	Higher managerial and professional occupations
1.1	Large employers and higher managerial occupations
1.2	Higher professional occupations
2	Lower managerial and professional occupations
3	Intermediate occupations
4	Small employers and own account workers
5	Lower supervisory and technical occupations
6	Semi-routine occupations
7	Routine occupations
8	Never worked and long-term unemployed

In addition, in the UK, individuals are further categorized, for the purpose of social classification, into ethnic groups of origin and gender. Chapter 9 details the differences between these groups and similarities within them when it comes to their educational experience. This chapter will outline some of the theoretical perspectives behind those issues but it is important at this stage to understand how society is stratified and the impact this stratification may have.

What is sociology?

Sociology (in the sense in which this highly ambiguous word is used here) is a science which attempts the interpretive understanding of social action in order thereby to arrive at a causal explanation of its course and effects. In 'action' is included all human behaviour when and insofar as the acting individual attaches a subjective meaning to it. Action in this sense may be either overt or purely inward or subjective; it may consist of positive intervention in a situation, or of deliberately refraining from such intervention or passively acquiescing in the situation. Action is social insofar as, by virtue of the subjective meaning attached to it by the acting individual (or individuals), it takes account of the behaviour of others and is thereby oriented in its course.

(Weber 1994)

What Max Weber is stating here is that modern society is not a purely natural state and that the 'actions' or 'inactions' of various groups have an impact on the fabric of society and the lives of individuals and groups made up of those individuals.

The sociology of education

Within the sociology of education there are two main schools of thought, functionalists or consensus theorists and Marxism or conflict theorists. Both theories see school as much more than a place where you receive an academic education. Instead, school is seen primarily as a socializing force, that is, it ensures that individuals develop into productive members of our society. The main differences between the theories concern the benefits of this socialization. Consensus theorists see it as a positive force within society, that we as individuals consent to a general overall view (ideology) which ensures that each of us can take our rightful place based upon our ability and dedication. There must be divisions in society in order for it to function properly. Conflict theorists also believe that there are divisions in society. However, instead of these being based upon ability and dedication, conflict theorists feel that they are based upon inequality. It is suggested that the ruling classes oversee the system of education in such a way that ensures those who share their ideological view (class-based) will succeed whilst those who do not will fail, and that, in order to achieve any success within the school system, we have to adhere to the dominant ideology. Conflict theorists believe that this ideology is not a shared one but one that has been developed from the top down and that the rest of society has been coerced into accepting it.

Functionalists or consensus theorists

Functionalism as a school of thought is so called because functionalist theorists feel that society has basic needs and that they need to be met in order for it to function correctly. They liken society to a biological organism such as the human body. We need every part of our body to be functioning correctly in order for us to survive. If, for example, our liver fails, then the rest of our body cannot bypass the organ but instead will fail. In a similar fashion, if the school system does not provide the socialization of our young people, in conjunction with other socializing forces such as the family, then society will collapse.

One of the pioneers of the functionalist movement was Emile Durkheim whose main works were developed in the late nineteenth century. He suggested that, at the time, society was in danger of breaking down and that the rules of social engagement were becoming confused and unclear. This, he felt, could cause the destruction of society. He called this condition anomie which means a breakdown of social norms and values leading to anarchy. This condition ensured no shared norms of behaviour existed and so it would be impossible for a society to form and function.

In *The Division of Labour in Society* (1893) Durkheim outlined his theory that societies developed from a mechanical system into an organic system In the mechanical system, individuals tend to have similar work tasks and similar goals. An example of this would be an agricultural society where the majority of workers are farm-based and each is reliant on the other to provide sufficient amounts and variety of foods for the whole. Therefore, in this society the ideology will be a shared one as we can clearly see the links between us and the rest of society. When society moves to a more complex arrangement, such as we have today, then the links between individuals become less clear. Different elements of society will be seen to be independent of each other and the idea of shared goals and ideology becomes more complex. It is at this stage that Durkheim believes there is a danger of anomie.

Different roles in society will carry greater or lesser rewards which can result in conflict between individuals. However, Durkheim believed that these rewards were necessary in order to ensure that society functioned correctly. He and other function-alists, such as Talcott Parsons, believed that school was a powerful force in ensuring that children were socialized into accepting their roles within society. Schools, according to Durkheim, acted as a secondary socializing force which enabled individuals to understand their role in a broader more complex society than that of their immediate environment and family.

This leads us to understand the two main relationships we encounter in our dealings with other individuals within society. First, affective relationships. These are relationships which are primarily based on love and affection, for many of us the ones we receive from family and close friends. Second, and more common in our day-to-day encounters, are instrumental relationships. These relationships are ones that contain a purpose such as in a shop or office. For these relationships there are certain shared rules which ensure that they run smoothly. Without education, functionalists argue, we would not understand those rules and either all of society would collapse or, as an individual, we would be excluded from the system. So, therefore, even though we adopt disparate roles in society, we all share a common value system which ensures that society functions.

Therefore, the role of schools, from a functionalist perspective, is not solely to provide a free education which examines knowledge unsullied by ideological bias. Instead the true purpose is to perform a number of key tasks. First, it should ensure that we have the necessary basic skills in order to perform our role, such as reading, increasingly, information communication technology skills and basic mathematics. The second task, and perhaps most crucial for our discussion here, is based on socializing us and ensuring that social order is maintained. This would entail manners, accepting hierarchical structures, working within the law, respect for elders and other shared norms and values which maintain the order of society. The third element is in preparing us for the world of work. This is partly linked to the maintaining of the social order element, for in work, as in society, we conform to certain rules but also we require the development of specialist skills and knowledge for certain jobs. So education would, through the teaching of, say, history, and in particular certain types of history, primarily British and with a bias towards British perspectives, ensure a spirit of patriotism in children. Furthermore, through subjects such as citizenship a sense of working within society could be fostered. Later on in the chapter we will discuss ways in which the socialization process within education is not primarily achieved through taught subjects but instead in the way in which the school is structured and managed.

Durkheim was not the only theorist who espoused these views and his work was developed further by, in particular, Talcott Parsons and Davis and Moore. In his work *The Social System* (1964), Parsons developed the theories of Durkheim and discussed how individual 'social actors' operated within the larger 'social order'. Parsons believed that our integration into society was not a natural process but instead was something which needed to be taught and learnt. He described many institutions in society as agencies of socialization which would together ensure that society and the individuals within it continued to function. School, of course, was considered to be a key agency in maintaining social order. Parsons, like Durkheim, believed that the system was meritocratic in that it favoured no individual but achievement was linked solely to ability and dedication.

Davis and Moore (1945) raised a similar point in terms of education being the proving ground for ability and that it acted as an agent of selection. Those who did well gained the roles which brought higher rewards in terms of social status and often, although not always, higher financial status. Their belief, therefore, was not only that education provided a function in maintaining control but that the system also fairly separated us into the roles to which we were most suited.

What each of the above theoretical perspectives suggests is that education is necessary to maintain social order and that, furthermore, each of us has an equal chance to succeed. They also put forward a crucial point which is that they believe society is generally positive for all sections of it. We all agree to the norms and values of society because it benefits all of us in some way. We may not all be given equal rewards and status but that is due to the importance of our roles and in any case we were all given a chance to succeed. To summarize the consensus viewpoint, we have a place in society, we know that place and act accordingly but that place is not pre-ordained but instead is based upon our own ability and dedication.

What the consensus perspective fails to fully account for are the inequalities we encounter within society. We have, in the UK, huge discrepancies in terms of wealth and educational achievement. Whilst consensus theorists would suggest that these are necessary and useful in creating ambition and a fully functioning society, the theory is less clear as to why those who tend to achieve generally are from the higher socio-economic groups and that those who do less well tend to be from the lower socio-economic groups. This, of course, is a generalization and more specific examples can be seen in Chapter 9. Nevertheless, broadly speaking, consensus theorists do not fully address power relations in society, who controls systems such as education and whether they could be used to maintain power and privilege in the hands of the few.

Conflict theorists

Conflict theorists also believe that the primary purpose of education is to socialize us into accepting norms and values in order to ensure the smooth running of society. However, while consensus theorists state that this is for the benefit of us all, conflict theorists state that we are being conditioned to accept as normal an unjust system. They see the primary role of education as maintaining the power base of the ruling classes and reinforcing the unjust class system. For conflict theorists, the system of education will not allow significant numbers of individuals from outside of the elite classes to succeed, as this would erode the power base of those in positions of power.

In order for this to be achieved, the whole of society needs to believe that maintaining social order is beneficial for us all. This cannot be solely achieved in the long term by force or by withholding services or goods but instead, in order to provide a stable and fully functioning society where those in lesser positions accept their roles, a form of social control must be developed. Gramsci (1971) suggested that through institutions like the media, family and schools, those in positions of power, namely governments and those who owned large industries, developed a concept of hegemony. Through this, the elite can govern in ways which suit their purpose whilst other groups believe that they too have a full say in the structure and belief system of that society. It is not enough, therefore, to impose rules, as that would be obvious coercion, instead, those rules must appear to be developed by all groups and be challengeable by all groups. For conflict theorists, the main problem lies in the fact that the structure and belief system of capitalism are not able to be challenged in any meaningful way as to do so would directly challenge the power of the elite groups. So, through an apparently free media, a supposedly democratic political system and an education system which, particularly within higher education, can be critical, it appears that we all have some say in the structure of society. However, conflict theorists would argue that all this is part of the deception and that the supposedly challengeable structure is anything but. Whilst we may be able to see small changes being made in the social structure, those changes will not challenge the overall structure which is designed to ensure the smooth handover of power from generation to generation of the ruling classes. You may have encountered the old political slogan, 'Whomever you vote for, the Government gets in.' This is what is meant by hegemony: a concept which gives the illusion of freedom and meritocracy in a system which is class-based and inherently biased in favour of those from the higher social classes. It is important to note though, as Apple does (2003), that hegemony is a process, not a thing and should not be seen as holding direct and total control over meanings. Instead hegemonic power is something which needs to be built and rebuilt; it is contested and negotiated (2003: 6). Whether this can be viewed as a suggestion that change can come via challenge, both intellectual and practical, or that the dominant ideology will merely shift to incorporate such challenges whilst maintaining overall control is a matter of debate.

Education, of course, is seen by conflict theorists as a primary tool in this deception. In much the same way as consensus theorists saw education as a socializing tool, conflict theorists see it as a tool which will socialize us or condition us into accepting an unfair system. Perhaps the most seminal and certainly the most famous of the conflict theorists is Karl Marx (1813–1883). Together with his compatriot Engels, Marx did not write specifically about education but his theories on the way in which the state maintained social order through deception pioneered the works of later sociologists who viewed education as a key tool in this form of control. In addition, his views can be indirectly applied to our modern system of education as later discussions in this chapter demonstrate. Marx stated that at the heart of society was production and that, under a capitalist society, production must make surplus profit which, rather than being shared among the workers, would instead be taken as profit by the owners of the companies, be they individuals or groups. This unfair system would, by definition, ensure that those who created the wealth, the workers, could not reap the full reward of their endeavours as to do so would result in a lack of profit. Marx and Engels stated that this system needed to be legitimized and naturalized by a system above it, thus suggesting that it was a natural order and beyond challenge rather than an engineered intrinsically unjust system. Marx saw these two elements as the economic infrastructure which ensured the power of the owners and the superstructure which supported, via ideological control, the status quo. Therefore, the profit-making production creates a superstructure of schools, religion, the family and mass media to ideologically condition us into accepting capitalist ideologies. This is done not through direct violence but through messages, both overt and covert, which suggest the current system is one that favours us all. One key message in this perspective is that schools are controlled by those in positions of power and, as such, the education system, rather than being a force for change, is engineered to favour those who will form part of the elite in later life. These individuals will be, almost without exception, from what we now class as the higher socio-economic groups. This control will manifest itself not in the subjects within education, but the content of those subjects, the status of different types of knowledge, the way in which those subjects are taught and the way in which individuals are assessed. In addition, control is exercised over the length of the school day, increasingly the structure of that day, at what age children start school and finish school and the amount of days they spend in school. Control also manifests itself in the training future teachers receive, what is included within that training and crucially what is deemed unnecessary. See Chapter 1 for more discussion on this subject. In essence, then, education is a highly controlled practice within formal institutions most notably schools and it is the purpose of that control which conflict theorists seek to question. As Marx put it: 'the ruling class will give its ideas the form of universality and represent them as the only rational universally valid ones' (cited in Apple 2004: 145).

Building on the works of Marx and Engels, Althusser (1984) stated that there were two main forms of maintaining social control in an unjust society. First, what he coined the repressive state apparatuses (RSAs). These elements, such as the army, the police force and system of law and order, are rough tools and whilst they can, for short periods, maintain order, that order is likely to be challenged as it is clear that they are repressing individuals and groups within society. Think of dictatorships in numerous countries worldwide which are supported by the threat or reality of force of such RSAs.

Far more subtle ways of control are those supported by the ideological state apparatuses (ISAs). These tools are far more important as the most effective way to ensure that there is no challenge to an unjust system is to convince the public that the system is just. Many of the chapters in the book have discussed ideology in detail so this is not the place for a lengthy discussion of its meaning, suffice to say that ideology is a system of values and beliefs which can be imposed, shared or given the illusion of being shared. Or as Althusser himself stated: 'the system of ideas and representations which dominate the mind of a man or a social group' ([1970] 1984: 32). Althusser suggested that the following were ISAs (Table 8.2).

Table 8.2 Ideological state apparatuses (ISAs)

- the religious ISA
- the educational ISA
- the family ISA
- the legal ISA
- the political ISA
- the trade-union ISA
- the communications ISA
- the cultural ISA (literature, the arts, sports, etc.)

Althusser stressed that one telling aspect of the ISAs were that many of them were privately owned or at least not under the direct control of the government, unlike the RSAs. This is a major indicator of how deeply hegemony has infiltrated the thinking of the population when even those institutions whose very role is to challenge, such as the trade unions, work within the system and as such become largely ineffective in achieving true change. As Althusser stated: 'No class can hold State power over a long period without at the same time exercising its hegemony over and in the State Ideological Apparatuses' (1984: 20). So if, as Althusser stated, ISAs such as schools maintain an unjust system, in what ways does this transmit itself?

Task 8.1   Stop, think & do

Consider in what ways the list of ISAs in Table 8.2 could develop hegemony and support an unjust system. Consider whether celebrity culture is a way of ensuring that individuals focus on less important aspects of life, thus preventing a challenge to the status quo.

Earlier in this chapter we examined how Davis and Moore believed schools acted as agents for selection in that school separated us into the roles we were most suited for. Whilst it is true that school and education generally is a competitive environment and that there will be winners and losers within the system, the question we must ask is whether the competition is a fair one in which all individuals have an equal chance of success.

Bourdieu (1977) outlined the theory of cultural capital and habitus to explain why certain students were more comfortable in and, therefore, more likely to succeed in the educational system. The theory that he outlined was one of cultural capital and the ways in which schools were a more natural environment for certain children, most notably those where education was valued and encouraged. Bourdieu stated that the systems within schools endowed those who entered with what they termed as the appropriate cultural capital. Schools are places which naturally value a willingness to learn and appropriate behaviour from the children in their care. Those children who see the value in education are more likely, therefore, to more smoothly integrate into the institution. As can be seen in Chapter 9, not all groups in society perform equally within the education system. You are far less likely to succeed if, for example, your parents' levels of qualifications are low and it is this type of discrepancy within the system that Bourdieu sought to explain. He felt that there are three main types of cultural capital that an individual can bring to an educational environment: the embodied state which includes the investment of time and influence by primary carers, often parents; the institutionalized form of educational qualifications and achievements; and the objective form of cultural goods such as books, resources and places to study, similar to concepts of material deprivation or affluence (Reay et al. 2005: 20). The theory suggests that those individuals who come to education from families which have previously succeeded within the education system will do well, and that, furthermore, the education system is primarily created, maintained and staffed by those who have done the same. Due to this, the cultural capital that the children of those groups bring to education results in a distinct advantage for them. Ultimately, the value systems, behavioural expectations and types of knowledge that are deemed important within the schools are similar to those they will encounter at home. Of course, this also results in the opposite being true for children from groups which have not succeeded as well within education and who, therefore, do not necessarily view success within it quite as crucially. In essence, the illusion of meritocracy is maintained as each individual receives a similar education and similar opportunities to succeed in exams but there is a fundamental advantage for those children whose cultural capital is more in tune with the ethos and culture of the school. As Bourdieu suggested, when the capital of a student links well with the field of an educational environment, then a student can feel like 'a fish in water'. However, when there is disjuncture between them, it can lead to feelings of isolation, discomfort and insecurity.

Examining similar instances of the culture that children bring to school, Bernstein (1971) introduced the concept of language codes that children from varying socio-economic backgrounds brought into schools, and how closely they matched the codes used within the school. Bernstein stated that there were two types of language codes 'restricted' and 'elaborated', the former being more commonly used by those from lower socio-economic groups and the latter by those from the higher socio-economic groups. In more recent years the terms have changed to 'dominated' codes and 'dominating' codes. The 'dominating' code is more commonly used within schools and those who enter school with a familiarity with the code are again at a distinct advantage within the system. The change in terminology was due to the fact that Bernstein never intended to suggest that one code was superior to another and that they could both be descriptive and discuss abstract concepts. As Labov (1969) stated, 'We could as easily expect the school to adapt its language to the child as expect the child to adapt his or her language to the school' (cited in Meighan and Siraj-Blatchford 2001: 335). This idea of the school adapting is core to our understanding of the conflict theory of education in that, at all times, we expect the pupil to adapt rather than the school, which ensures that those whose adaptation is smaller will continue to flourish in a system which suits their background. The 'dominating' language will be more descriptive and paint a picture for the reader, allowing them to visualize what is being described. The 'dominated' code, on the other hand, is more context dependent, it will also describe what is occurring but it will be more difficult for the reader to gain a sense of the overall situation. Within speech, however, it should again be stressed that Bernstein never suggested that one code was superior to another. In a similar fashion, non-standard English spoken by pupils from various minority ethnic groups or those from regions across the UK are often considered inferior as they do not match the language used within the educational system.

The hidden curriculum and conflict theorists

Many of the ways in which schools, from a conflict perspective, fail certain children are through the content of the official curriculum and the teaching methods employed (see Chapter 12 for a more detailed discussion around the official curriculum). This is not to be dismissed lightly as it demonstrates the value systems employed within and through education which form much of the basis for conflict theorists. However, whilst the official curriculum is of obvious importance, the ways in which we are socialized and learn which behaviour patterns are expected of us, often class- and gender-related, are often more effectively delivered through what Jackson (1968) coined the hidden curriculum. The hidden curriculum can be seen as all the messages that we gain from an educational experience which do not, at least implicitly, form part of the official curriculum. Therefore, whilst there are no actual lessons in appropriate gender behaviour, understanding and respecting hierarchy within schools and that knowledge is something to learn rather than create, we nevertheless take these and many more messages away from our educational experiences. Meighan and Siraj-Blatchford provide a more detailed list of messages that students gain through the hidden curriculum and include issues such as adults being more important than children, the Western world being more advanced and superior to the rest of the world and that passive acceptance of ideas is more desirable than criticism (2001: 65–6). As previously pointed out in Chapter 3, the hidden curriculum is not necessarily a simple and unintended by-product of the schooling process and instead can be viewed as a deliberate attempt to maintain social order through a series of covert and overt messages. The way in which the hidden curriculum can manifest itself are myriad. It can be in the teacher's attitude, the way in which they praise and admonish and the reasons for both of them. It can be in the way classrooms are laid out and the displays on the walls and in corridors. It can be in the uniform requirements, which prizes are given at the end of the year and which elements make up reports. In short, the ethos and direction of the institution are clearly defined through a series of messages which will be constantly reinforced in actions, words and decor.

Task 8.2   Stop, think and do

- Consider what knowledge you have retained from school.
- How much of the content of the subjects you studied at GCSE and A-level do you still recall? Would you feel confident in taking those exams again right now?
- In contrast, consider what other messages you received from school which may have been delivered in a less direct manner. Are the messages such as the ones listed above things that remain with you from your schooling?
- What other 'lessons' of this nature did you take from school?
- How would you describe the hidden curriculum of your current environment? Think of the ways in which this transmits itself.

The much admired and equally criticized work of Bowles and Gintis (1976) developed the concept of the hidden curriculum further and linked it to what they termed the 'correspondence principle'. Bowles and Gintis stated that the messages we gained from the hidden curriculum in schools corresponded closely with the world of work we would later encounter. This is part of what Hatcher (2001) would call the 'capitalist agenda for schools' in that the purpose of education is to create subservient workers within a capitalist economy. These workers will have the necessary knowledge to be productive but, far more importantly, they will also consider the working environment as a natural and unchangeable product which they should work within rather than seek to alter. For Bowles and Gintis, education corresponded to the world of work in a number of key ways. First, they stated that, in their study, grades related more to subservient personality traits rather than ability. In addition, the hierarchical nature of the educational environment in the way that the teacher is in charge and above her lie the deputy and the head teacher. Bowles and Gintis claim that an uncritical acceptance of these power relations will smooth the educational progress much as it would within a work environment. The idea of external rewards through the exam system and their role in gaining higher status employment also link education to school. In much the same way that much employment is unsatisfying and unrewarding with only the prospect of a wage making it worthwhile, the learning process is equally unrewarding with many children failing to enjoy school. However, the carrot remains in terms of external rewards, in one case, wages, in the other, exam results.

Whilst the importance of the work of Bowles and Gintis should not be underestimated, there are a number of criticisms of their work. Some of this focuses upon their reasoning and research methodologies but perhaps more tellingly criticism is levelled at the way in which they present children as uncritical and unquestioning adopters of the messages within the hidden curriculum. Bearing in mind that theorists such as Bowles and Gintis form part of what we class as the conflict theory of education, there is little evidence of conflict within their work. This has led to the likes of Apple (1999, 2002) and Giroux (2001) criticizing their work as being somewhat misleading. It is worth noting, though, that Bowles and Gintis (2001) reject such claims.

Such criticism as that above could not be levelled at Paul Willis who, in his seminal text *Learning to Labour: How Working Class Kids Get Working Class Jobs* (1977) discovered strong evidence of a rejection of school and the formulation of a counter-culture among working-class pupils. Willis followed a group of 12 boys for their last 18 months of school and into their first jobs. The 'lads', as Willis coined them, had clearly rejected the messages sent to them via the hidden and official curriculum. They had little respect for teachers and more subservient pupils and realized instinctively that the 'rewards' of good performance in school were not applicable to them as they had no prospect of succeeding within the system. This was not, as Willis states, a politically aware decision, and in fact the racism and sexism of the 'lads' were contrary to such an awareness, but instead the awareness was developed from observing those around them from similar backgrounds in their homes and the community. Their peers in this case obtained jobs primarily in semi-skilled and unskilled labour for which schools had little to offer. In fact, though, once Willis followed the 'lads' into their first jobs, he discovered that what was classed as a counter-culture within schools was the dominant culture within those workplaces. Therefore, the rejection of the school culture was borne out of the school culture having little relevance to their own. They also realised that academic qualifications were unlikely to be achieved within such a system which Willis argued was developed to exclude too many of their class from achieving. As he succinctly put it:

> Insofar as knowledge is always biased and shot through with class meaning, the working class student must overcome his inbuilt disadvantage of possessing the wrong class culture and the wrong educational decoders to start with. A few can make it. The class can never follow. It is through a good number trying, however, that the class structure is legitimated.

> (1977: 128)

What Willis means here is that to maintain an illusion of meritocracy, such as that suggested by the consensus theorists, some children from working-class backgrounds have to achieve, but the system will ensure that the numbers will be heavily restricted in order to maintain society's inequalities.

Conclusion

There is no doubt that there are clear indicators of how likely we are to achieve success within education. Broadly speaking, these indicators centre on our class status, ethnic origin and gender, all of which are discussed in more detail in Chapter 9. The main debate in the sociology of education is how engineered those differences are. The chapter has outlined a range of theoretical perspectives broadly separated into two main philosophies: the consensus theory, and the conflict theory.

The first, the consensus theory, suggests that we all have an equal chance within education, that education is a meritocracy. Any differences in achievement are not the fault of the system but instead education is a natural selection process which separates us into our most suitable future roles.

In contrast, the conflict theorists suggest that education is socially and politically constructed to exclude large numbers of, particularly, children from lower socio-economic groups. This is done through an official curriculum and a hidden curriculum which favours those children whose background, ethos and capital are more suited to the environment.

Both schools of thought believe that education primarily exists to socialize us into becoming productive members of society but that process can be seen by consensus theorists as positive and beneficial to all. Conflict theorists see this very differently, the socialization process is there to maintain and strengthen divisions ensuring that the economic base of society remains unchallenged.

Summary

1   Sociologists understand the system of education to play a key role in the socialization of individuals within society.

2   There are two main schools of thought on this process, conflict theorists, such as Marx, see it as a negative force which maintains divisions within society based on issues such as social class. In comparison, consensus theorists, such as Durkheim, see this as a positive force which socializes us into roles most suitable for the individual and therefore, society.

3   Education is one of the socializing agents within society, others include the family, religion and the media.

4   How the education system socializes us is via issues such as the hidden curriculum and a correspondence between school and the workplace.

5   This socialization process often leads to a negative educational experience for individuals from certain ethnic groups and lower socio-economic groups as discussed in Chapter 9, in this volume.

9 Education: Who Gets What?

In the previous chapter, issues concerning the role of education were discussed and differences in achievement in terms of class status, gender and ethnic origin were alluded to. In this chapter, an examination of the specific issues relating to these groups will demonstrate why the education system is so keenly debated and why accusations of a biased system cannot and should not be dismissed. The chapter will first outline some of the key issues specific to each area before concluding by drawing together relevant theoretical perspectives.

Introduction

Each of us belongs to a range of social classifications. We are separated by our sex, our class and our race. These social classifications can be seen as problematic. Whilst they clearly allow comparison of life chances between the classifications, which can highlight issues of inequality and thus seek to address them, their role in creating these inequalities needs to be considered. Being clearly identified as belonging to a social group, for example, females or working class, brings with it connotations. These connotations are based on the prejudices and stereotypical views each of us, in some way, hold. It is worth noting that all social classifications are engineered, that is, they are created artificially and do not necessarily reflect the individuals found within those groups. An example of this can be seen in the concept of gender. The term gender refers to the social differences between males and females. The term sex is used to describe the biological differences. The fact that separate terms are needed suggests that much of the perceived difference in behaviour and attitude is socially constructed in that males and females behave in certain defined ways not due to any biological reason but because they have been socialized in that manner. The work of anthropologists such as Mead (1935) have shown that gender differences inherent in Western society are challenged radically by other societies which, at the time, were free from global influences. In much the same way we should consider how natural differences in attitudes between varying racial groups and class groups might be and how much they are products of the socialization process discussed in Chapter 8.

By virtue of placing an individual within a social classification, you are labelling them not only with the title of that classification but also with all the history of that group and the prejudices held against that group by others. This level of prejudice should not be underestimated; there are many media and academic accounts of the difficulties in gaining employment by those whose names suggest they are not

English. Equally, the struggle for equal pay and status for women in today's society can in no way be said to have been achieved as yet.

Not only do others have prejudices against groups they do not belong to but individuals within those groups can begin to believe in and act out those social differences. Therefore, the battle for equality needs to be seen on two fronts, first, the attitudes of those who may, consciously or unconsciously, discriminate based on social classifications, and, second, the influence of the socialization process on the behaviour of those belonging to those groups. Examples of this latter issue can be seen in phrases such as 'boys will be boys' and in terms of narrow career choices concerning, for example, the gender groups.

In education, of course, this can impact on the achievement rates of individuals according to their social classifications and again reasons behind this need to be viewed from the dual perspective of internal and external expectations.

Task 9.1 Stop, think and do

This chapter will consider the different educational experiences of:

- boys and girls
- middle-class and working-class children
- Afro-Caribbean children and White children.

It will also consider ways in which our race, gender and class are interlinked issues.

- For each of these groups, write five words which you believe describes them and their attitudes towards education. What do your words suggest about the views we all hold?
- Can you create a list of jobs which are 'Male' and ones which are 'Female'?
- Why are jobs separated by gender? Would you consider working in a profession which is considered by most to be for the opposite sex to you? What do you believe would be the main issues in and out of the job if you did so?

External expectations – theoretical perspectives

Within any given group of people who attempt Task 9.1, there are likely to be some commonalities between the words chosen to describe the various groups. Each individual undertaking the task is likely to have their own view of acceptable or 'positive' behaviour which is likely to achieve educational success. Those views will have been developed from their own socialization process through the family, media, education and the other ideological state apparatuses that define us. The decisions taken as to how to describe each of the social groups listed above will largely depend on how different they are perceived to be from our own views, effectively the norms and values we hold. Therefore, each of the groups above will broadly have been assigned a label which stresses their difference from the perceived norm of society. This perspective is known as labelling theory. Labelling theory forms, in an educational setting, the basis of teacher expectations and the self-fulfilling prophecy.

Gender and education

Currently in many government publications and the educational press, much concern is expressed about the underachievement of boys within education. A range of theories on the lack of male role models, both in the classroom and at home, together with ideas of a male anti-school counter-culture continue to make headlines. However, the idea that boys are underachieving as a problem is seen only in relation to the achievements of their female counterparts, a telling point which raises important issues around how society views males and females.

Currently there is no doubt that girls are outperforming boys in the majority of subjects and at the majority of levels. However, whilst girls' performance in the more traditional male subjects of the physical sciences and mathematics has increased dramatically, the idea that females have always been significantly behind males overall in attainment is inaccurate as Figure 9.1 demonstrates.

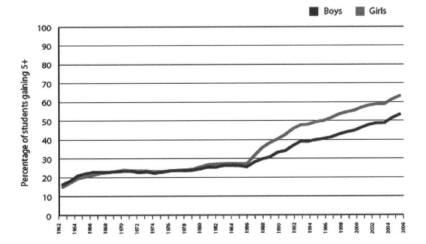

Figure 9.1 Percentage of school leavers achieving 5+ A–C (or Pass) O-level or A*–C GCSE by gender (1962–2006)

Source: (DfES 2007: 18).

As can be ascertained, historically, or at least since girls had similar educational opportunities to boys, there has been little difference in terms of O-level/GCSE pass rates. Although it should be noted that for reasons which are discussed later in the chapter, many of the girls' passes would be in lower status subjects such as home economics. Even taking that into account, there are two clear patterns emerging from the data above, first, that girls began to outperform boys more significantly after 1988, a year which saw both the introduction of the National Curriculum and the replacement of O-levels with GCSE examinations. The second issue to note is that both boys and girls show a steady upwards improvement in terms of achievement at this level. Therefore, the idea that boys are failing within the educational system is not fully supported by the statistical evidence which shows that boys, whilst not doing as well as their female counterparts, are, overall as a group, improving year on year.

Figure 9.1 only tells part of the story of achievement by gender as more telling differences are found in individual subjects. The following selection of subject results at GCSE level demonstrates this difference (Table 9.1).

Table 9.1 GCSE attainment by subject and gender (2006) (pupils gaining A–C passes at GCSE)

Subject	Boys (%)	Girls (%)	Gap (%)
D & T: Textiles Technology	38	70	32
Art and Design	59	78	19
English	55	69	14
Social Studies	48	62	14
Humanities	40	52	12
English Literature	61	73	12
French	58	69	11
German	63	74	11
Geography	63	69	6
History	63	69	6
Mathematics	55	57	2
Chemistry	91	91	0
Physics	92	91	−1
Biological Sciences	90	89	−1
Other Sciences	57	52	−5

Percentage figures relate only to pupils entered for each subject not overall group.
Source: adapted from DfES (2007: 21)'

As can be seen when examining results on a subject by subject basis, the gender achievement differential can vary significantly. Whilst it is clear, therefore, that gender impacts upon educational achievement, the reasons behind such results are not so well defined. Again it is worth commenting on the rhetoric of the debate which has a tendency to bemoan the underachievement of boys rather than celebrate the success of girls.

The education of girls

The rhetoric of boys underachieving is perhaps unsurprising given the history of unequal treatment of girls within education and society generally. This is an issue that globally is still a matter of major concern. The second of the Millennium Development Goals is to achieve universal primary education for all by 2015. Latest figures suggest that there are 72 million children out of school worldwide and that 57 per cent of them are girls. These figures should be regarded as an underestimate as it does not account for places where data are difficult to obtain. In addition, it only concerns enrolment in schools and not whether attendance is frequent and regular (UNDESA 2007).

In Chapter 2, there is a fuller discussion of the policy decisions which have shaped the education of girls and of more importance to this chapter are modern practices, which, it is suggested by many, favour girls, and the attitudes towards girls in education from society as a whole. These attitudes which have, and arguably still do, support this battle can be seen in the work of Newsom (1948) who stated that as the vast majority of girls will go on to be the makers of homes it was inappropriate for them to share the curriculum of boys' schools (cited in Martin 2004: 117).

The education of girls has historically prepared them for wifehood and mother-hood at the expense of academic achievement, a situation further developed by a marriage bar which excluded married women from many professions including teaching (Paechter 1998: 13). Furthermore, the curriculum in schools was differenti-ated according to sex with female pupils engaged in domestic subjects in their latter years to the detriment of the academic subjects within the boys' curriculum. Table 9.1 demonstrates how these attitudes are still influencing subject choice by gender, with the widest differences between boys' and girls' achievement being in the more creative and caring subjects whilst differences are less apparent in the Physical Sciences and Mathematics. It is still the case that subjects such as Education and Childcare are still primarily studied by females. Therefore, we can see that the history of females being treated as second class in education is still influencing both subject choice and the rhetoric of the debate which primarily focuses upon the underachieve-ment of boys.

Education was not the only public institution which differentiated between the sexes. For example, it was not until 1928 that women were allowed to vote at the same age as men. Furthermore, it was not illegal for women to be paid less than men when employed in the same job or even to be denied access to that job. The Sex Discrimination Act of 1975, together with the Equal Pay Act of 1970, ensured that discriminatory practices such as those above are now illegal. However, the relative lateness of these Acts shows how deeply ingrained in society discrimination based on sex was. Those attitudes are still prevalent today in terms of employment where women are on average paid 17 per cent less than men and part-time female workers are paid 38 per cent less than their male counterparts (Equal Opportunities Commis-sion 2007). It is against this background that the moral panic around boys' failure in education needs to be considered. The Acts alone, like most legislation, were insufficient to change attitudes and a range of texts from the mid-1970s onwards drew attention to the way education shaped and maintained differences based on gender. These differences were seen to be to the detriment of girls not only within the classroom but in terms of the messages they received on future roles within the workplace. Two of the most seminal texts of the period were Sue Sharpe's *Just Like a Girl* (1976) and Anne Oakley's *Sex, Gender and Society* (1975), both of which highlighted the marginalization of girls within education. This was done via both the official and the hidden curriculum. Subjects were gender-specific, girls were discouraged from taking subjects which were seen as traditionally male such as Mathematics and the Physical Sciences, and feminine behaviour was encouraged. It was argued that the underachievement of girls in education was engineered and supported by a system which favoured boys, an argument which current figures suggest had some validity.

Leaving aside the rhetoric and the fact that, year-on-year, boys' achievement is also rising, there is no doubt that girls do better in the majority of subjects at the majority of levels. This issue has led to debates on the content, delivery and assessment methods of the curriculum and whether those elements favour girls in their current formats. The Educational Reform Act of 1988 which introduced the National Curriculum had a major, if unintended impact upon girls' academic performance. First, it made a range of core subjects statutory and ensured that girls could not opt out of, or more likely be persuaded out of, subjects such as science. It also introduced league tables which have ensured the issue of achievement by gender remains high on the public agenda. Therefore, as girls were given greater opportunity within the educational system, we began to see their performance increase at a faster rate than the improvement of boys, resulting in the gender gap within the statistics. There is an ongoing debate on how boys' level of academic performance can be improved and, whilst it is crucial to constantly consider whether practices within education favour or disadvantage any particular group, it is again worth noting that the performance of boys, like girls, is steadily improving year on year. Later in the chapter we will examine some potential reasons for the discrepancies in achievement based on individuals' gender, race and class.

The impact of race

Obviously each of us as individuals belongs to more than one social group. As the discussion on gender demonstrated, fewer boys than girls are achieving the minimum levels of qualifications which society would deem as successful. Furthermore, behind the statistics is the unpalatable truth that over 30 per cent of children do not achieve that level after 11 years of compulsory schooling, an issue which should also feature highly in any discussion on achievement. It is insufficient to suggest that the learning styles of boys or the assessment process, for example, favours girls as this would fail to take into account the fact that not all boys 'fail' and we need to examine the statistics in more detail in order to understand that gender is only one aspect which impacts upon results and in reality may be a less crucial issue than other defining social classifications.

In 2006, 21 per cent of children in the state primary sector and 17 per cent of children within the secondary state sector were classified as belonging to a minority ethnic group (DfES 2006b). Overall as Table 9.2 demonstrates, there is a correlation between ethnicity and achievement at GCSE level but that correlation is related to specific ethnicities with various groups achieving at widely discrepant rates.

Table 9.2 Percentage of pupils achieving 5 A-C GCSE grades by ethnicity and gender (2006)

Ethnic origin	Boys	Girls
White British	53.0	62.3
Indian	67.1	76.6
Pakistani	45.4	57.9
Bangladeshi	46.7	58.5
Black Caribbean	36.5	52.9
Black African	45.2	56.7
Chinese	75.5	84.8

Source: DfES (2007).

Table 9.2 demonstrates that there is a complexity to the issue of ethnic minority achievement with Chinese and Indian pupils doing particularly well and Black Caribbean boys clearly achieving at levels well below the national average. Later in the chapter we will investigate how ethnicity and class status are often linked, which can go some way to explaining the differences within the figures. However, it is clear that there is major concern about the achievement rates of Black Caribbean boys in particular. This is by no means a new issue: in 1971, Bernard Coard published his short but seminal text, 'How the West Indian child is made educationally subnormal in the British school system. In the work, he highlighted how this group of children showed how the system failed to meet the needs of, in particular, recent immigrants to this country. Through a combination of cultural bias, such as that discussed in Chapter 8, an IQ test in which both the questions and the exam situation were alien to the child and low teacher expectations, West Indian children were deemed to be educationally sub-normal (ESN) and placed in special educational measures. Coard further suggests that historically British history has deemed Black people as educationally inferior, a view which justified slavery but is still given some credence today in limited circles. This perhaps at times subconscious view was supported by low scores in a biased IQ test which merely confirmed expectations. Coupled with this was the attitude towards the system which the Black children showed, an attitude which in many cases was largely negative. This is of course understandable when faced with a system which appears ill-equipped to deal with you at best and demonstrates blatant discrimination at worst. At the time when Coard was writing, the dominant ideology on race relations was one of assimilation slowly turning towards integration. The former suggested that immigrants would simply and naturally become British in their actions, thoughts and deeds. However, this approach was proving to be unworkable, for obvious reasons, and a move towards integration was beginning to gain momentum. It can be seen therefore, that in 1971 the idea of multicultural education or anti-racist education, both of which understand that one size does not fit all, was some way off, and it is fair to say that it has not fully been achieved in the current time.

Despite the importance of Coard's work and the excellent legacy it has left, the statistics in Table 9.2 demonstrate quite clearly that there is still much to be achieved in terms of equality of opportunity. Many of the issues which Coard highlighted are still an issue within the school system and in 2005 his work was included in a new volume *Tell It Like It Is: How Our Schools Fail Black Children*, in which the message as Mirza puts it, 'the more things change, the more they stay the same' (Mirza 2005: 111) is clear throughout. Still, Black children are far more likely to be excluded from school and are more frequently educated in Pupil Referral Units which Mirza likens to the special units Coard discussed nearly 40 years ago (Mirza 2005:113). The high levels of exclusion of Black children demonstrate that, despite a range of legislation, the experience of those children within the school system is not a particularly successful one. As Abbot (2005: 108) points out, when Black children enter primary school, their ability levels are similar to all other children; however, even at the Foundation Stage (end of reception class), they have fallen behind and as they progress through the system that gap in achievement widens at every stage.

The consensus of opinion as to why this is generally falls into two camps; first, a biased and unsuitable system staffed by teachers who hold stereotypical views for reasons similar to those that Coard outlined; second, an anti-school culture among Black children, in particular, boys. It is clear of course that the two elements are linked and each supports the other and the main debate is which issue causes the other. Regardless of this, the problems that Black boys face within education should not be underestimated and it is a major challenge facing the modern system of education. As Abbot (2005) further suggests, despite the seriousness of the situation, it is one that is not discussed often enough. 'You can discuss the underachievement of boys, but not how the system fails boys' (Abbot 2005: 109). The DfES point out that teacher assessments at Key Stages 2 and 3 underestimate the eventual performance of pupils from ethnic minority groups:

> Whilst all ethnic groups are less likely to achieve the expected level in the teacher assessment than in the test in English at Key Stages 2 and 3, there are larger than average differences between English teacher assessment and test results for Asian and Black pupils and for pupils for whom English is an additional language.

(DfES 2006b: 6)

Sewell (1997) demonstrates how the views of teachers and the structure of the system can negatively impact upon the educational experiences of Black boys. It is important to note that Sewell was not suggesting that teachers or indeed the schools are openly racist but more that they themselves are both projects of an over-arching society which sees Black boys as threatening and anti-school. Furthermore, the teachers in Sewell's study saw the home environment of those Black boys as unconducive to a successful educational experience. Sewell also commented on the relationship that Black boys had with the school and authority. In many ways, parallels can be drawn with the work of Willis (1977) which was discussed in Chapter 8. Sewell also found evidence of a counter-culture amongst Black boys. He stated that those children who did 'make it' paid the price of ignoring their peer group, ethnicity and anti-school sub-culture in order to do so. (Sewell 1997: 17).

Social class and education

Through examining the impact of gender and ethnicity upon educational success it is clear that they, by themselves, are not a clear indicator of likely achievement. In each of those varying groups there are students who clearly succeed at high levels and those who fail according to the way in which statistics are recorded. There is, of course, another major social classification to consider whenever we discuss educational attainment and that is the area of social class.

Educational discourses and statistics rarely use the term class, preferring instead to refer to socio-economic status (Hatcher 2004: 131). The most common criterion used to indicate that status in terms of schooling is eligibility for free school meals. While it may seem a mere matter of semantics to refer to socio-economic status rather than class, it does have the effect of changing the emphasis onto the individual and subsequently away from the group. This can at times be problematic for a more detailed discussion as individual success or failure is much easier to explain while still maintaining the illusion of meritocracy than large-scale failure of particular sections of society.

There is clear evidence, however, of a correlation between the socio-economic status of an individual and their likelihood of educational success. Whilst for each of those individuals the reasons for this and the experiences they face will never be exactly the same, it would be disingenuous to suggest that there is not commonality between those reasons and experiences. As such, a deeper understanding of the role that society and the education system play in this inequality must be considered. Many of those elements have been discussed in Chapter 8.

In 2002, 77 per cent of children whose families came from the Higher Professional section of the NS-SEC classifications (see Table 8.1) gained 5 or more A–C grades at GCSE level. In contrast, 64 per cent from the Lower Professional classification did so and the figures fell to 32 per cent for those whose families came from Routine or Other backgrounds (Babb et al. 2004: 12). The same authors also stated that lower socio-economic status was more likely to impact upon educational achievement in the UK than it was in other OECD countries.

The impact of class can also be found in other social indicators such as gender and ethnicity. While one in three children are in families that fall below the poverty line, that figure rises to nearly 70 per cent for Pakistani and Bangladeshi children and 41 per cent for Black Caribbean children (Sarda 2003, cited in Hatcher 2004). As can be ascertained, the relatively low levels of educational success achieved by pupils from those ethnic groups must be considered in terms of their socio-economic status as much as their ethnicity.

The impact of socio-economic status is not a new issue and it has been a matter of concern for a number of years. One of the main problems faced is an apparent inability to create and maintain solutions to this ongoing and deeply concerning state of affairs. This inability has been demonstrated by successive governments and a range of policies which ultimately have made little impact on the correlation between socio-economic status and academic success. Chapter 2 outlines some of the key policy changes in education over the last century. A number of these changes have been major ones in terms of attempting to narrow the achievement gap by socio-economic status. For example, we have moved away from the tripartite system of education and the selection at age 11 that the Butler Act of 1944 introduced. Through this Act, children were tested at age 11 in the eleven-plus exam and then placed in the school deemed most suitable for them. Those who performed academically well were placed in grammar schools; those who showed a technical or practical ability were meant to be placed in technical schools whilst all others were placed in secondary modern schools which aimed to provide a more general education. In reality, though, those schools were primarily segregated according to class status, thus fostering a tiered system which ensured that class differences were maintained and strengthened within the system. However, the move away from selection at age 11 and towards a more comprehensive system of education has not dramatically alerted the overall situation. Other initiatives such as the Widening Participation agenda within higher education (HE) have also sought to reduce the equality gap. Evidence of uptake of study within HE has demonstrated that those from the lowest socio-economic groups have not taken up the opportunity in HE in sufficient numbers to reduce the gap. In fact, that gap is currently widening. Even though more students from all groups are attending HE, the percentage difference between higher and lower socio-economic groups has widened from 24 per cent in 1991/92 to 31 per cent (DfES 2003). Additionally, the experience of those students entering HE with less suitable cultural capital is causing concern in terms of retention and success rates (Mufti 2006).

The general failure of policy in reducing the gap leads us to consider what are the main reasons for such figures. Hatcher (2004) suggests that current responses which either show that schools need to be pushed and encouraged to close the gap (school improvement agenda) or alternatively that schools themselves can do little to alter a system and society which predetermines success and failure are both incorrect. Hatcher states that it is instead the shaping of working-class culture by a class society which ensures a lack of successful school-based cultural capital amongst those students.

Throughout the chapter we have seen evidence that who you are in terms of gender, ethnicity and socio-economic status correlates with the likelihood of academic success in the current education system. We have looked in previous chapters at the history and policy of education together with the curriculum studied and the purpose of education; all of these elements have influenced the current system and it is worth remembering that the system is not organic and instead has developed to meet the needs of society via the political ideologies of the policy-makers.

In considering why a student's background can influence their achievement levels, we need to consider not only what influences that student within the system but also outside of that system within the home, the community and the wider society they engage in.

Parental involvement and the home environment

The impact parents can have on the educational progress of a child has been known for some time. In 1967, the Plowden Report built on a range of research which demonstrated the correlation between parental interest and the educational progress of the child. Nor is the role that parents play in their child's education lost on national government. Through initiatives such as Sure Start, for families with children under 4, and information sources including *The Parents' Magazine* and the DfES website, the government seeks to ensure that as many parents as possible have access to resources that can facilitate them in supporting their children's education. Recent proposals to increase the power of parents have also been included in various educational policies. The qualification levels of a child's parents and their career have proved to be a good indicator of academic success for the child. This has led to suggestions that as those parents have succeeded in the education system and that, furthermore, it has provided them with their current lifestyles, they are more likely to see the value of education and aid their child's development, that in some way they care more about the education of their child. This of course would suggest that the parents of those children who do not perform well have a less developed interest in their child's education. This is not necessarily the case. While it is true that increased involvement correlates with higher levels of success, the issue is more complex than that. The idea that parents from lower socio-economic groups do not have an interest in their child's education is an over-simplified suggestion and evidence from Topping and Wolfendale (1985) is just one of many examples which show that parents of all class groups have an interest in the education of their child. The main difference lies in the ideologies they have around education as a positive or negative force, ideologies which have been shaped by their own experiences. Furthermore, issues of cultural capital and an awareness and knowledge of the system ensure that parents who have previously succeeded in the system are able to navigate their way through its intricacies much more effectively.

Role models and counter-culture

In discussions on the achievement of boys and students from minority ethnic groups, the lack of appropriate role models is often presented as a major cause for concern. Male educational role models in the school, home and community can be conspicuously absent for boys from lower socio-economic groups and in particular Black Caribbean boys. This has a dual effect in that there are few who understand the particular needs of these children who then adopt a counter-culture unsuitable to successful academic performance as evidenced by the work of Sewell (1997) and Willis

(1977). It should be noted that this counter-culture is a response to a system which is not designed to meet their needs as they see little or no evidence of past achievement amongst those they would respect. Much of this is due to increased levels of single, predominately female parents coupled with a lack of male teachers within the primary school. There is also a wider issue of a narrow curriculum which does not promote such role models in a positive manner. As Abbot (2005: 109) states: 'Black boys need men in the classroom. They simply do not see reading or educational attainment as masculine or cool.' Abbot further links this issue to that of White working-class boys. While there are male role models, they rarely come from similar backgrounds to those most at risk in the system.

A narrow curriculum?

Although there are a range of schools and new types of schools are often developed and promoted such as Academies, generally through initiatives such as the National Curriculum and the National Numeracy and Literacy Strategies, it is fair to say that there is a one-size-fits-all philosophy in the state education system. As Murphy et al. (2006) state: 'Moreover, the one-size-fits-all aspect of the strategy as a pedagogy to be applied in all classrooms nationally, … does little to take into account the prior experience, background, interests and individuality of both teacher and pupil' (2006: 35).

In Chapter 1, we discussed the narrowing of the standards for teacher training which have led to new teachers not always being aware of or equipped to deal with the differing needs within their classrooms. A continual narrowing of curricula together with enforced pedagogy is unlikely to meet the disparate needs of a multi-cultural, class-driven society.

Labelling theory and the self-fulfilling prophecy

Each of us is influenced by a range of experiences, media images, our upbringing and the capital that has been invested in us over the years. Teachers are no exception. These influences can impact upon the expectations held about varying groups of learners and the individuals that make up those groups. Think back to the Stop, Think and Do activity you were asked to undertake earlier in the chapter (Task 9.1). What do the words you chose suggest about the ways in which we view certain individuals? The concept of labelling is not a new one. Becker (1952) discussed how teachers held a view of the 'ideal pupil', a pupil who would be interested and hard working. In addition, they would be compliant and unproblematic. The problem arises when a child does not fit that narrow and culturally biased viewpoint. The label of problematic, uncooperative, unacademic etc. can be attached to a child and this label is further reinforced by the messages given by those around him. The child then comes to accept and work within this label, making it extremely difficult for them to change that expectation of them. Labels can be attached not only by a child's behaviour but through the background of the parents, their appearance and their acceptance of the hierarchies within the system.

Rosenthal and Jacobson (1968) demonstrated that lower or higher expectations held about a child will ultimately prove to be correct, not, however, because of any insight into a child but because through reinforcement of a label the child will come to accept that they are naughty, stupid, bright or good. This concept is known as the self-fulfilling prophecy and goes some way to explaining the inequalities in achievement found within the system. Effectively, we imagine that certain children will perform at a higher level and that belief is apparent through our actions and the messages sent to that child. Those messages and actions will ensure that the prophecy becomes reality. Of course this prophecy can be negative as well as positive.

Task 9.2 Stop, think and do

- How were you viewed within education? Were you seen as an 'ideal pupil' or not?
- How did this manifest itself?
- What impact do you believe it had upon you?

Conclusion

As individuals, we belong to certain social classifications based upon our gender, ethnicity and social status. We may strongly believe that we are not defined by them but most evidence would suggest that this is not the case and that all of these aspects make us who we are through a complex socialization process. There is no doubt though that there is a strong correlation between our social characteristics and how likely we are to do well within the education system. The statistical evidence presented in this chapter paints a disturbing picture of a system which fails to adequately meet the needs of large sections of society. For a system to claim to be based upon meritocratic principles, this is deeply concerning.

This chapter and Chapter 8 have sought to explain some of the potential reasons behind such issues. It would be naïve to suggest that there is one reason or that there is a simple solution, because both would be incorrect. However, each of the potential reasons has some validity and a combination of them all goes some way towards an explanation. Awareness is a start but it is solutions that will ultimately make a difference. We must realize that the education system is not fully addressing the needs of all of society and it is this challenge that has to be at the forefront of current and future debates.

Summary

1 Gender, class and ethnicity largely determine the nature of the education that individuals receive. However, we cannot view these social factors in isolation from each other as in combination they can create further issues.

2 These social factors should not be underestimated in terms of their impact upon educational experiences and achievement, and social class, in particular, is a major determinant of an individual's chances of success within the educational environment at all levels.

3 There are a wide range of theories which can help us to understand the situation some of which are internal to the individual but many which are external.

4 An understanding of how these theories combine allows us to analyse the barriers that certain individuals face in education.

5 Ultimately, it is essential that we understand the challenges that individuals face if we are truly to develop an education system that allows each individual to reach their full potential.

Section 4

Inside the School

10 Early Years Education

Introduction

Since 1999, Early Years workers have been faced with a stream of legislation and other initiatives, some of which can appear to contradict others. This chapter attempts to explain the context in which these policies have been formed and to consider their implications for current and future practice.

Concepts of childhood and models of early childhood provision

People from various societies and eras can have very different understandings of just what childhood is. While it is clear that children are small and physically immature compared with adults, their role within society and the obligations of society towards them have varied greatly (Wyness 2006). We need to agree, then, on the meaning and purpose of childhood before we can decide how children are best cared for.

Until the second half of the nineteenth century, it was widely believed that children were much like adults, but merely smaller and less physically robust. Campaigners such as Fielden believed that children were being made to work harder than was good for them, but saw no intrinsic problem in employing them for physical labour (Fielden 1836). This view gradually changed during the middle part of the century, possibly as a result of a series of social investigations and reports that revealed just what life was like for the working class. There was certainly a change of attitude after education was made compulsory in England in 1870. For the first time, childhood as a time for learning, rather than earning, was common to all classes, and as the economic value of children declined, so they came to be regarded more sentimentally (Zelizer 1985).

Another change was the emerging science of physiology. Particularly critical was the identification and study of cells, which demonstrated that cellular activity was particularly vigorous in children. From this observation came the idea of physical maturation, as opposed to mere growth. The systematic study of children's physiology gradually separated them from adults, and this was supported by work that was taking place in other fields. Combe's *Principles of Physiology* (1842) drew on statistics of infant mortality which had been published in the *First Annual Report of the Registrar-General* and showed that mortality patterns in children differed markedly from those of adults (Steedman 1994).

We should be cautious about regarding the development of attitudes towards children as one of continuous progress. Aries (1973) is among those who have suggested that the history of childhood is one of gradual emergence from brutality and abuse, and that only in relatively recent times did adults have any real conception of childhood as qualitatively different at all. Pollock, on the other hand, believes that the evidence of four centuries of parents' diaries suggests that the treatment of children has alternated between harsh and mild according to the religious climate of the time (Pollock 1983).

One modern-day view suggests that:

> In the twentieth century ... Western childhood has become a period in the life course characterised by social dependency, asexuality, and the obligation to be happy, with children having the right to protection and training, but not to social or personal autonomy.
>
> (James et al. cited in Wyness 2006: 9)

This contrasts strongly with societies in which children take paid employment, act as carers, get married, and even fight alongside adult soldiers. The implication of this definition is that childhood is a time for play and for freedom from responsibility, whereas adulthood involves the need to work and, in particular, to provide for children.

Legislation concerning children has often been passed in an attempt to keep up with current concerns, and the Children Act 1989 (DES 1989) was the result of a number of influences (Allen 1992). There was an awareness that the existing laws affecting children were unsystematic and, in some cases, contradictory, and several reviews were undertaken in the 1980s. There had also been cases where failures in practice had led to the deaths of children; in particular, there were child death inquiries into the cases of Tyra Henry, Jasmine Beckford, and Kimberley Carlile. Parents and others were concerned at the way in which local authorities had exercised their use of Wardship and Care Order proceedings in cases of alleged child sexual abuse, most notably in Cleveland in 1987. Finally, the United Nations Convention on the Rights of the Child came into force in 1989 and was legally binding on all countries that ratified it. The result was to help shape the values which underlay the Children Act 1989 (MacLeod-Brudenell 2004).

The guidance accompanying the Children Act 1989 emphasized the link between child care and education, stating that 'the aim should be to offer 3 and 4 year olds in daycare settings experiences comparable in quality with those offered to children attending school' (cited in Cohen et al. 2004: 54). Nothing much changed in practice at this stage, but it is clear that the emphasis was on the benefits which day care could offer to the child, rather than on providing a childminding service for mothers. This was in keeping with the principle, set out at the very beginning of the Act, that 'when a court determines any question with respect to the upbringing of a child, the child's welfare shall be the court's paramount consideration' (Allen 1992).

The Children Act 1989 aimed to alter the balance of power between individual families and the state. In particular, it was intended to protect families from the arbitrary exercise of authority. The underlying assumption was that the best interests of children were served by being cared for within their own families, and good reason had to be established for deviating from this pattern. Child protection policy was built on the assumption that most families functioned reasonably satisfactorily, and that attention needed to be concentrated on those children who were deemed to be at risk of coming to harm. It was recognized that relationships between agencies had evolved differently in different parts of the country, and also that every case in which a child came to be at risk was unique and demanded individual consideration. The Act, therefore, demanded that child protection policies be flexible, allowing each case to be examined on its merits (Allen 1992).

An important new concept was that of parental responsibility, which abolished the earlier idea of the child as an object over which adults had certain rights and sought to replace it with a system in which rights were more explicitly balanced by duties. In particular, it aimed to do away with the 'winner takes all' aspect to child custody proceedings (Allen 1992).

While the Act set out clearly the rights of children and the role of parents, it was less specific about the duties of local authorities. Although it did provide for the establishment of family centres 'as they consider appropriate', it left the precise scope of their activities somewhat open. Likewise, it laid upon councils a general duty:

a. to safeguard and promote the welfare of children within their area who are in need; and

b. so far as is consistent with that duty, to promote the upbringing of such children by their families.

(Advisory Centre for Education 1992: 13).

This approach fitted with the ideology of the Conservative government of the day, which was simultaneously libertarian, believing in a minimal role for the state, and socially conservative in that there was a desire to support traditional family structures. Since its rejection of the Black Report on health inequalities in 1980 (Townsend and Davidson 1982), the government had dealt with deprivation and, in particular health inequalities, on the basis of the 'behavioural-cultural explanation'. This stresses the responsibility of the individual to take positive action to improve their own circumstances, for example, by changing their diet, taking more exercise or working for better qualifications. Whilst promoting the freedom of individuals from state interference in their lives, it suggests that those who make 'bad' choices do so because they possess a deficient system of culture and values. The behavioural-cultural explanation has thus been described as a victim-blaming approach (Kirby 2000).

The 1944 Education Act had made the provision of nursery schools the responsibility of local authorities, but gave them discretion as to just what level of service they would provide. Only in 1989 did the Children Act require local authorities to make provision for children in need and for those not yet in school. This was still non-specific as to numbers; it was the 1998 Education Act which required local authorities to enable all 4-year-olds to have five half-days of free provision. This began to be extended to 3-year-olds from 2000 (Broadhead 1994).

Meanwhile, other forms of provision had been emerging outside the state sector. From the 1960s, playgroups became increasingly common, and after 1998 these were incorporated into the mainstream of provision. The 1990s saw increasing numbers of women returning to work and needing care for their children. This led to a rapid expansion in the number of private nursery places and childminders (Broadhead 2004).

In the 1980s and early 1990s, school governors and head teachers began to recognise the high monetary value which many funding formulas assigned to 4-year-olds. There was increasing pressure on parents to admit their 4-year-olds to reception classes, and it is estimated that by 1995 around 75 per cent of this age group were attending school (Broadhead 2004).

In 1994, there was a new initiative in the form of nursery vouchers which could be used to pay for care in any approved setting, whether in the private, voluntary, or state sector. The aim was to provide a mixed economy market which would maximize parental choice. The first pilot schemes began in 1996, but the experiment was cut short by the Labour victory in the 1997 General Election (Cohen et al 2004).

In 1997, the newly-elected Labour Government asked the Chief Medical Officer, Sir Donald Acheson, to conduct an inquiry into inequalities in health (Acheson 1998). Acheson's conclusions argue that the major cause of deprivation and social inequality was the result not of individual choices but of structural and material factors. This explanation links poverty to factors such as poor housing, dangerous working conditions, and poor diet, all of which lead to stress which can cause mental health problems, unemployment, and family breakdown as well as being linked to higher levels of smoking and alcohol intake. It has also been noted that working-class people tend to receive less education and advice about health-related issues. The implication of this explanation is that co-ordinated action by the state is needed to address problems such as housing quality, low wages, and information about the availability of health, education, and social services (Kirby 2000).

In May 1998, the government announced its National Childcare Strategy. The aims were to support families, in particular by enabling parents and carers to meet others in a similar position and possibly to improve their parenting skills; to enable more women to take paid employment, thus helping strengthen the economy; and to promote children's development by helping them to become happy and confident, and to prepare them for school.

In order to achieve this, the plan was to provide good quality childcare for all children aged 0–14 years, including playgroups, out-of-school clubs, and support for childminders. In order for this to be possible, it would be necessary to train 50,000 new childcare workers and to increase the benefits paid to parents to help them afford the childcare they needed, as well as providing additional funding to support the new facilities. One other aspect was the need to involve employers, in particular by working towards more 'family-friendly' policies (DfEE, 1998c).

The Effective Provision of Pre-School Education Project (EPPE) showed that children who attended pre-school settings from the age of 2 years made better social, emotional, and intellectual progress than those who remained at home. Children from deprived backgrounds, and especially boys, gained the most advantage. Once the children started primary school, however, the advantages diminished. There was no significant impact on behaviour by the age of 7, and intellectual development showed no significant difference by the age of 11. The report states 'the impact of pre-school operates through a stronger start to school and NOT through increased capacity to learn more in subsequent years' (Sylva 2004: 57). There was also no evidence that greater levels of provision automatically brought greater benefits. Children who had attended pre-school full-time showed no improvement over those who attended part-time, whilst those who had extensive experience of group care before the age of two years showed increased levels of anti-social behaviour at ages three and five years.

This research suggests, then, that a sophisticated approach needs to be taken to providing early years care. It can certainly be of benefit in preparing children for the primary classroom, but the evidence does not appear to support the sort of full-time provision which would be needed to help mothers to take employment.

As a part of this process of expansion, Sure Start was established in 1999. This had the aim of improving children's health, education, and emotional development. What distinguished it from previous schemes was its commitment to involving parents in planning and running its services and its sensitivity to cultural differences and local needs (Schneider et al 2007). Sure Start Local Projects (SSLPs) were targeted at designated disadvantaged areas, with the aim of using early intervention to support children's development and strengthen families and communities, thereby breaking the cycle of deprivation and reducing poverty (Cohen et al 2004). This targeting was intended to concentrate the newly-available resources on those areas which were in most need, but this raised problems. Whereas mainstream providers applied eligibility criteria which were based on need, the strictly geographical organisation of SSLPs could lead to anomalies whereby families who were 'in need' but had the wrong postcode were deprived of access to services to which other households were entitled (Edgley, cited in Schneider et al 2007: 122–3).

In 2003, the then Chancellor of the Exchequer, Gordon Brown, cited Sure Start as an illustration of the new localism which the government favoured. It was, he said: 'a genuine break with the recent past: services, once centrally funded and organised, can and should now be led, organised and delivered by voluntary, charitable and community organisations' (Brown 2003).

A year later, however, in 2004, the government responded to the 'postcode lottery' by what has been described as the 'mainstreaming' of Sure Start. The Ten Year Childcare Strategy (HMT et al. 2004) promised a Sure Start Children's Centre for every community by 2010 – in other words, there was a shift from targeted to universal provision (Schneider et al. 2007). This shift was, moreover, accompanied by an end to the generous and ring-fenced funding that had supported the SSLPs for the first five years. Children's Centres now became the responsibility of local authorities, with a consequent loss of funding and autonomy (Leighton, cited in Schneider et al 2007:

87). They were given a set of targets to achieve, and those in the most deprived areas, the very areas where local autonomy and parental involvement had been championed, had the most detailed targets (Sure Start 2008).

These changes followed the publication in 2003 of the Green Paper *Every Child Matters* (DfES 2003a), which formed the basis for the Children Act 2004 (DfES 2004a). This was published following the conclusions of the Laming Enquiry (Laming 2003) into the death of Victoria Climbié at the hands of her great-aunt and the aunt's boyfriend. There was a strong sense that the system for protecting children had failed, and that drastic reform was needed (Stepney 2006). For the first time, there was a set of common goals towards which all bodies and agencies involved with working with children should be aiming. The five desirable outcomes for all children were: being healthy; staying safe; enjoying and achieving; making a positive contribution; and achieving economic well-being (DfES 2003a: 6–7).

Under national guidance *Working Together to Safeguard Children* (DfES 2006a), it was stated that child protection should work within a broader framework of safeguarding and promoting the welfare of children in general. Thus the notion of certain children being 'at risk' was broadened, and child protection was superseded by the new safeguarding children approach, which included children who were disabled or suffering social exclusion (Barker and Hodes 2007). The Every Child Matters agenda thus transfers the focus of attention from those children who are most at risk of harm to attempting to intervene directly to meet the needs of all children.

Some investigators have questioned the notion that all children are potentially at risk of harm, and indeed have suggested that current policies feed a climate of fear. Clements (2006) points out that the number of children deemed to be 'at risk' actually fell from 32 per 10,000 in 1995 to 23 in 2004–5, and that perhaps social services have been doing a better job than the newspapers give them credit for.

To improve the collection and sharing of information about children, the government is establishing a new information-sharing database called ContactPoint. The system will maintain a file on every child in England, containing a range of information including the child's name, address, date of birth, and a unique identifying number; the name and contact details for the child's parent or carer; contact details for services working with the child; and a means to indicate whether a practitioner working with a child is a lead professional and if they have undertaken an assessment under the Common Assessment Framework (ECM 2007).

It is estimated that at least 330,000 users will have legitimate access to this information (Ward 2007). Foucault described the panoptic approach, by which a person was kept under constant scrutiny in order 'to induce in the [subject] a state of conscious and permanent visibility that assures the automatic functioning of power' (Foucault 1977: 201). This might be a useful viewpoint from which to consider ContactPoint.

The problem which faces the authorities is that of multi-agency working: when a child is being seen by schoolteachers, a GP, a health visitor, and maybe a social worker, there continue to be real difficulties in maintaining effective communication between the various disciplines. For further discussion of this, see Chapter 12 in this volume.

There are risks inherent in making unrealistically high demands of the child protection system. An enormous emphasis has been placed in recent years on information gathering and information sharing, and it is doubtful whether the possession of more detailed information will lead to a better service being provided (Beckett, C. 2007). In the great majority of cases, the limiting factor is lack of resources. In particular, in 2007, the co-director of the Association of Directors of Children's Services, John Coughlan, observed that a shortage of suitably qualified social workers was placing vulnerable children at risk. He pointed out that workers in this field face low salaries, high levels of stress, and constant criticism over cases where social workers have failed to protect children in their care (Hill 2007).

The new approach presents dangers to the relationship between parents and professionals, and also between children and professionals. Mothers with post-natal depression have been known to keep it secret for fear of having their children taken from them, and Eileen Munro has observed that children who cannot be assured of confidentiality by an advocate will be more likely to conceal their problems (Beckett, C. 2007).

The risk is that we are developing a culture of fear, in which 'agencies act to "cover their backs" rather than in the best interests of children' (Beckett, C. 2007: 209). Increasing numbers of children are being taken into public care annually in England and Wales. At the same time, increasing surveillance and information-sharing are being used to monitor and even coerce parents who are seen to be making 'bad' choices. As Fitzpatrick (2001: 192) states,

> The paternalism of the classic welfare state has fused with the disciplinary and correctional systems that had lain more or less dormant since the time of the Victorian Poor Law. Social control, social surveillance and social welfare are becoming increasingly hard to distinguish.

Task 10.1   Stop, think and do

- How has 'Every Child Matters' changed the priorities involved in safeguarding children?
- What are the advantages and disadvantages of targeting attention specifically on those children who are deemed to be most at risk?
- According to Lord Laming's report, what were the principal causes of Victoria Climbié's death? To what extent did a lack of information play a part?

Investment in Early Years inside the school

Just as we need to decide on the objectives which Early Years settings should be aiming for, we need to determine which settings are best suited to achieving these objectives. The current age at which a child must enter full-time education in

England is during the term after their fifth birthday (DfES no date). It is by no means clear why this should be the case. This law originates with the 1870 Education Act, which stated that compulsory attendance could be required from an age of not less than five years. Many voluntary schools at this time considered 7 years an appropriate age for starting, but large numbers of children aged 3–6 years were attending elementary schools, usually divided into babies (3–5 years) and infants (5–7 years). A survey conducted in 1870 estimated that a third of all children attending school were aged between 3 and 6 years (Whitebread 1972: 40). By 1900, more than 50 per cent of 3- and 4-year-olds, and even many 2-year-olds, were attending infant schools, and in 1905 a report called for the introduction of a system of national nurseries which would care for young children in a way that was distinct from the experience offered by schools. This case was made again and again, notably in 1919, 1929, 1931, and most particularly in 1945, when the experience of day nurseries operated during the Second World War convinced the Ministry of Health that while nursery education would be of benefit to children aged between 2 and 5 years, full-time day care should be regarded as the exception, and thus mothers of young children should be positively discouraged from going out to work (Moss and Penn 1996).

The debate about school starting age had little to do with children's readiness to learn. In favour of the case that they should start later was the idea that 6 and under was 'simply too tender an age for compulsory attendance', and that many parents preferred to keep their children at home at this age (Whitebread 1972: 40). The case for starting at 5 or even earlier was twofold: first, children were safer at school than at home; second, there was a demand that education not encroach too far on the business of earning a living, and so it would be best for education to start and finish early. While the pressure is now to maximize, rather than minimize, the time which children spend in education before seeking employment, it remains the case that one strong argument for increasing the provision of Early Years care and education is the belief that too many households are not doing enough to meet children's developmental needs (Furedi 2001). This is a very different matter from saying that the primary school is the best place to do this.

Setting the starting age for compulsory schooling at 5 years distinguished Britain from practice in both Europe and the United States. The curriculum for babies and infants was distinct from that prescribed for 7–13-year-olds, a position that remained largely unchallenged until the Plowden Report suggested that 8 years would be a better age for transition to more formal learning, although little has come of this proposal (Whitebread 1972).

Sharp (2002) shows that there is a lack of conclusive evidence concerning the benefits of starting school at different ages. The best available evidence suggests that teaching more formal skills early (in school) gives children an initial academic advantage, but that this advantage is not sustained in the longer term. There are some suggestions that an early introduction to a formal curriculum may increase anxiety and have a negative impact on children's self-esteem and motivation to learn. The long-term impact of different early childhood curricula would seem to be an important topic for further research. Furthermore, there are disadvantages to delivering the Foundation Stage in primary rather than nursery settings, including poorer staffing ratios, fewer facilities for outdoor play, a less active, more sedentary style of teaching and learning, and more teacher-led and fewer child-centred activities. Finally, although starting formal schooling early produced short-term gains, the best long-term results were achieved by children who started school at 6 or even 7 years.

Plans for the expansion of the Early Years workforce and its continuing training and development depend on recruiting and retaining increasing numbers of Early Years workers. It has long been recognized that status and pay are important factors in this. In 2000, the Education Secretary, David Blunkett, acknowledged the importance of setting pay at a level which would enable Early Years providers to compete for skilled workers, and yet a few months later a report found that half of pre-school assistants were paid just half the minimum wage. There has long been a distinction between primary teachers, who are necessarily graduates, and nursery workers, fewer than 40 per cent of whom had a first degree in 1997 (Browne 2004).

With the introduction of the Foundation Stage for 3–6-year-olds in 2006, and the expansion of nursery provision, there was a need not just to expand the workforce but to develop a new kind of Early Years worker who could operate across a variety of settings. The result was the introduction from 2001 of the new Early Years Sector-Endorsed Foundation Degree, which would confer the status of Senior Practitioner. This would form a link in the career pathway from Level 3 (CACHE Diploma, NVQ3, and equivalent qualifications) to Qualified Teacher Status (QTS) (DfES 2002).

Before the new status gained widespread understanding and recognition, it was made obsolescent by the new approach which followed the publication of *Every Child Matters: Change for Children* (DfES 2003a), *The Ten Year Childcare Strategy* (HMT et al. 2004), and the plans for a new Early Years Foundation Stage. The result of these initiatives was the introduction of a new type of practitioner, the Early Years Professional (EYP). The purpose of the EYP is to lead delivery of the Early Years Foundation Stage curriculum, whatever the setting. This is a higher level qualification than Senior Practitioner, being on an equivalent level to QTS. EYPs should be working in all full-time day care settings by 2015, and in order to support the training of so many practitioners the government has established a Transformation Fund to assist employers with the costs they will face (CWDC 2006).

As well as creating the post of Early Years Professional, the government has invested in the development of classroom support staff. In particular, Higher Level Teaching Assistants work under the direction of a teacher to support both individual pupils and whole classes. The development of this and other initiatives is supported by the Training and Development Agency for Schools (TDA 2008). For them to succeed, there will need to be a sustained improvement in the pay of many Early Years workers.

Following the Childcare Act 2006 (DfES 2006b), the government committed £680 million to the development of Extended Schools over the period 2006–8. This would include after-school activities including study support, clubs and activities, and, in primary schools, childcare both before and after school; support for parents and families; and community access to learning facilities. The aims include improving attainment, reducing exclusion rates, and improved access to community facilities (Teachernet 2007). In addition, Beverley Hughes, Minister for Children, Young People and Families, has expressed the hope that the availability of additional childcare will enable more parents to take paid employment (Sure Start 2005). The effect of extended schools on children in the Early Years Foundation Stage has yet to be evaluated; given that the EPPE study cited above showed no benefits to be gained from full-time, rather than part-time, attendance, it remains to be seen just how children of this age will respond to an even longer school day.

Task 10.2 Stop, think and do

From what you have read, and from your own experience, at what age do you think that children should start formal schooling? Give reasons for this answer.

Do you feel that:

- working in Early Years can lead to a rewarding and well-paid career?
- the pay is not so good, but the job makes up for it in other ways?
- it is a useful stepping stone in your personal and career development?

Parents are increasingly being asked to choose between caring for their children at home and sacrificing vital earnings, or expecting them to spend up to ten hours per day in education and care settings. What would you choose for your child, and is there any way round this dilemma?

The meaning behind different curriculum models

For a broader discussion of curricula, see Chapter 12. The content and structure of a curriculum are defined by its purpose. Lauder et al. (2006) looked at education in the context of preparation for participation in the wider world. In particular, they consider social integration (enabling people to fit in and join in), the transmission of culture and values, the promotion of social equality (by making opportunities available to all), encouraging the use of opportunities to enable individuals to fulfil their potential, and the demands of the 'knowledge economy' and the need to compete with overseas economies.

This view is to a large extent dominated by the requirement that the curriculum prepares the individual to serve the needs of society at large. This is all well and good as long as those who determine society's needs are themselves following a moral agenda. Education could equally be (and has been) used, for example, 'to limit the pupil's scope for criticism ..., to ensure political conformity and obedience or even to promote racist or religious intolerance' (Kelly 2004: 3). It is, therefore, important not to ignore the need to promote the development of the individual child. Guidance from the DfEE and QCA in 1999 includes the need to 'promote pupils' spiritual, moral, social and cultural development' (White 2004: 3–4). The extent to which a curriculum promotes the development of critical, confident children can be linked to whether it prepares them for conforming to, reforming, or transforming society (MacNaughton 2003). Which of these qualities is most desirable is a question that must be decided by society itself.

Collier (1959: 82–4) summarized the objectives of education as being good personal relationships, creative initiative in a group setting, a sense of public duty, co-operation with superior authorities, adult learning, a personal sense of duty, and integrity.

He was concerned that Great Britain was facing a period of rapid social and economic change, including increasing economic competition from abroad, and that the education system needed to prepare the population to be able to meet these challenges. The key to this was to develop people's social, civic, and private virtues. Note that these objectives stress particular personal qualities rather than the development of specific skills. He objected in particular to the trend in scientific and technical education towards a narrow concentration on facts at the expense of intellectual creativity. He showed that the standard of attainment expected of and achieved by students of these subjects had risen markedly since the 1920s, but held that the effect was 'to crowd out more human and general studies from the pupil's thinking. He knows that his future career depends largely on his results in the examinations, and that these rarely give much credit to general education' (Collier 1959: 225). Nearly 50 years later we are hearing these same complaints.

The Plowden Report (DES 1967) followed this line of thinking, suggesting that the role of the primary teacher should be more supportive than directive, and that, if provided with a rich environment, then children would flourish of their own accord. The problem with this approach, as Cullingford (1989) indicates, is that it fails to specify just what children are supposed to be learning. This fear lay behind the campaign for a national curriculum which would ensure that schools were teaching 'proper' subjects. By 1989, there was a widespread assertion that primary schools were not doing enough teaching of English and maths, and yet the evidence showed that these subjects dominated the school day. It was, therefore, a matter of continuing discussion as to just what purpose primary education was to serve.

Whatever the model chosen, there follows the question of whether (and if so, how) to assess pupils' progress. Preparation for testing can become an end in itself as test results come to be used for an increasing range of purposes, including judging the effectiveness of the institution and the staff within it (Duffy, cited in Pugh and Duffy 2006: 85). This concentration on the needs of the institution, rather than on those of the individual child, can be furthered by pressure from primary schools to prepare Foundation Stage children for the very different demands of Key Stage 1.

The Foundation Stage was introduced in 2000, and contained six areas of learning (DfEE 2000). These are personal, social, and emotional development; communication, language and literacy; mathematical development; knowledge and understanding of the world; physical development; and creative development. It displays elements of both developmental and social imperative models. It contained guidance as to what might be expected of children at particular ages, and 'stepping stones' which indicated ways in which they might make progress. The early learning goals indicate the child's likely attainment by the end of Reception Year. It has been shown that, in practice, less emphasis is placed on physical development, understanding the world, and creative development than on the first three areas. In particular, by the reception year, the main effort is placed on following the national literacy and numeracy strategies, despite many practitioners believing that the early learning goals for these areas are unachievable. There is a widespread view that children of this age are not developmentally ready for these challenges, and that the 'standards agenda' and preparation for statutory testing have replaced the needs of children as educational priorities (Duffy, cited in Pugh and Duffy 2006: 84).

In 2002, the Curriculum Guidance for the Foundation Stage was supplemented by the publication of *Birth to Three Matters*, which was to be regarded as a framework rather than a curriculum, which is to say that it provided guidance for practitioners working with children aged under 3 years but was intended to be flexible (Duffy, cited in Pugh and Duffy 2006: 81). The guidance was organized into four strands: a strong child; a skilful communicator; a competent learner; and a healthy child. Crucially, it was not formally assessed or monitored, and is much more person-centred than the Foundation Stage. To that extent, it can be seen as a stepping-stone towards the approach taken by Every Child Matters.

The Early Years Foundation Stage (EYFS) will replace Birth to Three Matters and the Foundation Stage from September 2008 (DfES 2007). Its aim is to help young children achieve the five Every Child Matters outcomes: be healthy; stay safe; enjoy and achieve; make a positive contribution; and achieve economic well-being. Its content is divided into four strands: a unique child; positive relationships; enabling environments; and learning and development.

Although these are not identical to the four strands found in *Birth to Three Matters*, the approach is similar. Unlike the Foundation Stage, the EYFS will not form a part of the National Curriculum, although it will continue to reflect the national literacy and numeracy strategies. Thus, despite its softer tone, it will have the potential to continue the narrowing of the Early Years curriculum which was occurring even before the introduction of the Foundation Stage.

Early years and play

Play is one important way in which children come to understand the world around them. It gives them an opportunity to use their imaginations to examine and experiment with new concepts they have encountered in their exploration of the world around them – they experience real things and real people, and then represent both real and imagined things and people in their play (Ouvry 2003). Friedrich Froebel (1782–1852) was the first Western authority on the value of play, regarding it as the highest form of learning. His work was followed in Britain by educators such as Margaret Macmillan and Susan Isaacs, whose work continues to inform British Early Years policy (Bruce 2001).

According to the DfES (2007: 7) 'Play underpins the delivery of all of the Early Years Foundation Stage.' One key item of practice guidance for the EYFS states that practitioners must plan to meet the needs of children from ethnic minorities, however, and there is a view that the great emphasis on play is a cultural phenomenon of the Western world (Bruce, 2001). We cannot assume that all parents will be happy with a play-based curriculum for their child, and even many educators still believe at some level that effective learning only happens when children are still, quiet, and calm, using pencil and paper and supported by a teacher (Ouvry 2003).

One aspect that is receiving increasing attention, particularly in the Early Years, is outdoor play. It provides space and allows children to move freely; it enables them to learn safely about assessing and taking risks; and it provides learning opportunities that cannot be provided indoors. As a result, it has been shown to improve behaviour and, more controversially, to serve the needs of young boys in particular (Ouvry 2003). As Browne (2004) points out, in Britain in 2002 around 2 per cent of the Early Years workforce were male. Although children are individuals and exhibit a wide range of behaviours, there is some evidence that a predominantly female workforce relates more easily to what are perceived as more articulate and compliant girls than to the louder, more boisterous behaviour exhibited by many boys (Jones 2003; Ouvry 2003). It could, therefore, be argued that outdoor play can provide an environment in which such behaviour can be displayed in an acceptable fashion.

As well as promoting children's general development, active play can help tackle specific problems such as the decline in children's physical fitness. Fears for children's safety have reduced the opportunities for children to play out of doors, while new technologies provide increasingly sedentary opportunities for play in the home. Decreasing levels of physical activity among children are leading to concerns about increasing levels of childhood obesity. There is a danger, though, that physical play might come to be seen by children as more of a health and fitness regime imposed by adults than as adventure and fun (Wood and Attfield 2005). Once again, it is important that this activity be made genuinely child-centred.

Task 10.3   Stop, think and do

- Think about a work placement you've been in: how often was successful play interrupted by the need to get on with 'work'?
- There has been a marked increase in the giving of homework to young children, along with demands that parents become more involved in supporting their children's learning, particularly with regard to literacy and numeracy. Which parents are most likely to engage with this approach, and how can it be made to fit with the Sure Start agenda of supporting struggling or uninvolved parents?

Summary

1. The past ten years have seen a series of new educational initiatives for the early years, some of them contradictory, some superseded before they have had time to become established.
2. There has been a paradigm shift by which childhood is no longer seen as a time of innocence, but of constant vulnerability to harm.
3. Policies are as likely to be introduced in response to a politically significant event as because there is research evidence to support them.
4. The Early Years Foundation Stage has a more child-centred approach than the previous Foundation Stage.
5. The main reason for children joining the school reception class at the age of 4 years is because schools benefit financially from this policy.
6. An early start to schooling eases the transition to Key Stage 1, benefiting teachers, but offers no lasting benefit to children.
7. Full-time day care assists parents but offers no lasting developmental benefits to children, and can be detrimental to children under 2 years old.
8. In order to be sustainable, measures to expand and upgrade the Early Years workforce must be supported by improvements to their status and pay.
9. There is a long way to go before we achieve the child-centred system of Early Years care and education which the rhetoric proclaims.

11 Inclusion
A case for special treatment

Until fairly recently the education of children with special needs was considered as quite a separate issue from mainstream educational provision. However, over the past 30 years there has been a major change in the way the needs of young children are met due to a shift in educational philosophy and in policy that now emphasizes inclusion of children with special educational needs in mainstream education and care settings (Pugh and Duffy 2006).

This chapter will begin with a consideration of models of disability and their associated educational discourses which gave rise to segregated schooling for those with special educational needs (SEN). It will go on to outline landmark educational policies which led to a rethinking of the treatment of children with educational difficulties within the UK and prompted a move from segregation to integration and finally to inclusive education. An overview of the debate concerning inclusive education will serve as a springboard for consideration of whether current education policy on SEN in the UK is fit for purpose or whether there is need for a further rethinking and overhauling of special education.

Models of disability

As will be highlighted below, concern over SEN provision and practice in the UK has resulted in part from a lack of clarity in both the literature and policy documents regarding the very definitions of disability and special educational needs (Farrell and Ainscow 2002; Warnock 2005). The term SEN is not static and, as Beveridge (2002) points out, it can be regarded as a socio-historical and cultural construct which changes over time depending on social, political and economic attitudes and expectations.

The medical model of disability

In the nineteenth century what is called the medical model dominated attitudes to disability. Any behaviours perceived as subnormal or abnormal were defined as a 'pathology of difference' (Clough 2005: 11). In other words, disability was defined in terms of a pathology or science of disease and seen as a deficit or lack *within* the individual which could be diagnosed and, in some cases, treated. External factors such as poverty, health and social expectations which could have an impact upon behaviour and psychological orientation were not considered as affecting a person's ability to function in terms of accepted social and educational norms (Kellett 2004).

Historically, the medical model of disability defined four categories of pathological difference: idiot, imbecile, feeble-minded and moral defective. The dominance of this model resulted in a lack of educational provision for children with educational difficulties in early education policy, such as the 1870 Education Act (the Foster Act) and the 1872 Scotland Act. When disability was considered in educational terms in 1898 by the Departmental Committee on Defective and Epileptic Children, only those diagnosed as feeble-minded or morally defective were deemed educable within special educational institutions. Imbeciles and idiots were excluded from educational provision (Kellett 2004).

The legacy of the medical model of disability has been far-reaching. The 1944 Education Act (the Butler Act) introducing the eleven-plus based on intelligence quota (IQ) tests and the tripartite system (see Chapter 2), still held that many children were uneducable with mainstream educational provision. Children assessed as having an IQ below 50 were diagnosed as severally mentally subnormal and excluded from schools, while those with IQs 20 per cent or more below the perceived standard IQ, though categorized as educationally subnormal, were seen as educable within remedial classes of secondary modern schools (Bartlett and Burton 2007).

As the 1944 Act defined ability on the basis of IQ tests, the educational categorizations assigned to children were seen as permanent and unchanging. Furthermore, due to the medical model's emphasis on labelling, such terms as defective, subnormal, remedial and maladjusted dominated educational discourse until the Warnock Report (DES 1978) called for a redefining of educational difficulties.

The medical model then defines educational difficulties against a trajectory of perceived normal development. It diagnoses an inherent lack in the individual, be it physical, sensory or mental, and it uses labels to categorize disability. The implication is that the disability is permanent or that, at best, it can be normalized to some degree by means of adaptation. There is little acknowledgement of ability or individuality.

The link between the medical model of disability and segregated specialist education is clear. As Hall points out, this model sees the child and her/his impairment as the problem:

> All of the adjustments must be made to the lifestyle and functionality of the child. Hence a range of prosthetic devices will be offered, along with a separate educational environment and transport to facilitate attendance. The notion that the world might need to change hardly arises because the child has and is the problem.

(1997: 74)

The focus on diagnosis and categorization of the medical model, and the educational discourses which result from it, have led many to reject this model, not least because its insistence of permanent labelling can have impact on the social and psychological well-being of an individual. As Brantlinger (2006: 233) points out, labelling an individual as disabled can create an imposed and fragmented sense of identity. Labelling can be seen as a political issue by which privileged social groups maintain their status by creating socially accepted norms (Becker, cited in Brantlinger 2006: 233). Those defined as being or behaving outside of the norms are seen as deviant and are stigmatized with labels. Pressure is asserted upon them to adapt and conform to the social definition of normality. However, the issue of labelling within the special needs arena presents a conundrum. Though the negative impact of labelling may be accepted and excessive use of labels may be rejected, as it can lead to additional support and funding for a child with SEN, it is still felt by some that the medical model has its benefits (Waller 2005).

The social model of disability

In contrast to the medical model, the social model of disablement is concerned with social attitudes and with environmental barriers (Allan 2006). The notion is that it is the attitudes of non-disabled people and/or the physical and economic barriers faced by disabled people which create the disability. The social model resists medical diagnosis and labelling and sees the problem as a social one, not as an impairment located within the individual. The social model of disability calls for a broadening of the concept of *education* which places the person first and then considers the need arising from their disability.

Two important government policies, the 1994 Disability and Discrimination Act (DfE 1995) and the revised 2001 Disability Discrimination Act (DfES 2005a), validate the social model of disability in line with human rights issues (see below). The emphasis is on inclusion of individuals with disablement in all aspects of society rather than on exclusion and segregation which are implicit in the medical model.

Numerous educational policies have sought to move from segregated schooling of those with educational difficulties towards this inclusive model. The Special Needs and Disability Act (SENDA) (DfES 2001c) and the Special Needs Code of Practice (DfES 2001b) make it unlawful for any institution, including an educational provider, to treat a disabled person less favourably than an able-bodied person. The institution is legally required to make appropriate and reasonable adjustments to accommodate the needs of the disabled person. In other words, if a disabled person is at a substantial disadvantage, the educational provider must take reasonable steps to prevent exclusion. This may include changes to policies and practice and changes to course requirements, delivery and assessment. Physical features of buildings may need to be altered and interpreters and other support workers may be employed.

While the social model of disablement now seems to be favoured above the medical model by disabled people and their advocates, the medical model, as pointed out above, still has support from some educationalists, parents and children (Waller 2005). The medical model focuses on early identification of need, high-quality diagnosis and recommendations for placement, management and monitoring. Issues related to the availability of specialist equipment, specialist teachers, a curriculum pitched at the appropriate level and services located in one place, mean that segregated, special schools may be viewed as providing the best education for learners with certain disabilities.

SEN on the agenda

Though the 1944 Education Act did provide education for those diagnosed with less severe educational needs – the educationally subnormal, the moderately physically handicapped and the remedial child, those categorized as severely disabled or mentally subnormal were excluded from the education system. It was not until the 1970 Education Act (Handicapped Children) and the 1974 Education Act (Mentally Handicapped Children) (Scotland) that all children with special educational needs were considered to have the right to education (Kellett 2004). Thus the 1970s saw an increase in special schools within the UK.

The Warnock Report (DES 1978)

The Warnock Committee was set up in 1974 to review special education provision in the UK. The Warnock Report (DES 1978), and the subsequent 1981 Education Act (DES 1981), were the turning point in public and professional opinion concerning special education.

The Warnock Report set out several recommendations for policy on the education of disabled children. First, the Report called for a change in educational discourse and labelling. As such terms as educationally subnormal and handicapped were seen as stigmatizing to a child, the Report advocated use of educational difficulty and the term special educational need was coined. Though it could be argued that this was a case of replacing one label with another, it was a definite move away from the medical model of disablement and the concept of a pathology or syndrome.

The Report focused on assessment of special educational needs rather than on diagnosis and it set out a five-stage assessment process. Input from educational professionals as well as a medical professional was incorporated into the procedure and, for the first time, weight was given to parental views and information concerning their disabled child and his/her needs. Warnock's five-stage framework begins with school-based assessment, followed, if necessary, by multi-agency assessment with input from medical professionals in progressively specialized areas of physical and mental disability. The process results in a Statement of Special Needs for a child for which a local educational authority (LEA) is legally bound to make provision.

This statementing process is very similar to that made statutory by the 1994 SEN Code of Practice, though the Code of Practice in its five-stage procedure not only requires parental involvement and consultation, but also input from the child intended to encourage responsibility for learning and to raise confidence (DfEE 1994).

The Warnock Report estimated that for a variety of social, developmental, physical and psychological reasons, one in five children would require special educational provision at some stage in their school career. In other words, it was suggested that at any point in time 18–20 per cent of a school's population could be identified as having a learning difficulty. For this reason it was recommended that all but severely disabled children be educated in ordinary schools and that provision be made within the curriculum to meet their needs.

Though the Warnock Report represents a landmark change in attitudes to and provision for special educational needs, the recommendations were for integration rather than inclusion of those with learning difficulties within ordinary educational institutions. It was advocated that those assessed as having a special need be educated in special classes within the same institution as non-disabled learners, not within mainstream classrooms. Furthermore, the Report envisaged that those with severe needs would still be educated in segregated settings.

Warnock defines different types of integration. Locational integration is full-time placement in special classes within an ordinary school and functional integration is partial or full-time placement within mainstream classes. Functional integration, however, even on a full-time basis, cannot be described as inclusion as it requires the child with learning difficulties to adjust its learning capabilities to the mainstream curriculum and not vice versa. Finally, Warnock recommended social integration, that is, mixing with other children outside of the classroom during breaks, meal times and other appropriate extra-curricular activities, for all SEN children placed within ordinary schools.

The Warnock Report put SEN and the need to cater for diversity of learners' needs on the government agenda. The Report and subsequent government policy radically changed the conceptualization of SEN provision in the UK. Over the following decades, the emphasis on redefining SEN provision increased considerably. In the 1980s and 1990s, there was a considerable decline in the number of children in special schools and a gradual increase in the proportion of children identified as having a special need, but being educated in mainstream settings. However, in the movement towards inclusive education in line with the social model of disability, there was still a long way to go.

From integration to inclusion

The 1981 Education Act on SEN (DES 1981) in response to the Warnock Report, made the five-stage statementing process statutory and shifted more responsibility on to LEAs to provide education for disabled learners. Children assessed with SEN could be educated in ordinary schools if certain conditions were met. These conditions were that the institution was able to meet the child's specific needs through efficient use of resources and that the education of other children would not be adversely affected. The Act, however, did not directly outline how SEN policy, provision and practice should be co-ordinated. The means of providing for those with learning difficulties within the school curriculum was not specified with clarity. The 1988 Education Reform Act (DES 1988) which introduced the National Curriculum sought to provide a balanced curriculum for all learners. However, as will be discussed below, there was still a failure to indicate how the needs of those with learning difficulties could be met and further strategies had to be developed and implemented.

In 1994, a seminal document from the United Nations education agency, the Salamanca Statement (UNESCO 1994), called for an international consensus on inclusion and diversity in education. The 1994 Disability and Discrimination Act (DDA) (DES 1995) attempted to bring UK legislation in line with the social model of disability advocated in the Salamanca Statement. However, as education was not an explicit factor in the DDA, the Act prompted a growing debate about continued discrimination against disabled people in the education system.

It could be argued that it was not until the 2005 Disability Discrimination Act (DfES 2005a) that the rights of disabled people to engage with equality in all public sector organisations and institutions in the UK were fully endorsed and protected. Under this legislation all public bodies, including education institutions, are required to eliminate unlawful discrimination against disabled people and to promote equal opportunities and positive attitudes towards disabled people.

When New Labour came to power in 1997 with their manifesto for improvement of educational provision and standards, they did not overlook SEN. The Green Paper *Excellence for All Children: Meeting Special Educational Needs* (DfEE 1997b) set out the government's plans for the delivery of SEN. The paper cited the benefits felt by all when all children, including those with disabilities, are included in the school community as equal partners.

Following a year of consultation on the 1997 Green Paper, the government published a White Paper, Special Educational Needs Programme for Action (DfEE 1998b), which purported to advocate delivery of SEN in line with the Salamanca Statement, that is, the promotion of inclusion and education for all. However, although increases of funding to support the development of inclusive education started to come from central government, the 1998 White Paper still asserted the need for special schools for a minority of learners. This double-edged approach set the tone of New Labour's policy on special needs education and sent out mixed messages to educationalists.

The 2001 Special Educational Needs and Disability Act (SENDA) (DfES 2001c) and the associated Special Educational Needs Code of Practice (SENCOP) (DfES 2001b), which took effect in January 2002, replaced the 1994 Code of Practice. SENDA strengthens the rights of the disabled child to be educated in the mainstream, making it illegal for educational institutions to discriminate against a disabled person in admission arrangements and provision of education. SENCOP established the government's strategy for identification, assessment and provision for SEN which replaced the five-stage model of the 1994 Code and is still current.

In a sense, SENCOP seeks to consolidate measures which previous policies related to inclusion and catering for diversity in the mainstream classroom have advocated. Initially, the needs of all children, including those with learning difficulties, must be provided for by a flexible teaching approach and a differentiated curriculum. SENCOP states that if an SEN child is still making little or no progress in response to such approaches, the first intervention strategy – School Action – should be implemented. School Action involves the drawing up of an Individual Education

Plan (IEP) for the child through discussion and consultation between the school's special needs co-ordinator (SENCO), the mainstream teacher, the parents or guardians, the child and the head teacher. The IEP will outline short-term targets and learning objectives for the child and must be monitored and updated regularly by the SENCO and class teacher. Involvement of the parents and the child seeks to ensure that the process is transparent and that all parties take responsibility for the child's progress.

The reasoning behind the legal requirement for IEPs is questionable because the level of transparency and parent/pupil participation is not clearly defined in the policy and may be very loosely interpreted in some situations. Moreover, as Ainscow (1999) points out, IEPs may place a great strain on resources and create budget problems. It could be suggested that as schools now have the responsibility to manage their own budgets and allocate funding for SEN (see below), there may be a reluctance to move a child requiring special provision onto School Action. Finally, Ainscow (1999: 199) notes that IEPs 'had gone badly wrong' in some schools and have, in fact, become, particularly in secondary schools, 'a way of marginalizing some pupils'. Such problems with IEPs may present a further barrier to inclusion, rather than a solution.

The next stage in the procedure, School Action Plus, is implemented if progress is still not being recorded. This may involve providing support for a child from a teaching assistant (TA), from an outside agency such as a speech and language therapist or the school may subscribe to a support programme provided by an independent agency locally or nationally. Finally, a formal statement of SEN may be made. Statements must be annually reviewed and there must be plans for young people with SEN to make the transition from school to school, to college, training and employment.

New Labour's educational policy has created self-managing schools and changed the role of the local authority to that of a facilitator and funding middle-man allocating monies from central government to schools and overseeing schools' budget plans and expenditure (DfES 2005b). Schools now have ultimate responsibility for managing SEN provision and assigning funding and resources to it. This has the advantage of reducing bureaucracy, but it may also have detrimental effects. Due to financial constraints, school management may be reluctant to fund expensive intervention strategies and the needs of some children may be overlooked or poorly catered for.

As mentioned above, some have criticized current government policy for its lack of clarity in SEN categorization which may lead to a child not receiving the support appropriate to meet her/his needs (Warnock 2005). However, Armstrong (2005) suggests that SENCOP as it outlines five classifications of SEN may, in fact, be returning to a labelling system which is more in line with a medical model of disability than with a social and inclusive model. Such arguments highlight a fundamental issue in the inclusion debate. Although there is a general level of agreement among educationalists, politicians and the general public that inclusion is a morally acceptable educational ideology, tensions exist concerning the validity of its practical application in an absolute way (Clough 2005).

The inclusion debate will be explored in more detail below. First it is necessary to consider further developments in recent government policy which have contributed to this debate.

One of the most important, and perhaps most controversial, policies of recent years which aims to improve educational outcomes for all children and young people, including disabled children, is *Every Child Matters* (DfES 2003a) (see Chapter 10) and *For Scotland's Children* (SE 2001). *Every Child Matters* (ECM), working alongside the 2004 Children Act (DfES 2004a) and *Every Child Matters: The Next Steps* (DfES 2004b), state the government's strategy to develop a multi-agency approach for the care and education of children and young people by integrating children's services. As many disabled children's needs are complex and cross traditional service boundaries, they are one of the groups who stand to gain the most from the ECM agenda if its implementation is successful.

Three more important policy documents published in 2004/2005 support the government's ECM agenda and aim to further strengthen provision for children with special or specific needs. *Choice for Parents, the Best Start for Children: A Ten Year Strategy for Childcare* (HMT et al. 2004) sets out the government's plan to invest in childcare and the Early Years sector to meet the needs of all families. For families with children with disabilities/SEN the aim is to provide affordable and appropriate childcare with flexible working times for parents.

Removing Barriers to Achievement: The Government's Strategy for SEN (DfES 2004c) outlines the government's strategy for enabling children with special educational needs to realize their potential by supporting educational institutions by the removal of barriers which prevent them from succeeding in the mainstream. Similar to previous documents, it aims to reduce bureaucracy and to improve specialist provision through a multi-agency approach. Furthermore, it states the government's intention to implement changes in initial teacher training (ITT) and to resource continuing professional development for qualified teachers (CPD) in order to provide them with the strategies to take a flexible approach to pedagogy and curriculum which will enable them to include SEN children in the mainstream classroom.

Finally, in 2007, the strategy *Aiming High for Disabled Children: Better Support for Families* (HMT and DfES 2007) was launched with the intention of 'transforming' the lives of disabled children. The foreword to the document states that it is the culmination of the government focus on disability and that together with the ECM agenda it will help disabled children fulfil their potential. The report outlines the government's intention to invest large sums of money in three specific areas in order to achieve this end. First, the strategy seeks to improve access and empowerment for SEN learners and their families by making entitlements and assessment transparent and by including them fully in designing the provision. There is also promise of individual budgets for families. Second, it intends to provide more responsive services and timely support by making disabled children a priority at local and national level and providing a Transition Support Programme to adulthood. Finally, the strategy promises to improve quality and capacity by allotting more funds to maximize mobility, access to educational institutions and independence for disabled young people and to allow families access to flexible childcare so that parents can work.

It could be argued that the government's ECM agenda and related strategy and policy documents are being presented as the panacea to resolve the issue of inclusive education and catering for diversity in the education system. As yet, it is too early to estimate the successes and failures of this agenda. Nevertheless, caution should be applied when asserting that this multi-agency approach is the magic bullet for providing equal opportunities and improving educational outcomes for all children, including those with learning difficulties.

Anning (2006: 10–13) summarizes findings from a number of evaluation studies of earlier multi-agency and integrated services for children. She states that across several studies similar sets of issues arise regarding the setting up and maintaining of the services. Professionals from different specialist backgrounds found it difficult to 'tune into' each other's ways of working and many acknowledged distress and a sense of deprofessionalization as their previous professional identities were questioned and destabilized. Moreover, she found that there were tensions related to what she terms 'the status of versions of knowledge' (2006: 11). In other words, professionals with different training, different levels of experience and expertise, and different levels and types of qualifications, both academic and vocational, often found it difficult to adjust to an integrated, non-hierarchical setting. Some refused to let go of previous high status, while others failed to realize the value of their experience and expertise. Anning noted that tensions frequently resulted in conflicts which needed to be carefully managed to ensure that the integrated services functioned effectively. She concludes that such findings need to be fed back into planning for the reshaping of children's services in line with the ECM agenda. Furthermore, she adds that in order for ECM to become an effective reality, major workforce reform and training obstacles need to be overcome and there needs to be a 'radical reappraisal of staff training, development, career opportunities and salaries for those charged with developing children's services' (2006: 15).

It is clear that much has been done since the Warnock Report to move from an educational ideology of segregated schooling for those with learning difficulties to a more inclusive system. Nevertheless, in the UK a system of partial inclusion still exists and the debate concerning inclusive education to which we now turn is far from over.

Task 11.1   Stop, think and do

- Having read the sections above, produce a timeline or a flow chart tracing the move from segregated special education to inclusive education.
- In the process of constructing your timeline, identify key issues that brought about change in SEN provision and explain why you think the changes occurred.

The inclusion debate

The shift in educational philosophy regarding people with special educational needs over the past 30 years has centred on the idea of equality of opportunity and the valuing of difference in keeping with the social model of disability and human rights issues highlighted in the Salamanca Statement (UNECSO 1994) and the United Nations Convention on the Rights of the Child (UN 1989). This move towards inclusivity and diversity has been an international phenomenon, particularly in the West.

If we regard the inclusion debate as a human rights issue (Waller 2005), there are implications concerning the very existence of special schools. The social model of disability and the issue of human rights suggest that all children should have the right to choose mainstream education and that all schools should accept all children. This, by default, suggests that special schools should close. If this were to happen, we would have a reversal of the current situation. At present, many parents have to fight for their child with SEN to be educated in the mainstream, as more special schools close, the situation may arise in which some parents may have to fight for a place in a special school.

The term inclusive education is somewhat elusive and, as Clough (2005: 6) points out, this highly contested term has come to mean different things to different groups of people. In very broad terms it can be described as the right of all children to be educated in the mainstream, that is, to participate fully in the mainstream curriculum and in all aspects of the institution's activities. Many see inclusion as a process of change through which barriers to participation are removed or reduced so that those who have been excluded are included (Booth and Ainscow 1998). Barton (1998: 85) highlights the fact that this does not just mean inviting previously excluded learners into educational institutions and closing down segregated provision. The process of inclusion means that mainstream systems must change in all aspects – physical and environmental, curriculum, teaching and leadership.

It is this process of change which is often the bone of contention in the inclusion debate. Politicians, academics and educationalists are concerned with how the appropriate changes can be made to the education system to cater for the potential infinite diversity of full inclusion. Moreover, some have contested whether the process of change to a fully inclusive education system is possible in practical terms or even, in fact, desirable (Farrell 1997).

Advocates of inclusive education would assert that, given commitment and support, inclusive education is a more efficient use of educational resources, that segregation teaches children to be fearful, ignorant and breeds prejudice and that inclusion has the potential to reduce fear and to build friendship, respect and understanding. However, there are many who still question the practicality of full-scale inclusion. While it is recognized that those with moderate learning difficulties develop improved social skills from attending mainstream institutions and that diversity benefits all within an educational setting, some feel that there is still a place for segregated special institutions for learners with severe difficulties (Croll and Moses 2000).

Two of the main concerns regarding the process of change to an inclusive education system are the lack of adequate training for mainstream practitioners to support a variety of specific needs and lack of provision within the National Curriculum to cater for diverse abilities. These concerns are not new and are related to the conditions outlined by the Warnock Report and the 1981 Education Act for the education of SEN learners in mainstream settings: that the mainstream institution is able to meet the learner's specific needs and that the learning of other pupils is not disrupted.

The disruptive behaviour of some learners with SEN may lead practitioners to feel that inclusion is to the detriment of their mainstream peers. This issue of teachers' concerns with the behaviour of SEN children was highlighted by Tomlinson (1982: 80):

> Teachers in normal schools may be willing to accommodate the "ideal" child with special needs in their classroom – the bright, brave child in a wheelchair – they will still want to be rid of the actual "average" child with special needs – the dull, disruptive child.

Clough and Nutbrown (cited in Kellett 2004) conducted research into the attitude of Early Years practitioners towards inclusion and found that while many thought the concept of inclusion acceptable in theory, they were afraid of the additional responsibilities of educating some children, for example, those with emotional behavioural difficulties and those on the autism spectrum.

It appears that many mainstream practitioners feel that they lack the skills and the resources to provide for some categories of SEN effectively. As noted above, the current system in which school management must resource SEN provision from school budgets may affect funds allocated to staff training and specialist resources. Ainscow (1999: 5) states that in some mainstream settings in England there is a 'proliferation of largely untrained classroom assistants who work with some of the most vulnerable children'.

Specialist schools, funded by central government, may remove some of this financial requirement from schools. Conversely, it could be argued that employing SEN professionals in mainstream schools is a better use of the limited funds available for SEN provision, rather than maintaining specialist schools which can be a huge drain on the education budget.

Funding issues aside, the attitude of educationalist professionals towards inclusion may indicate that there remains a long way to go in deconstructing practitioners, approaches to SEN and inclusion. In other words, it could be suggested that at a fundamental level the concept of inclusion is still perceived in terms of barriers and hindrances rather than of needs and solutions.

Research has criticized special educational training within ITT. Allan (2006: 29) states that student teachers are introduced to SEN in a series of 'regulated chunks of traditional special education knowledge'. This suggests that ITT training in SEN is somewhat tokenistic. Student teachers may be given the appropriate language to discourse about SEN in line with politically correct policy and practice and may be able to adapt on a surface level to diversity in the classroom. However, due to a lack of deep level education about specific learning difficulties which encourages critical deconstruction of traditional SEN definitions, their knowledge may not go beyond a superficial awareness of need.

Allan goes on to suggest that current ITT practice means that newly qualified teachers receive the message that they will never know enough about students' needs to cater for them appropriately so that they 'come to regard their responsibilities towards disabled students with guilt, fear, and the sense they will inevitably let them down' (2006: 29).

As mentioned above, the government strategy for SEN, *Removing Barriers to Achievement* (DfES 2004c), stresses the need for ITT providers to improve undergraduate and CPD training in special educational needs. It could be suggested that the nature of ITT and CPD training needs to be overhauled and that funding needs to be provided for continual training and professional development of all practitioners who work with SEN learners: class teachers, teaching assistants, SENCOs, head teachers.

Training should focus on critically deconstructing socially constructed definitions of ablement and normality, not on defining and assessing disability. Rather than delivering 'chunks' of surface knowledge about specific SEN conditions and strategies for coping with diverse conditions in the classroom, educational practitioners should be encouraged to critically deconstruct, to question and unpick, definitions of normalcy. Brantlinger (2006: 244) believes that critical inspection and introspection can make norms transparent so that they can be challenged and modified. She asserts that this process can lead people to see that some norms are themselves dysfunctional and that some normative practices create inequalities. This focus on questioning definitions of ableness and normalcy, can lead to acceptance and understanding of diversity in line with the social model of disability and with true inclusive education.

The National Curriculum implemented in 1989 was introduced by the 1988 Education Reform Act (DES 1988) with the intention of providing all pupils with equal access to a balanced curriculum. However, some felt that the initial document did not have appropriate programmes of study and educational objectives for diversity among the needs of pupils, particularly those with learning difficulties (Fletcher-Campbell 1994). The National Curriculum was revised in 1999 and a Statutory Inclusive Statement was incorporated with guidelines for adapting programmes of study to meet diversity in mainstream schools. The Statement proposes that the needs of all individuals and groups can be meet by: setting suitable learning challenges, responding to pupils' needs and overcoming potential barriers to learning and assessment (National Curriculum Online 2007). The responsibility rests with teachers and institutions to adapt pedagogy and assessment in ways that cater for diversity in the mainstream classroom. While it could be argued that this is a positive factor as it recognizes the professionalism of educational practitioners, ultimately the issue returns to effective ITT and CPD. In order to make the guidelines work in reality, practitioners need the training and confidence to modify their practice appropriately and effectively.

Current government policy of inclusion has come under criticism from Warnock herself in her 2005 article Special Educational Needs: a new look (Warnock 2005). Policy documents have been accused of providing confused and changing definitions of SEN and inclusion. It is suggested that this is causing the closure of special schools and forcing some children into mainstream schools when it is not in their best interests to be there, resulting in distress for pupils and parents. She believes that the potential adverse effect on the learning of others by the inclusion of children with SEN is hard to gauge and that in reality children with certain special needs do in fact frequently disrupt and undermine teaching and learning. Arguing that the concept of inclusion has become muddled and has been taken too far as a worthy ideal, Warnock is calling for inclusion to be rethought. The comments of Warnock have angered some disability groups who have seen this as a dramatic U-turn.

A recent review of SEN provision in the UK by the House of Commons Education and Skills Select Committee (HCESC 2006) concluded that government policy on inclusion is not resulting in the closure of special schools. The report states that inclusion is a broad concept that covers a wide range of issues both within and between schools and should not be taken by local authorities to imply the closure of special schools. However, the inquiry did identify difficulties in policy, practice and provision and the recommendations suggested do, in fact, seem to concur with Warnock's claims that the current policy is confused and in need of review. The report calls for more clarity in policy documents to ensure that the concept of inclusion in terms of full integration of all pupils within educational settings is more fully understood. It highlights the need to resolve the contradiction over whether the number of special schools is likely to decrease or whether numbers are likely to remain static. Furthermore, it recommends the development of a national SEN framework, outlining the minimum standards for the range of provision that should exist in very area and a radical review of the statementing process. The government resists the call for fresh look at SEN. *Aiming High for Disabled Children* (HMT and DfES 2007) reaffirms their belief that disabled children will benefit the most from the ECM agenda which, along with its related strategies, will transform the lives of disabled children and their families.

As noted above, though educational provision in the UK has come a long way from segregated specialist provision for those with SEN, there still exists a partially inclusive system. Many children with learning difficulties are educated in the mainstream, though special schooling is often allocated for those with severe difficulties. Moreover, along the continuum from segregation to inclusion a variety of arrangements may be in place. Some SEN learners are placed in specialist schools on a short-term basis and reintegrated into the mainstream after a period of intensive support. Others may be educated part-time in special schools and part-time in the mainstream. Furthermore, within ordinary schools some SEN learners are regularly removed from the classroom and supported by teaching assistants or other specialists on a one-to-one or small group basis. As Kellett (2004: 158) points out, from a strictly inclusive perspective, even this arrangement is problematic as it creates an exclusive learning situation.

Task 11.2 Stop, think and do

- Find out all you can about one or more of the following disabilities: Asperger's syndrome, attention deficit hyperactivity disorder (ADHD) and hearing/sight impairment.
- Consider the educational, physical and social needs of the learner.
- Consider the advantages and disadvantages of the individual being educated in the mainstream.

Conclusion

Fundamentally, the inclusion debate is fuelled by tension between a morally accept-able educational ideology and its practical application. Some have suggested that an overzealous ideological insistence on equality and inclusion can lead to an oversight of the individual needs of a child (Warnock 2005). In such a situation, lack of clear categorization of need for fear of stigmatization may undermine the effectiveness of inclusive education (Armstrong 2005). Moreover, Farrell (2004) has implied that the debate surrounding SEN and inclusive education may become a political and policy struggle in which the child itself is essentially overlooked. As Allan (2006: 33) points out, such a struggle results in 'unproductive politics in which the opposing sides will inevitably beg to differ'.

'Responsible inclusion', according to Allan, means 'opening our eyes' (2006: 38). This involves a fundamental shift in thinking about disability across all sectors of society leading to the questioning of normalcy rather than emphasizing categoriza-tion of difference. In order for this to become a reality within the education system, SEN policy and practice needs to be rethought. Policy must not degenerate into unproductive political struggle and ITT and CPD must focus on respect for the diversity and the individual needs of all learners. If labels must be used to ensure that learners receive the appropriate provision, these labels must be continually decon-structed and challenged. Policy-makers and educationalists must not be blinded to the fact that labels are socio-historical and cultural constructs. Such an approach would go some way to allowing professionals to make decisions concerning SEN provision on a child-by-child basis (Allan 2006: 243) and would lead to the possibility of a more inclusive system in line with social models of disability and human rights issues.

Summary

1. The Warnock Report put the issue of special educational needs on the political agenda and has had a substantial influence on the SEN debate instigating a move from segregated to integrated provision.
2. Since the Warnock Report, numerous governmental policies have focused on the issue of SEN and moved towards inclusive education in an attempt to bring the education system in line with UN dictates on the rights of the disabled child to be an equal member within mainstream educational institutions.
3. The psycho-medical model of disability defines disability in terms of impairment and seeks to diagnose special needs in order to secure support and funding.
4. The social model of disability places an individual's needs first and seeks to remove social and environmental barriers which may cause disadvantage and inequality within society.
5. Inclusive education works in tandem with social models of disability and with human rights issues.
6. The debate concerning the extent to which inclusive education should and can be implemented highlights a discrepancy between inclusion as a sound moral ideology and the problems related to its practical implementation.
7. Two of the main concerns regarding inclusive education are ensuring that educational practitioners have the appropriate training and ensuring that SEN learners are provided for within the mainstream curriculum.
8. The government proposes that disabled learners will benefit most from the ECM agenda, however, there are concerns with multi-agency services.
9. At present in the UK there is still a partially inclusive education system.
10. In order to bring about a more inclusive system, a rethinking of current policy and provision may be required.

12   Ideology and the Curriculum

What is a curriculum?

Task 12.1   Stop, think and do

- Think about what you understand by the term 'curriculum'.
- Read the following definitions of curriculum. Which do you agree with?

A curriculum as a package of ideas, together with the manner in which it is delivered (its pedagogy).

(Matheson, C., 2004: 20)

The curriculum is the totality of the experiences the pupil has as a result of the provision made.

(Kelly, 2004: 8)

A curriculum is the formation and implementation of an educational proposal to be taught and learned within the school or other institution and for which that institution accepts responsibility at three levels: its rationale, its actual implementation and its effects.

(Jenkins and Shipman, 1976: 53)

Curriculum is the questioning of authority and the searching for complex views of human situations.

(Marsh, 2004: 4)

- Write your own definition of curriculum in less than 40 words.

The word 'curriculum' has its origins in Latin meaning a racecourse or a course to be run and from this a course of study (Ross 2000: 8; Marsh 2004: 3). However, as this book will have made clear, providing a concise and straightforward definition of the key concepts in the field of Education Studies is far from simple. This is no less the case with the term 'curriculum'. Goodson (1990: 47) described the curriculum as 'a slippery concept' one that is 'perennially elusive and multi-faceted'. The reason for this difficulty in providing a simple definition of the term is that understanding the curriculum involves understanding what is taught, why it is taught and how it is taught (Husbands, cited in Bartlett and Burton 2007). Understanding the what, why and how of the curriculum means exploring fundamental questions related to a society's very definition of education and knowledge. As Smith (cited in Brisard and Menter, 2004: 199) points out, the curriculum advocated by any society is the strongest statement of its beliefs in the purpose of education, of the values it holds dear and of what it strives to be.

Ross (2000: 8) proposes that the curriculum 'is a definition of what is to be learned'. It could be argued, however, that this definition is too vague and that it begs more questions than it answers. In other words, this definition does not concern itself with how and why the content of the curriculum is selected, nor with how the content is to be delivered, that is, what pedagogy is to be employed. Kelly (2004) acknowledges the difficulties in defining an educational curriculum, not least due to the fact that education itself is problematic and requires further examination (see Chapter 1 and Chapter 3). He warns against too narrow a definition of curriculum which may encourage people to equate a curriculum merely with a particular timetable or syllabus of subjects to be delivered within an educational institution, be that a school, college or university. In this sense, the definition offered by C. Matheson (2004: 20) above is too narrow.

In seeking to define curriculum, Kelly uses the term 'total curriculum' (2004: 4–8). For Kelly, the total curriculum is the totality of experiences that the learner has. This includes not just the knowledge which is intentionally transmitted, but, moreover, and perhaps more importantly, things that the student learns due to how the learning process is organized, planned and delivered.

Furthermore, Kelly, in keeping with the definition of curriculum proposed by Jenkins and Shipman (1976: 53) above, asserts that an adequate definition of a total curriculum must go even further. Deploring what many, including Young (1971), identified as the unquestioned nature of valid knowledge, of knowledge selection and of curriculum planning, Kelly states that any worthwhile definition of curriculum must include an overall rationale for the educational programme to which the curriculum belongs. In other words, a total curriculum is an explanation and justification for a particular educational ideology and questions concerning the nature, purpose and development of a curriculum are inevitably tied to an exploration of attitudes to the nature and purpose of education itself.

For the purposes of this discussion, an educational curriculum will be defined as the knowledge and skills delivered to, and/or acquired by the learner, whether intentional or unintentional, and the manner in which they are delivered to, and/or acquired by, the learner. In line with Kelly (2004), a broad definition of curriculum is advocated, involving both content and pedagogy and encompassing both the experience of the learner and the curriculum planner's rationale for the total curriculum and its effects. The definition suggested here incorporates the first three offered in Task 12.1 above. The validity of the fourth definition will be considered below.

Different types of curricula

Curriculum models

Three curriculum models will be considered here: content-based, objectives-based and process-based. Table 12.1 illustrates the defining characteristics of these curricula models in terms of content and content selection, purpose, teaching methodology or pedagogy and associated ideologies as outlined in Chapter 3.

Table 12.1 Characteristics of curriculum models

Characteristic	Content-based curriculum	Objectives-based curriculum	Process-based curriculum
Content/Content selection	Selection based on belief in objective value or truth of knowledge Knowledge organized into separate units/subjects Knowledge hierarchically organized	Selection based on need to deliver skills/competencies necessary to achieve assessed objectives Knowledge secondary to achieving objectives	Selection based on ability to promote developmental processes Knowledge secondary to processes
Purpose	To transmit true knowledge To allow equality of access to true knowledge To maintain status quo	To achieve assessed objectives To train learners for roles in society	To promote a series of developmental processes To learn how to learn To know how to know To question knowledge and social structures
Pedagogy	Traditional transmission-based teaching Teacher-centred	Traditional transmission-based teaching Teacher-centred	Teacher as facilitator Child-centred
Associated Ideology	Elitist Conservative/ neo-liberal	Revisionist Technocratic/utilitarian Conservative/neo-liberal	Social democratic/ Legalitarian Post-modern

Ross (2000) employs a useful extended analogy from gardening to describe the three major curriculum models. He draws his analogy from David Eccles' discussion of English educational curriculum in the House of Commons in March 1960 which was in response to Crowther Report on 15–18 education (DES 1959). Eccles declared that the government would begin to take more interest in what was being taught in schools and would open up 'the secret garden of the curriculum' (Ross 2000: 1). Using this garden metaphor to begin his discussion of the English curriculum, Ross identifies three major models: the Baroque garden, the Dig-for-Victory garden, the Naturally Landscaped garden.

The Baroque garden has strongly demarcated beds or areas, each with its own form of cultivation and function. There is a strict hierarchy in terms of value associated with each area and ideals of balance, symmetry and regularity are emphasized. These characteristics can be seen in the classic content-based curriculum of clearly bounded subjects, restricted in number, balanced against each other, but generally considered in a hierarchical organization, in which some forms of knowledge, such as language and literacy and science, are considered more valuable than others. As in the highly organized Baroque gardens of seventeenth- and eighteenth-century Europe, the contents of such curricula are valued for their traditional, aesthetic and inbuilt or intrinsic value.

The Dig-for-Victory garden, somewhat like an allotment, is cultivated for use, that is, for utilitarian purposes – production of food, leisure or recreational manual labour. Similarly, the objectives-based curriculum selects content which will allow the development of skills and competencies which are useful to the individual and/or to society. In order that the curriculum provides maximum usefulness, objectives are pre-specified and content and pedagogy are selected to meet these outcomes. Cost effectiveness is a major concern here and has an impact on resources, staffing and approaches to delivery.

The Naturally Landscaped garden is intended to mirror nature and to allow plants to grow unhampered by human formality or organization. The analogy to the process-based curriculum can be illustrated by reference to the ideas of Rousseau as laid out in *Emile* ([1762] 1979) which are summarized in Chapter 3. The process-based curriculum focuses on the all-round academic, social and moral development of the learner. Content is selected to promote processes which allow for such development rather than on the acquiring of knowledge itself. The education is supposedly learner-centred and the teacher acts as facilitator. Ross (2000: 4–5) points out, however, that such natural learning is somewhat of an illusion. Just as Rousseau's hypothetical education of Emile was in fact highly structured and controlled by the tutor, so the landscape garden is constrained and shaped by the attitudes and opinions of the designer to give the illusion of naturalness.

Typology of curricula in educational institutions

The above discussion has focused on academic and theoretical explorations of curriculum models. It is also useful to outline more practical typology of curricula as realized in educational institutions.

As something is to be taught and learned, very educational institutions will have a planned or official curriculum, which is set out in syllabi and timetables. However, any exploration of curriculum must acknowledge the fact that what is planned by teachers or national planners is often very different from the received or experienced curriculum. This gap between what is planned and what is received or experienced by the learners may exist for a great variety of reasons, both social and personal, and may be intentional or unintentional on the part of the curriculum designers and deliverers. However, as this is in fact the reality of the learners' experiences, teachers and planners must be aware of it and must take responsibility for it.

Besides the planned and experienced curriculum, we must also consider the formal and informal curriculum. The formal curriculum, like the planned or official curriculum, is that which is verified by state and school and is set out in timetabled subjects/units. The informal curriculum, sometimes termed extracurricular activities, is the learning that occurs, often on a voluntary basis, outside of lessons or class time, through a variety of activities, sports, hobbies, clubs, societies, trips.

The hidden curriculum (see Chapter 8, in this volume)

In general terms, the hidden curriculum is everything that a learner learns above and beyond the official or planned curriculum. The hidden curriculum includes all the socializing behaviours, attitudes and values that the learner picks up from how teaching and learning is organized and delivered. The learner picks up these social messages from the school buildings, teacher expectations, teachers' interaction with learners, kinds of knowledge valued, language used within the learning environment, attitudes to different sectors of society displayed within the learning institution (see Meighan and Siraj-Blatchford 2001: 65–100, for a detailed discussion of the hidden curriculum). Jackson (1968), who was the first to use the term hidden curriculum, alluding to the traditional 3Rs of education – reading, writing and arithmetic – identified a further 3Rs that must be learnt in order to survive in an institution – rules, routines and regulations. It is from these 3Rs that the hidden curriculum of education is derived, for example, the rules within many educational institutions coupled with the teacher expectations and behaviour, may teach that some sectors of the institution's population, male or female, white or black, are more valued than others; that the voice of authority is always to be trusted; that passive acceptance of rules and routines is preferable to resistance or questioning. Kelly's (2004) total curriculum involves all of the curriculum types identified above.

Those who approach the curriculum from the critical perspective, such as Apple (2004), stress the fact that the hidden curriculum was not originally hidden. Early curriculum planners in the USA, the UK and other countries, used the curriculum overtly to preserve the status quo and balance of power, to establish nationhood and to achieve a consensus view of acceptable socialization and social behaviour (Flinders and Thornton 2004). At the turn of twentieth century great social upheavals in the West, such as industrialization and economic growth, immigration, the suffrage movement and the development of free state education, led to a concern about the stability of nations and a desire for standardization. This in turn resulted in the development of common-sense rules for curriculum selection and school organiza- tion based on efficiency, economic utilitarianism and a desire for social control in expanding and diversifying societies. Once the perceived appropriate social behaviour and values had been established as the consensus, this overt socializing function of the curriculum became hidden although it lingers in the 3Rs and the very fabric of education – in building, texts, timetables – what Meighan and Siraj-Blatchford (2001: 69–70) call the 'ghosts' of educational institutions.

Bowles and Gintis (1976: 131) developed the concept of the hidden curriculum to include what they termed the 'correspondence principle'. The correspondence principle holds that the 3Rs taught by most schools corresponds to the social relations and the expected behaviour of the workplace in Western society today. In other words, the 3Rs can be seen as a preparation in attitude for the workplace. This idea of education as direct preparation for work is generally considered as character- istic of the objectives-based curriculum and the revisionist/technocratic approach to education. However, each of the curriculum models discussed here and the associated educational ideologies involve socializing to some extent. The content-based curricu- lum and elitist approaches to education prepare learners to be leaders or followers and the process-based curriculum and democratic view of education aim to equip learners with the ability to become active members of a socially egalitarian state.

Core or common curricula

A core or common curriculum can be defined as a state, centrally-controlled, statutory curriculum in terms of content and often pedagogy. Many countries in the West and globally, such as the USA, France, Greece and Japan, have had a core curriculum for many years, in fact since national state education was introduced. The extent to which the state controls both the content and the delivery of the curriculum varies from country to country. The UK did not have a core curriculum as such until the 1988 Education Reform Act (DES 1988) introduced the National Curriculum for England and Wales and so institutions had some degree of freedom over what was taught and how it was taught. However, it must be noted that even before the introduction of the National Curriculum, institutions were subject to external pressures such as national examinations and inspections which did influence curriculum content and pedagogy.

There are a variety of arguments in favour of a core curriculum, many of which are related to the idea of equality of educational provision. If knowledge is considered to be objectively valid and true, it could be argued that all learners have the right to access this universal knowledge and so have entitlement to the same curriculum content. Moreover, from a social and political perspective, it could be argued that all learners have the entitlement to access a balanced curriculum so that they receive the same educational experiences and opportunities which will prepare them to meet the demands of, and succeed in, the workplace and society in general.

On the other hand, it could be suggested that the arguments in favour of a core curriculum are, in fact, only a defence of the traditional content-based curriculum or of the objectives-based curriculum. The argument above presupposes objective truths and hence the validity of some knowledge and skills above others. However, if we consider knowledge as socially constructed (see below), we must consider *whose* valid knowledge is selected for the core curriculum. Rather than allowing all learners access to knowledge and skills which are valid to them and their socio-historical and cultural contexts, a core curriculum, by promoting the knowledge of those controlling the curriculum – politicians, educators, philosophers – may in fact alienate some sectors of the society by making their view of knowledge wrong. In other words, content selection for a core curriculum may indoctrinate learners to accept one view of knowledge, may sustain social hierarchies and promote inequality.

Within a process-based model of curriculum, the concept of core can be understood in a different way. The common characteristic of a core curriculum may be based, not on content and pedagogy, but on an overall aim: to develop learners holistically, to equipped them with the critical skills to learn how to learn and to question and explore their social reality. In this case, content and pedagogy of a curriculum may be negotiated by institutions, by teaching bodies and by the learning community.

The creation and validation of knowledge

The debate about the creation and validation of knowledge revolves around a basic dichotomy. Rationalists or absolutists, such as Plato (see below) and Descartes (see Chapter 5, in this volume) and more recently Hirst (1965), believe that there is knowledge which is objectively and universally true, which is out there somewhere, and, therefore, is valid. Earlier advocates of this approach to knowledge believed that universal truth was God-given, though more recent absolutists assert that knowledge is secular, scientific and factual.

Opposed to absolutist ideas of knowledge is the view that knowledge is not objectively true, but that it is subjective and based upon interpretation of experience. Knowledge may be considered as subjective whether it is accessed through the senses as believed by empiricists such as Locke (see Chapter 3, in this volume), or through an individual's relation to his/her social, historical and cultural context and to what knowledge and skills are deemed to be important and useful within that context.

The early work of the educational philosopher Paul Hirst (1965) was very influential in terms of curriculum content and organization in the English-speaking world. Hirst argued that there is universally true knowledge which is not historically or culturally based. He suggested that there are a number of basic forms of knowledge, such as mathematical, physical scientific, literary and artistic, each of which has unique content and concepts, though all are related via complex networks. Hirst believed that these forms of knowledge are manifested in the world through public symbols and that access to these symbols allows an individual access to universal knowledge.

The work of Hirst provides philosophical justification for a content-based curriculum of subjects which are organized into discrete units, hierarchically structured and which are seen as true beyond social and cultural context. In a sense, the selection of contents for the curriculum is given and unquestionable, for rejection of the contents advocated would mean rejection of the truth. However, if we believe that there is no universally true knowledge, this justification is invalid. In fact, as content-based curriculum is the descendant of the traditional elitist curriculum, justification for this curriculum model could be seen as no more than a reliance on established tradition and a desire for those in power, the elite, to maintain their control over the curriculum.

In stark contrast to this absolutist approach to knowledge and curriculum, the sociologist Michael Young in the 1970s championed the view that knowledge is socially constructed and this view is accepted by many today. Young (1971) argued that knowledge is best understood, not through philosophical analysis, but through the study of the sociological conditions in which it is created and validated. The idea that knowledge is not permanent, that it is continually created, recreated and validated by societies within particular socio-historical and cultural contexts is not new. We need only to consider how historically what is considered true knowledge at one time changes, for example, how Darwinism replaced previously held religious views about the origins of humanity and how quantum physics is today challenging such fundamentally held truths as time and space. No doubt absolutists would argue that this reflects, not the creation of new knowledge, but the continual quest of humanity to uncover the universal, fundamental truths. However, it could be suggested that it is humanity's own evolution which creates the new knowledge, that ultimately there is no end-goal of permanent, universal truth, just a gradual realization of the human potential.

Whatever our view of knowledge, it must be conceded that curriculum designers must engage in a process of content selection and that this process inevitably involves value judgements about knowledge. It has been suggested that prior to critical approaches to curriculum studies, the processes by which curriculum content was selected, organized and assessed were largely unquestioned (Young 1973: 339).

Ralph Tyler (1949) is often cited as one of the main proponents of the objectives-based model. Tyler believed that curriculum planners needed to clearly define the desired outcomes or objectives of education in terms of specific behaviour, skills or competencies which learners needed to be successful in society. Use of objectives is justified as they provide a measure, a standard, by which attainment in knowledge and skills can be tested. However, to reduce the educational curriculum and knowledge to a set of tick-box objectives is highly questionable, not least because, as many would assert, human knowledge and understanding are not condensable into discrete, linear units (Golby 1989). Tick-box objectives may serve to measure basic skills, but beyond that they seem redundant.

A comparison could be drawn between the process-based model and the objectives-based model in that in neither case is curriculum content selected due to a belief in its inbuilt or intrinsic value. Here, however, the comparison ends. In the objectives-based model there is an end-goal of discrete assessable objectives and the objectives and the content of the curriculum are usually specified by a body external to the education process such as a government organization, an examination board or a commercial or industrial authority.

On the other hand, the overall aim of the process-based model is the life-long development of the individual learner. This model advocates that knowledge is selected on the basis of its appropriateness to provide the individual learner with the necessary experiences and activities which will promote his/her development. This implies that curriculum content cannot be externally imposed, but must be a process of continual negotiation between teacher and learner.

Some advocates of the process-based curriculum (Kelly 2004), would also adhere to a postmodern view of knowledge. Postmodernism, sometimes termed relativism, is a highly controversial philosophy and has been described and debated at length elsewhere (see Harvey 1991; Hicks 2004). A brief overview will serve here in order to relate postmodernism to curriculum studies.

In very general terms, Postmodernism asserts that no knowledge is given, absolute or permanent. All knowledge is socially created and is relative to socio-historical and culture context. Knowledge and truth, therefore, are a set of ideas and opinions relative to a particular context and as such is an ideology. Defined in this way, no ideology – no single account of knowledge and truth – can be better, superior or more right that any other. In postmodern terms, all ideologies and the knowledge and truth which they embody, are relative to each other. Furthermore, postmodernism believes that as all versions of knowledge are ideologies, they are closely bound to politics and power. Those who control knowledge and knowledge distribution hold power within a society (Lyotard 2004).

In terms of the curriculum, those in control of knowledge selection are in effect imposing their ideology, their view of knowledge and truth, on society through the education system. Postmodernism sees the issue of knowledge selection for the curriculum as highly dangerous. At the very least, planners and recipients of the curriculum must be conscious of the changing and relative nature of knowledge and the potential political and power implications. Further to this, a truly postmodern approach to education would seek to equip learners with the skills to question and critically evaluate knowledge, the very knowledge included in the curriculum.

We can see how postmodernism aligns with the process-based curriculum model, as both see the aim of the learning process as the development of critical thinking, the ability to question and contest assumed opinions and beliefs, rather that the acquisition of knowledge or the achieving of objectives.

The postmodern view of power and social control in relation to knowledge selection for the curriculum is held by many who approach curriculum studies from the critical perspective. When the selection of content for a curriculum – no matter what model – is in the hands of those in power who are external to the actual education process, the curriculum becomes a reflection of the forms of knowledge, the ideology, of the dominant class and can be used as a political tool of social control (Gramsci 1971). However, not all of the critical school, such as Apple (2004), would hold with the postmodern view that all educational ideologies and all knowledge is relative and, therefore, that none is to be favoured above another.

Both the critical approach and the postmodern perspective involve the fourth definition of curriculum given at the beginning of this chapter. Learners, deliverers and planners of curricula must continually question, contest and challenge knowledge creation and selection, curricula and pedagogy and, in fact, education itself and its relation to society and power hierarchies.

The development and purpose of a curriculum

In order to understand the rationale behind the development of a curriculum model, it is beneficial to consider things in reverse. In other words, the end clarifies the means. If we identify the purpose of the curriculum (the end), then the rationale for its development (the means) becomes apparent. Of course, whether either the ends or the means are considered valid or justified depends on an individual's or a society's ideology of education. In this section we do not intend to provide a detailed chronology of curricula development. Rather we will outline the perceived purposes of each curriculum model, both by those who advocate and those who criticize it, then we will briefly consider how each model developed (for a detailed discussion of the development of curriculum models in the West and in the UK, see Moon and Murphy 1999; Ross, 2000).

Historically, the origins of curriculum debate and development in Europe and, due to European influence, internationally, are traceable to the work of Greek philosophers such as Plato (427–347 BC). Plato's views on education are clearly outlined in his work *The Republic* ([c.375 BC] 2003) which is an account of a hypothetical society. In *The Republic*, Plato describes society as constructed on three levels, each of which has a role in maintaining the overall smooth functioning of the society. He suggests that there are three different natural dispositions in the human which assign him/her to one of those groups within society – Guardians or philosophical leaders, soldiers or workers.

The purpose of education is to prepare people for their purpose and role within the sector of society to which they are naturally inclined. As each group has a different role to play, the type of education they should receive will differ in terms of content and pedagogy. The curriculum for leaders should be traditional and geared towards academic and high-status knowledge. The education of soldiers should be based on development of physical skills and military acumen, while workers should be practically trained.

The content-based curriculum has its origins in the Platonic approach to education. The Platonic purpose of the model, the education of the elite who were to be Guardians or leaders in society, still prevails today. Indeed, until the twentieth century, this curriculum model was the reserve of the elite public schools in England and elsewhere where the ruling class were educated.

Traditionally, the purpose of this curriculum was seen as a means of passing on refined cultural heritage and as a means of allowing learners access to pure forms of valued knowledge which would equip them with the ability to rule and lead with wisdom and understanding. More modern critical interpretations of the content-based curriculum see it as a political tool through which the dominant culturally elite seek to control societies via the transmission of their ideology and their cultural symbols, such as valued literary texts and refined musical tastes (Wexler 1976).

The content-based curriculum developed from the Platonic ideal, through the church-controlled medieval university system into the elite public school system. By the turn of the twentieth century it had become so entrenched in tradition due to its historical origins, its exclusivity, its alliance with power and its association with true knowledge, that it became, almost by default, the basis for general state education in many countries. Despite the development of the other two curriculum models and despite assignment of different curricula to different sectors of society as occurred in the tripartite system in the UK post-1944 (see Chapter 2, in this volume), the content-based model remains that which is aspired to and most valued (Skilbeck 1976).

In the UK, as in many other countries such as France and the USA, the content-based curriculum forms the basis of the core or common curriculum. The National Curriculum for England and Wales is organized into hierarchy discrete subject areas, with core and foundation subjects. The justifications for the curriculum are that it allows all pupils access to a balanced curriculum of traditionally valued knowledge and access to a common cultural heritage. As was mentioned above, however, in increasingly plural societies, such justification begs questions because it inevitably involves the selection and promotion of a specific interpretation of cultural heritage above others with the potential result of subjugation, segregation and alienation of some sectors of society.

The turn of the twentieth century saw major social, political and cultural upheavals in the West. With such changes there was a desire to maintain stability, while promoting economic growth in many countries. The developing state education system was seen by many as the arena for socializing the different factors in society into accepting the standards of the ruling class. This led to interest in objectives-based curricula.

The influential American educationalist, Bobbitt (1918), advocated an industrial and utilitarian approach to curriculum. The purpose of the curriculum was clear – to train an efficient workforce in order to eliminate waste and maximize output of both public resources and potential workforce. His model of curriculum was basically a deficit model in that the planners were to observe the skills and abilities current workers lacked and then devise a set of educational objectives which would enable learners to gain these skills and abilities. The curriculum content and pedagogy were to be planned to meet these objectives.

This approach to curriculum, however, is based on many dubious assumptions. In the first place, planning begins with a description of adult deficiency and education is seen purely as a preparation for adult life. In other words, the child is somehow taken out of the equation. Moreover, there is an assumption that different sectors of society, or different social classes, require different skills and abilities to function usefully in society and, therefore, require different curriculum content and pedagogy. In other words, this model is a form of behaviour moulding (Kelly 2004: 59–61) and, by assigning different curricula to different sections of society serves to create and maintain social hierarchies.

There is no place within this model for either the valuing of knowledge and learning for their own sake, or for the development of the individual in terms of his/her unique capacities. Here the individual is secondary to the needs of the community. Furthermore, as Eisner (2004) points out, objectives cannot always measure the outcome of the educational process as learning does not necessarily proceed in a linear, step-by-step fashion, nor can achievement in some subject areas, particularly in creative and expressive activities, be measured by quantifiable objectives. In these areas judgements of quality are more useful than quantifiable objectives which seek to measure against a set standard.

Despite the shortcomings of a strictly objectives-based model, this approach to curriculum has maintained its foothold since the work of Bobbitt and those who followed him such as Tyler. In fact, besides a brief interlude into more process-based approaches to learning in the 1950s and 1960s, objective models go hand-in-hand with content-based models, and have dominated curriculum planning in much of the Western world. As Moon (1990) points out, commenting on developments in education across the industrialized world in the 1980s, through comparing the UK specifically with France and the Netherlands, concern with educational decline or crisis as related to economic shortcomings led to a full-scale revival of objectives-based models and increasing government intervention in curriculum planning.

The purpose of the process-based curriculum model is to develop the individual, socially and morally, as well as academically, and, in a more general sense, to establish a socially democratic society. John Dewey ([1916] 1997) is often cited as one of the forefathers of this approach. Dewey asserted that child-centred education is vital for producing and maintaining a democratic society. The education process should teach social democracy in practice not as a goal to be strived for. In other words, Dewey believed that via the experience of democracy while in the education system, in terms of experiencing equal valuing and development of her/his unique abilities and skills, a learner would be prepared to promote and value a socially democratic society.

During the 1950s and 1960s process-based curriculum models were popular in the UK and elsewhere. The Plowden Report (DES 1967) was very influential in the UK in terms of promoting child-centred education, particularly in primary education, encouraging learning through play and favouring a curriculum of activity and experience. Studies of secondary school education in 1970s identified the use of interdisciplinary curricula, a movement towards group and individual work rather than traditional forms of class teaching and a change in the teacher's role from that of expert transmitter of knowledge to that of a facilitator, structuring the pupils' own discovery of knowledge (Rubinstein and Simon 1972: 123).

However, the ascent of the process-based curriculum was short-lived. Worldwide recession in the 1970s led to the equation of poor economic performance with what was perceived as informal teaching and a failure of the education system to equip learners with the skills and knowledge to be efficient members of society. A series of 'Black Papers on Education' were published which began the assault on process-based education (Cox and Dyson 1969, 1970) which was echoed in Prime Minister James Callaghan's famous Ruskin College speech (1976) and its claims that students were spending too much time studying subjects which were not directly related to economic success and usefulness. Boyson (1975) suggested that progressive ideas about education had resulted in a breakdown of the curriculum in English schools and called for school to be made more accountable through a nationally enforced curriculum. This movement away from the process approach to curriculum eventually led to the introduction of the National Curriculum in England and Wales (DES 1988).

Political directions and the role of the curriculum

Since the 1980s there has been a general trend in international politics, particularly in the West, towards capitalist neo-liberalism (McMurty 2000). Neo-liberalism (see Chapter 3) involves the introduction of the market forces of private investment, choice, diversity and competition into areas of public life, such as the education and health services, which previously were state-funded and managed in many countries. The general global march towards neo-liberal politics, which has been largely unquestioned, has been questionably seen as a healthy form of modernism in which social structures and systems are immune to the constraints of government interference (Cole 2007).

However, such arguments in favour of neo-liberal policies when applied to the education system are somewhat contradictory. In many countries, including the UK, neo-liberal politics have been coupled with increasing state intervention in education, specifically with the introduction, or reestablishment and reformation, of a core curriculum. In the UK, prior to the introduction of the National Curriculum for England and Wales by the Conservative Government in 1988 (DES 1988), there had been no direct government intervention in curriculum planning. The level of government involvement in the education curriculum continued and increased as New Labour took up the mantle of neo-liberalism with the introduction of the primary strategies for literacy and mathematics (DfEE 1998a, 1998c) and their subsequent developments, the combined primary strategy and the Key Stage 3 strategy (DfES 2001a, 2003b).

We do not intend here to engage in a lengthy analysis of the UK's core curriculum, as this has been done in detail elsewhere (see White 2004). Nevertheless, it is useful to place curriculum developments in the UK within the global context. In 1992, a research project at Stanford University in the USA analysed the primary curricula of over 70 countries and found a surprising level of movement towards international conformity in terms of the subjects taught and the percentage of teaching time allocated to subjects (Meyer et al. 1992). Moreover, Hatcher and Hirtt (1999: 13) commented on the 'gradual homogenisation of education systems in the advanced capitalist countries ... under the pressure of the business agenda'. This global homogenization of educational curricula has been towards the neo-liberal principles of economic efficiency and the production of an effective workforce to support a country's position in international markets.

Rather than allowing more freedom and diversity within the curriculum, it seems that neo-liberalism has actually involved an increase in government interference in the educational curriculum. There appears to be a set of double standards at work here. In the UK, the neo-liberal market policies of choice and diversity when applied to the education system appears to be no more than a superficial choice of educational institution: Academy, specialist school, Foundation school (see Chapter 5, in this volume), rather than a real choice in terms of educational curricula. The core curricula and the recommended pedagogy currently advocated in the UK appear to be a political tool to establish and reinforce neo-liberal politics as the common-sense consensus.

Assessment types

Task 12.3 Stop, think and do

- List the types of assessment you have experienced in the education system at school, college and university.
- What are the benefits and disadvantages of these forms of assessment?
- Can you think of any other forms of assessment which would be useful?
- Rank the assessment types listed in descending order of formality.

Assessment obviously plays an important role in the education process. Assessment enables the progress of the learner to be monitored and the final level of achievement to be identified. It also provided the means for the teaching and learning process to be evaluated and, if necessary, adapted and refined. Moreover, levels of attainment as recorded in assessment figures, such as Standard Attainment Tests results (SATs), GCSE results, and degree classifications, allow comparison to be made between educational institutions. Before turning to a brief discussion of the role of assessment within the current education system, let us consider different assessment types (for a more detailed discussion of assessment types, see Kelly 2004: 126–31).

Assessment may be formative in the sense that the actual experience of undertaking the assessment is a learning experience through which the learner's knowledge is substantiated and research, presentation, communication and organizational skills are consolidated and developed. Formative assessments are usually not included in the eventual overall grading of a learner's attainment, but are intended to inform further learning by highlighting areas of strengths and weaknesses. Formative assessments vary in type, from written essays to verbal presentations and may be formal or informal. Conversely, summative assessment is not traditionally regarded as having any learning value in itself. It is usually undertaken at the end of a period of learning in order to generate a grade that reflects the student's level of attainment. The traditional unseen examination is often presented as a typical form of summative assessment, though other forms of assessment, such as written coursework, may be used summatively.

Ideally, the type of assessment chosen in any course of learning will depend on the reasons for assessment, be they formative or summative, and the actual nature of the knowledge and/or skills to be assessed. In order to cater for different learners' reactions to different types of assessment, it is generally considered to be advantageous for both assessed and assessor that a variety of assessment types are included in any one course of study. The assessed learner may fare better, for example, at either examinations, coursework or verbal presentation, so a combination of assessment types may provide the assessor with a better indication of the learner's level of attainment.

Assessment over content

The neo-liberal education policy relies heavily on standards by which education institutions can be judged and compared in order to allow for competition. Developments in the education system within the UK since the introduction of the National Curriculum with its regime of Ofsted inspections, SATs, targets and league tables clearly provide the standards by which institutions can compete and be compared. This system is intended to help parents and learners choose between educational institutions based on league table ranking. However, deciphering league tables is a far from simple process. Since their introduction in 1992 as part of the Citizens' Charter (Cabinet Office 1992), league tables for schools have been adapted to include value added figures – recording the difference between the baseline of pupils' abilities and their final achievement in SATs or GCSEs. There are current moves to include complex value added figures which measure the progress of each individual pupil, but also take account of other factors affecting achievement, such as ethnicity, gender, poverty and special needs. If parents take valued added figures, complex value added figures and also Ofsted reports into account when choosing a school, they may be faced with conflicting and confusing information.

Moreover, performance indicators – tests, league tables and targets – termed the 3Ts of education (Kelly 2004: 53), have created a hierarchical, tiered education system at all levels from nursery schools to universities. This has resulted in increased funding and oversubscription for some institutions while others have suffered from lower levels of government and private investment and falling numbers on roll.

At present, pupils in the UK are assessed summatively during statutory education at least three times to provide the government with the figures for their league tables. Currently, SATs are statutory in English, Mathematics and Science at the end of Key Stage 2 (Year 6) and Key Stage 3 (Year 9). At the end of Key Stage 4 (Year 11) pupils must take public examinations in the form of GSCEs or other qualifications such as GNVQs.

It could be suggested that neo-liberal education policies have resulted in 'assessment–led education reform' (Hargreaves, 1989: 99). In the UK, and in most other Western countries (Moon 1990) knowledge for the curriculum is selected on the basis of its ability to help pupils attain assessable objectives, so that assessment figures can be collated into tables. In other words, knowledge is only considered to be valid if it can be tested and quantified. It would appear that, in light of the current neo-liberal trends in education policy, a fourth model of curriculum must be identified – the assessment-based model.

The implications of an education system and educational curricula which are planned and delivered on the basis of assessment criteria and targets are far-reaching. If education and knowledge are valued only in so far as they are a means to achieve assessment targets, then the system could be schooling learners not to value anything for its own sake, but merely as a means to achieve definable and quantifiable ends. In this sense neo-liberalism may be encouraging learners of all ages to have no interest in their own development, nor in questioning and exploring their understanding of the world they live in. Rather it encourages them to see education as one aspect of human interaction which as a totality amounts to no more than a process of compliance to externally imposed goals in order to succeed in social competition.

Summary

1. In order to understand the nature of curriculum a broad definition must be sought, including the totality of the learning experience, the formal and informal, planned and received curricula.
2. It is important to recognize the difference between the planned or the official curriculum and the experienced or received curriculum.
3. Traditionally three curriculum models have been identified – content-based, objectives-based and process-based.
4. The hidden curriculum of education institutions teaches the 3Rs – rules, routines and regulations – which prepare learners for the workplace.
5. Many countries in the world have a core or national curriculum controlled directly by the government. In the UK, this did not exist prior to 1988.
6. There are two basic points of view on the creation and validation of knowledge. Some believe that universally true knowledge exists and that this knowledge is not created, but is uncovered. Others assert that knowledge is created and validated within a specific socio-historical and cultural context. The second view is the most commonly held.
7. Within any society the validation of one form of knowledge valued by those in power via its inclusion in the educational curriculum can be seen as a means of social control.
8. Current global trends in neo-liberal politics favour a curriculum which allows market forces – choice, diversity, private funding and competition – to be realized within the education system.
9. The effect of neo-liberalism on the education system is producing curricula which are superficially content- and objectives-based, but are, in reality assessment-based.

References

Abbot, D. (2005) Teachers are failing Black boys, in B. Richardson (ed.) *Tell It Like It Is: How Our Schools Fail Black Children.* London: Bookmarks.

Acheson, D. (1998) *Independent Enquiry into Inequalities in Health: Report.* London: Stationery Office.

Adams, R. (1991) *Protests by Pupils Empowerment, Schooling and the State.* London: Falmer.

Adnett, N. and Davies, P. (2003) Schooling reforms in England: from quasi-markets to co-operation? *Journal of Education Policy,* 18(4): 393–406.

Advisory Centre for Education (1992) *The Children Act and Education: A Guide for Parents and Schools on the Children Act 1989.* London: ACE.

Ainscow, M. (1999) *Understanding the Development of Inclusive Schools.* London: Falmer Press.

Allan, J. (2006) Failing to make progress? The aporias of responsible inclusion, in E. A. Brantlinger (ed.) *Who Benefits from Special Education? Remediating (Fixing) Other People's Children.* Mahwah, NJ: Lawrence Erlbaum Associates. Inc.

Allen, N. (1992) *Making Sense of the Children Act.* 2nd edn. Harlow: Longman.

Althusser, L. (1984) *Essays on Ideology.* New York: Verso Books.

Anning, A. (2006) Early Years education: mixed messages and conflicts, in D. Kassem, E. Mufti and J. Robinson (eds) *Education Studies: Issues and Critical Perspectives.* Maidenhead: Open University Press.

Apple, M. (1989) The politics of common sense: schooling, populism, and the new Right, in H. Giroux and P. McLaren (eds) *Critical Pedagogy, the State and Cultural Struggle.* New York: State University of New York Press.

Apple, M. (1999) *Power, Meaning, and Identity.* New York: Peter Lang.

Apple, M. (2002) Does education have independent power? Bernstein and the question of relative autonomy, *British Journal of Sociology of Education,* 23(4): 607–616.

Apple, M. (2003) *The State and the Politics of Knowledge.* New York: Routledge.

Apple, M. (2004) *Ideology and Curriculum,* 3rd edn. London: RoutledgeFalmer.

Apple, M. and Teitelbaum, K. (2006) John Dewey, in J. A. Palmer (ed.) *Fifty Major Thinkers on Education: From Confucius to Dewey*. Abingdon: Routledge.

Aries, P. (1973) *Centuries of Childhood*. Harmondsworth: Penguin Books.

Armstrong, D. (2005) Reinventing 'inclusion': New Labour and the cultural politics of special education, *Oxford Review of Education*, 31(1): 119–34.

Arrow, K. (1953) *Social Choice and Individual Values*. 2nd edn. New York: Wiley.

Babb, P., Martin, J. and Haezewindt, T. (2004) *Focus on Social Inequalities*. London: TSO.

Bailis, L. N. (2000) *Taking Service-Learning to the Next Level: Emerging Lessons from the National Society for Experiential Education's National Community Development Program*. Washington, DC: National Society for Experiential Education.

Baker, D.P. and LeTendre, G.K. (2005) *National Differences, Global Similarities World Culture and the Future of Schooling*. Stanford, CA: Stanford University Press.

Ball, S. (2008) *The Education Debate*. London: Policy Press.

Ball, S., Rowe, R. and Gewirtz, S. (1996) School choice, social class and distinction: the realization of social advantage in education, *Journal of Educational Policy* 11(1): 89–112.

Bandura, A. (1963) The role of imitation in personality. *Journal of Nursery Education*, 18(3).

Bandura, A. (1977) Self-efficacy: Toward a unifying theory of behavioural change. *Psychological Review*, 84: 191–215.

Banks, O. (1955) *Parity and Prestige in English Secondary Education*. London: Routledge and Kegan Paul.

Barber, M. (2007) *Instruction to Deliver*. London: Politicos.

Barker, J. and Hodes, D. (2007) *The Child in Mind: A Child Protection Handbook*. London: Routledge.

Baron-Cohen, S. (2003). *The Essential Difference: Men, Women and the Extreme Male Brain*. London: Penguin.

Bartlett, S. and Burton, D. (2007) *Introduction to Education Studies*, 2nd edn. London: Sage.

Barton, L. (ed.) (1998) *The Politics of Special Educational Needs*. Lewes: Falmer Press.

Becker, H. (1952) Social class variation in the teacher–pupil relationship, *Journal of Educational Sociology*, 25.

Beckett, C. (2007) *Child Protection: An Introduction*, 2nd edn. London: Sage.

Beckett, F. (2007) *The Great City Academy Fraud*. London: Continuum Books.

Benn, C. (1992) *Keir Hardie*. London: Hutchinson.

Benn, C. and Chitty, C. (1997) *Thirty Years On: Comprehensive Education Alive and Well or Struggling to Survive?* London: Penguin.

Benn, M. and Millar, F. (2006) *A Comprehensive Future: Quality and Equality for all Our Children*. London: Compass.

Bernstein, B. (1971) *Class, Codes and Control*. London: Paladin.

Bernstein, J. S. (1992) Beyond the personal, in Renos K. Papadopoulos (ed.) *Carl Gustav Jung: Critical Assessments* London: Routledge.

Beveridge, S. (2002) *Special Educational Needs in Schools*. London: Routledge.

Blair, T. (2005) Speech delivered at the City of London Academy on 12 September 2005. www.pm.gov.uk/output/Page8181.asp (accessed 25 June 2006).

Bobbitt, F. (1918) *The Curriculum*. Boston: Houghton Mifflin.

Booth, T. and Ainscow, M. (eds) (1998) *From Them to Us: An International Study of Inclusion in Education*. London: Routledge.

Bourdieu, P. (1977) *Outline of a Theory of Practice*. Cambridge: Cambridge University Press.

Bourdieu, P. (1986) *Distinction: A Social Critique of the Judgement of Taste*. London: Routledge.

Bowles, S. and Gintis, H. (1976) *Schooling in Capitalist Amercia: Educational Reform and the Contradictions of Economic Life*. London: Routledge and Kegan Paul.

Bowles, S. and Gintis, H. (2001) *Schooling in Capitalist America Revisited*. e\Papers\JEP-paper\Sociology of Education.tex.

Boyd, R. D. and Myers, G. J. (1988). Transformative education. *International Journal of Lifelong Education*, 7(4): 261–284.

Boyson, R. (1975) *The Crisis in Education*. London: Woburn Press.

Bradshaw, J., Sturman, L., Vappula, H., Ager, R. and Wheater, R. (2007) *Achievement of 15-year-olds in England: PISA 2006 National Report (OECD Programme for International Student Assessment)*. Slough: NFER.

Brantlinger, E. A. (2006) Conclusion: whose labels? Whose norms? Whose needs? Whose benefits? In E. A. Brantlinger (ed.) *Who Benefits from Special Education? Remediating (Fixing) Other People's Children*. Mahwah, NJ: Lawrence Erlbaum Associates.

Brettingham, M. (2008) Class of 1858. *The Times Educational Supplement Magazine*, Issue 14, 8 February.

Brisard, E. and Menter, I. (2004) Compulsory education in the United Kingdom, in D. Matheson (ed.) *An Introduction to the Study of Education*. 2nd edn. London: David Fulton Publishers Ltd.

Broadhead, P. (2004) *Early Years Play and Learning: Developing Social Skills and Cooperation.* London: RoutledgeFalmer.

Brown, G. (2003) A modern agenda for prosperity and social reform: speech made to the Social Market Foundation at the Cass Business School, London, 3.2.2003. www.hm-treasury.gov.uk/newsroom_and_speeches/press/2003/press_12_03.cfm#Top (accessed 18 March 2008).

Brown, M. (1999) Problems of interpreting international data, in B. Jaworski and D. Phillips (eds) *Comparing Standards Internationally Research and Practice in Mathematics and Beyond.* Oxford: Symposium Books.

Brown, P. (1997) The third wave: education and the ideology of parentocracy, in A. Chadwick and R. Heffernan (eds) (2003) *The New Labour Reader.* Cambridge: Polity Press.

Browne, N. (2004) *Gender Equity.* Maidenhead: Open University Press.

Bruce, T. (2001) *Learning Through Play: Babies, Toddlers and the Foundation Years.* London: Hodder & Stoughton.

Bruner, J. S. (1960). *The Process of Education.* Cambridge, MA: Harvard University Press.

Cabinet Office, Office of Public Service and Science (1992) *Citizens' Charter: First Report: 1992.* London: HMSO.

Callaghan, J. ([1976] 1996) The Ruskin College speech, in J. Ahier, B. Cosin and M. Hales (eds) *Diversity and Change: Education, Policy and Selection.* London: Routledge/Open University.

Carr, W. and Harnett, A.(1996) *Education and the Struggle for Democracy.* Maidenhead: Open University Press.

Child, D. (2007) *Psychology and the Teacher.* London: Continuum.

Children's Workforce Development Council (2006) *Early Years Professional Prospectus.* Leeds: CWDC.

Chitty, C. (2004) *Education Policy in Britain.* London: Palgrave Macmillan.

Clements, D. (2006) *Every Child Matters – but so does our privacy.* www.spiked-online.com/index.php?/site/article/1889/ (accessed 28 March 2008).

Clouder, C. and Rawson, M. (2003) *Waldorf Education: Rudolf Steiner's Ideas in Practice.* Edinburgh: Floris Books.

Clough, P. (2005) Routes to inclusion, in P. Clough and J. Corbett, *Theories of Inclusive Education: A Student's Guide.* London: Paul Chapman Publishing.

Clough, P. and Corbett, J. (2000) *Theories of Inclusive Education: Student's Guide.* London: Sage.

Coard, B. (2005) How the West Indian Child is made educationally subnormal in the British school system: the scandal of the Black Child in schools in Britain, in B. Richardson (ed.) *Tell It Like It Is: How Our Schools Fail Black Children*. London: Bookmarks.

Cohen, B., Moss, P., Petrie, P. and Wallace, J. (2004) *A New Deal for Children? Re-forming Education and Care in England, Scotland and Sweden*. Bristol: Policy Press.

Cole, M. (2007) The State Apparatuses and the Working Class: Experiences from the UK; Educational Lessons from Venezuela, paper presented at the annual conference of the British Education Studies Association (BESA) Bath Spa University, July.

Collier, K.G. (1959) *The Social Purposes of Education*. London: Routledge and Kegan Paul.

Condorcet, (1976) *Condorcet: Selected Writings*. Ed. K. Baker, London: Macmillan Publishing Co.

Cosin, B. (1972) *Ideology*. Milton Keynes: Open University Press.

Cox, B. and Dyson, A. (eds) (1969) *Fight for Education: A Black Paper*. London: Critical Quarterly Society.

Cox, B. and Dyson, A. (1970) *Black Paper Two: The Crisis in Education*. London: Critical Quarterly Society.

Croll, P. and Moses, D. (2000) Ideologies and utopias: education professionals' views of inclusion, *European Journal of Special Needs Education*, 15(11):1–12.

Cullingford, C. (ed.) (1989) *The Primary Teacher: The Role of the Educator and the Purpose of Primary Education*. London: Cassell Educational.

Dale, I. (ed.) (2000) *Labour Party General Election Manifestos, 1900–1997*. London: Politicos.

Davies, I. (1969) Education and social science, *New Society*, 8 May.

Davis, K. and Moore, W. (1945) Functional theory of stratification: some principles of stratification, *American Sociology Review* 10: 242–9.

Dearing, R. (1997) *Higher Education in the Learning Society: Report of the National Committee of Inquiry into Higher Education* (the Dearing Report). London: HMSO.

Denessen, E., Drissena, G. and Sleegers, P. (2005) Segregation by choice? A study of group group-specific reasons for school choice, *Journal of Educational Policy* 20(3): 347–68.

Department for Children, Schools and Families (DCFS) (2008) *GCSE and Equivalent Examination Results in England 2006/07 Revised*. London: DCSF.

Department for Education (DfE) (1988) *Education Reform Act*. London: HMSO.

Department for Education (DfE) (1992) *Choice and Diversity: A New Framework for Schools*. London: DfE.

Department for Education and Employment (DfEE) (1988) *Meeting the Childcare Challenge: A Summary.* Sudbury: DfEE Publications.

Department for Education and Employment (DfEE) (1994) *The Code of Practice on the Identification and Assessment of Children and Special Educational Needs.* London: DfEE.

Department for Education and Employment (DfEE) (1997a) *Excellence in Schools.* London: DfEE.

Department for Education and Employment (DfEE) (1997b) *Excellence for All Children: Meeting Special Educational Needs.* London: DfEE.

Department for Education and Employment (DfEE) (1998a) *The National Literacy Strategy: Framework for Teaching.* London: DfEE.

Department for Education and Employment (DfEE) (1998b) *Special Educational Needs Programme for Action.* London: DfEE.

Department for Education and Employment (DfEE) (1998c) *Meeting the Childcare Challenge: A Framework and Consultation Document,* London: HMSO.

Department for Education and Employment (DfEE) (1998d) *The Implementation of the National Numeracy Strategy. The Final Report of the National Numeracy Task Force.* London: DfEE.

Department for Education and Employment (DfEE) (2000) *Curriculum Guidance for the Foundation Stage.* London: QCA Publications.

Department of Education and Science (DES) (1995) *The Disability Discrimination Act.* London: HMSO.

Department of Education and Skills (DfES) (2001a) *The Key Stage 3 National Strategy.* London: DfES.

Department for Education and Skills (DfES) (2001b) *Special Educational Needs Code of Practice.* London: DfES Publications.

Department of Education and Skills (DfES) (2001c) *Special Educational Needs and Disability Act (SENDA).* London: HMSO.

Department for Education and Skills (DfES) (2002) *Senior Practitioner: New Pathways for Professionals.* Nottingham: DfES Publications.

Department for Education and Skills (DfES) (2003a) *Every Child Matters.* London: HMSO.

Department for Education and Skills (DfES) (2003b) *Excellence and Enjoyment: A Strategy for Primary Schools.* London: DfES.

Department for Education and Skills (DfES) (2004a) *The Children Act.* London: HMSO.

Department for Education and Skills (DfES) (2004b) *Every Child Matters: The Next Steps.* London: HMSO.

Department for Education and Skills (DfES) (2004c) *Removing Barriers to Achievement: The Government's Strategy for SEN*. Nottingham: DfES Publications.

Department for Education and Skills (DfES) (2004d) *Primary Strategy Learning Networks: An Introduction*. London: HMSO.

Department for Education and Skills (2005a) *The Disability Discrimination Act*. London: HMSO.

Department for Education and Skills (DfES) (2005b) *Higher Standards, Better Schools for All: More Choice for Parents and Pupils*. London: DfES.

Department for Education and Skills (DfES) (2006a) *Working Together to Safeguard Children*. London: DfES.

Department for Education and Skills (DfES) (2006b) *The Children Act*. London: HMSO.

DfES (2007) *Practice Guidance for the Early Years Foundation Stage*. Nottingham: DfES Publications.

DfES (no date) *Tackling it Together: Frequently Asked Questions*. www.dfes.gov.uk/ schoolattendance/faq/#faq9 (accessed 29 March 2008).

Department of Education and Science (DES) (1959) *15 to 18* (the Crowther Report). London: HMSO.

Department of Education and Science (DES) (1967) *Children and Their Primary School* (the Plowden Report). London: HMSO.

Department of Education and Science (DES) (1978) *Special Educational Needs. Report of the Committee of Enquiry into Education of Handicapped Children and Young People* (the Warnock Report). London: HMSO.

Department of Education and Science (DES) (1981) *The Education Act*. London: HMSO.

Department of Education and Science (DES) (1988) *The Education Reform Act*. London: HMSO.

Department of Education and Science (DES) (1989) *The Children Act*. London: HMSO.

Department of Health (DH) (1989) *The Children Act 1989*. London: HMSO

Descartes, R. ([1637] 1960) *Discourse on Method and Meditations*. trans. L. Lefleur. New York: Macmillan.

Dewey, J. ([1916] 1997) *Democracy and Education*. London: Free Press.

Dewey, J. (1938) *Experience and Education*. New York: Collier Books.

Dörnyei, Z. and Murphey, T. (2003) *Group Dynamics in the Language Classroom*. Cambridge: Cambridge University Press.

Dowker, A. (2006). What can functional brain imaging studies tell us about typical and atypical cognitive development in children? *Journal of Physiology*, 99: 333–41.

Durkheim, E. ([1893]1947) *The Division of Labour in Society*. New York: Free Press.

Edwards, J. R. and Harrison, R. V. (1993) Job demands and worker health: three-dimensional re-examination of the relationship between person-environment fit and strain. *Journal of Applied Psychology*, 78(4): 628–48.

EOC (2007) *Sex & Power: Who Runs Britain?* Manchester: EOC.

Eisner, E. W. (2004) Educational objectives – help or hindrance? in D. J. Flinders and S. Thornton (eds) *The Curriculum Studies Reader*, 2nd edn. Abingdon: RoutledgeFalmer.

Erikson, E.H. (1963) *Childhood and Society*. New York: Norton.

European Commission (1994). *Growth, Competitiveness, Employment: The Challenges and Way Forward into the 21st century* (*White Paper*). Luxembourg: European Commission.

Every Child Matters: Change for Children (ECM) (2007) *About ContactPoint*. www.everychildmatters.gov.uk/deliveringservices/contactpoint/about/ (accessed 28.3.2008).

Farrell, P. (1997) The integration of children with severe learning difficulties: a review of the recent literature *Journal of Applied Research in Intellectual Disabilities*, 10(11): 1–14.

Farrell, P. (2004) *Special Educational Needs: A Resource for Practitioners*. London: Paul Chapman Publishing.

Farrell, P. and Ainscow, M. (eds) (2002) *Making Special Education Inclusive*. London: David Fulton Publishers Ltd.

Fielden, J. (1836) *The Curse of the Factory System*. London: A. Cobbett.

Fitzpatrick, T. (2001) *Welfare Theory: An Introduction*. Basingstoke: Palgrave.

Fletcher-Campbell, F. (1994) *Still Joining Forces? A Follow Up Study of Links between Ordinary and Special Schools*. Slough: NFER.

Flett, K. (2006) *Chartism After 1848: The Working Class and the Politics of Radical Education*. London: Merlin.

Flinders, D. J. and Thorntons, S. (eds) (2204) *The Curriculum Studies Reader,* 2nd edn. Abingdon: RoutledgeFalmer.

Foot, P. (2005) *The Vote: How It Was Won and How It Was Undermined*. London: Viking.

Foucault, M. (1977) *Discipline and Punish*. Harmondsworth: Penguin.

Foucault, M. (1980) *Power/Knowledge: Selected Interviews and Other Writings, 1972–1977*. C. Gordon (ed.) New York: Pantheon.

Freire, P. ([1970] 1996) *Pedagogy of the Oppressed*. trans. M.B. Ramos. London: Penguin Books Ltd.

Freire, P. (1973) *Education for Critical Consciousness*. trans. M. B. Ramos, L. Bigwood and M. Marshall. London: Sheed and Ward.

Furedi, F. (2001) *Paranoid Parenting: Abandon Your Anxieties and Be a Good Parent*. Harmondsworth: Allen Lane.

Galton, F. (1874). *English Men of Science: Their Nature and Nurture*. London: Macmillan and Co.

Gardner, H. (1983). *Frames of Mind: The Theory of Multiple Intelligences*. New York: Basic Books.

Gardner, P. (1984) *The Lost Elementary Schools of Victorian England*. London: Croom Helm.

Glazer, S. (2005) Gender and learning: are there innate differences between the sexes? *The CQ Researcher,* 15(19): 445–68.

Gewirtz, S., Ball, S. J. and Bowe, R. (1995) *Markets, Choice and Equality in Education*. Buckingham: Open University Press.

Giddens, A. and Stanworth, P. (eds) (1974) *Elites and Power in British Society*. Cambridge: Cambridge University Press.

Giroux, H. (2001) *Theory and Resistance in Education: Towards a Pedagogy for the Opposition*. Westport, CT: Greenwood Press.

Golby, M. (1989) Curriculum traditions, in B. Moon, P. Murphy and J. Raynor (eds) *Policies for the Curriculum*. London: Hodder & Stoughton.

Goleman, D. (1995). *Emotional Intelligence: Why It Can Matter More than IQ*. New York: Bantam Books.

Goodson, I. (1990) Curriculum reform and curriculum theory: a case of historical amnesia, in B. Moon (ed.) *New Curriculum – National Curriculum*. Milton Keynes: Open University Press.

Gopnik, A. (2005). How we learn. *The New York Times.* 26/01/06 www.nytimes.com/2005/01/16/education/edlife/EDSCIENCE.html. (accessed 16.4.08).

Gramsci, A. ([1929–35] 1971) *Selections from the Prison Notebooks*. London: Lawrence & Wishart Ltd.

Green, A., Preston, J. and Janmaat, G. (2006) *Education, Equality and Social Cohesion: A Comparative Analysis*. London: Palgrave.

Gribble, D. (1998) *Real Education: Varieties of Freedom*. Bristol: Libertarian Education.

Gurian, M. and Ballew, A. C. (2003) *The Boys and Girls Learn Differently: Action Guide for Teachers*. San Francisco: Jossey-Bass.

Hall, J. (1997) *Social Devaluation and Special Education*. London: Jessica Kingsley Publishers.

Hall, S. (1998) The toad in the garden: Thatherism among the theories, in C. Nelson and L. Grossberg (eds) *Marxism and the Interpretation of Culture*. Urbana, IL: University of Illinois Press.

Hargreaves, A. (1989) *Curriculum and Assessment Reform*. Milton Keynes: Open University Press.

Harvey, D. (1991) *The Condition of Postmodernity: An Enquiry into the Origins of Cultural Change*. Oxford: Blackwell Publishing Limited.

Harvey, D. (2005) *A Brief History of Neoliberalism*. Oxford: Oxford University Press.

Hatcher, R. (2001) Getting down to business: schooling in the globalised economy, *Education and Social Justice*, 3(2): 45–59.

Hatcher, R. (2004) Social class and school, in D. Matheson (ed.) *An Introduction to the Study of Education*. London: David Fulton.

Hatcher, R. and Hirtt, N. (1999) The business agenda behind Labour's education policy, in M. Allen, C. Benn, M. Cole, R. Hatcher, N. Hirtt and G. Rilowski (eds) *Business, Business, Business: New Labour's Education Policy*. London: The Tufnell Press.

Head, B. (1985) *Ideology and Social Science: Destutt De Tracey and French Liberalism*. Boston, MA: Kulwer Academic Publisher.

Hicks, S. R. C. (2004) *Explaining Postmodernism: Skepticism and Socialism from Rousseau to Foucault*. Tempe, AZ: Scholargy Publishing.

Hill, A. (2007) Social worker crisis puts children at risk, *The Observer*, 7. October 2007, www.guardian.co.uk/society/2007/oct/07/childrensservices.socialcare   (accessed 19 March 2008).

Hill, D. and Cole, M. (2004) *Schooling and Equality: Fact, Concept and Policy*. London: Routledge.

Hindess, B. (1988) *Choice, Rationality and Social Theory*. London: Unwin Hyman.

Hirst, P. H. (1965) Liberal education and the nature of knowledge, in R. D. Archanbauld (ed.) *Philosophical Analysis and Education*. London: Routledge.

HM Treasury, DfES, DWP and DTI (2004) *Choice for Parents: The Best Start for Children: a Ten Year Strategy for Childcare*. Norwich: HMSO.

HM Treasury (HMT) and Department for Education and Skills (DFES) (2007) *Aiming High for Disabled Children: Better Support for Families*. Norwich: HMSO.

Hobson, P. (2006) A. S. Neill, in J. A. Palmer (ed.) *Fifty Modern Thinkers on Education: From Piaget to the Present*. Abingdon: Routledge.

House of Commons Education and Skills Committee (HCESC) (2003) *Secondary Education: Diversity of Provision*. London: The Stationery Office.

House of Commons Education and Skills Select Committee (HCESC) (2006) *Special Educational Needs*. Third report of Sessions 2005–6, Volume 1. HC 478–1. London: The Stationery Office.

Humphries, S. (1981) *Hooligans or Rebels? An Oral History of Working-Class Childhood and Youth 1889–1939*. Oxford: Basil Blackwell.

Hunt, F. (ed.) (1987) *Lessons for Life: The Schooling of Girls and Woman, 1850–1950*. Oxford: Basil Blackwell.

Hursh, D. (2008) *High-Stakes Testing and the Decline of Teaching and Learning: The Real Crisis in Education*. New York: Rowan & Littlefield.

Hursh, D. (in press) No Child Left Behind, really? in D. Kassem and D. Garratt (eds) *Exploring Issues in Education*. London: Continuum.

Illich, I. ([1971] 2004) *Deschooling Society*. London: Marion Boyars Publishers Ltd.

Jackson, P. W. (1968) *Life in Classrooms*. New York: Holt, Rinehart & Winston.

Jenkins, D. and Shipman, M. D. (1976) *Curriculum: An Introduction*. London: Open Books.

Johnson, D. and Salle, L. (2004) *Responding to the Attack on Public Education and Teacher Unions: A Commonwealth Institute Report*. CA: Menlo Park.

Johnson, R. (1979) Really useful knowledge: radical education and the working class, 1790–1848, in J. Clarke, C. Ritcher and R. Johnson (eds) *Working Class Culture Studies in History and Theory*. London: Hutchinson University Library.

Johnson, S. (1999) International Association for the Evaluation of Educational Achievement Science Assessment in Developing Countries, *Assessment in Education*, 6(1): 57–73.

Jones, G. (2003) *Killing Monsters: Our Children's Need for Fantasy, Heroism, and Make-Believe Violence*. New York: Basic Books.

Jones, K. (2003) *Education in Britain 1944 to the Present*. London: Polity.

Jones, K. et al. (2008) *Schooling in Western Europe: The New Order and its Adversaries*. London: Palgrave.

Kassem, D. (2006) Education of looked-after children: who cares? In D. Kassem, E. Mufti and J. Robinson (eds) *Education Studies: Issues and Critical Perspectives*. Maidenhead: Open University Press.

Kassem, D., Mufti, E. and Robinson, J. (eds) (2006) *Education Studies: Issues and Critical Perspectives*. Maidenhead: Open University Press.

Kellett, M. (2004) Special needs and inclusion in education, in D. Matheson (ed.) *An Introduction to the Study of Education*, 2nd edn. London: David Fulton Publishers Ltd.

Kelly, A. V. (2004) *The Curriculum: Theory and Practice*, 5th edn. London: Sage Publications.

Kelly, G. (1955) *The Psychology of Personal Constructs*. New York: W. W. Norton.

Kirby, M. (2000) *Sociology in Perspective*. Oxford: Heinemann.

Klahr, D. (2000) *Exploring Science: The Cognition and Development of Discovery Processes.* Cambridge, MA: MIT Press.

Knight, C. (1990) *The Making of Tory Education Policy in Post-War Britain, 1950–1986.* London: Falmer Press.

Labour Party (1980) *Private Schools: A Labour Party Discussion Document.* London: The Labour Party.

Laming, Lord (2003) *The Victoria Climbé Inquiry*, CM 5730. London: Department of Health.

Larrian, J. (1979) *The Concept of Ideology.* London: Hutchinson University Library.

Lauder, H., Brown, P., Dillabough, J. and Halsey, A. H. (2006) *Education, Globalization, and Social Change.* Oxford: Oxford University Press.

Law, S. (2006) *The War for Children's Minds.* Abingdon: Routledge.

Locke, J. ([1693] 1996) *Some Thoughts Concerning Education.* Indianapolis, IN: Hackett Publishing Co.

Lowndes, G. (1969) *The Silent Social Revolution,* 2nd edn. Oxford: Oxford University Press.

Lyotard, J-F. (2004) *The Postmodern Condition: A Report on Knowledge.* trans. G. Bennington and B. Massumi. Manchester: Manchester University Press.

MacDonald, K. (2006) England: educating for the twenty-first century, in D. Kassem, E. Mufti and J. Robinson (eds) *Education Studies: Critical Issues and Perspectives.* Maidenhead: Open University Press.

MacLeod-Brudenell, I. (ed.) (2004) *Advanced Early Years Care and Education.* Oxford: Heinemann Educational Publishers.

MacNaughton, G. (2003) *Shaping Early Childhood: Learners, Curriculum, and Contexts.* Maidenhead: Open University Press.

Manton, K. (2001) *Socialism and Education in Britain 1883–1902.* London: Woburn Press.

Marsh, C. J. (2004) *Key Concepts for Understanding Curriculum,* 3rd edn. London: RoutledgeFalmer.

Martin, J. (2004) Gender in education in Matheson, in D. Matheson (ed.) *An Introduction to the Study of Education.* London: David Fulton.

Marton, F. and Saljo, R. (1976) On qualitative differences in learning I: Outcome and process, *British Journal of Educational Psychology,* 46: 4–11.

Marx, K. and Engels, F. ([1845–7] 1970) *The German Ideology.* London: Lawrence & Wishart Ltd.

Massey, A., Green, S., Dexter, T. and Hammett, L. (2002) *Comparability of National Tests over Time: Key Stage Test Standards Between 1996 and 2001: Final Report to the QCA of the Comparability Over Time Project*. London: QCA.

Matheson, C. (2004) Ideology in education in the United Kingdom, in D. Matheson (ed.) *An Introduction to the Study of Education*, 2nd edn. London: David Fulton Publishers Ltd.

Matheson, D. (2004) What is education? In D. Matheson (ed.) *An Introduction to the Study of Education*, 2nd edn. London: David Fulton Publishers.

McCormack, S. (2006) Montessori: the startling success of progressive teaching methods, *The Independent,* 17 August.

McIntosh, A. (1981) When will they ever learn? In A. Floyd (ed.) *Developing Mathematical Thinking*. London: Addison-Wesley Publishers.

McLaren, P. (1989) On ideology and education: critical pedagogy and the cultural politics of resistance, in H. Giroux and P. McLaren (eds) *Critical Pedagogy, the State and Cultural Struggle*. New York: State University of New York Press.

McMillan, M. (1904) *Education through the Imagination*. London: Swan Sonnenschein & Co.

McMurty, J. (2000) Education, struggle and the Left today, *International Journal of Education Reform*, 10(2): 145–62.

Mead, M. (1935) *Sex and Temperament in Three Primitive Societies*. New York: William Morrow & Company.

Meighan, R. (1995) *The Freethinkers' Pocket Directory to the Educational Universe*. Nottingham: Educational Heretics Press.

Meighan, R. (2000) *Natural Learning and the Natural Curriculum*. Nottingham: Educational Heretics Press.

Meighan, R. and Siraj-Blatchford, I. (2001) *A Sociology of Educating,* 4th edn. London: Continuum.

Meyer, J., Kamens, D. and Benavot, A. (1992) *School Knowledge for the Masses: World Models and National Primary Curricular Categories in the Twentieth Century*. London: Falmer.

Mezirow, J. (1997) Transformative learning: theory to practice, *New Directions for Adult and Continuing Education,* 74: 5–12.

Miller, R. (2004) Educational alternative: a map of the territory, *Paths of Learning*, 20, Spring: 20–7.

Mirza, H. (2005) The more things change, the more they stay the same: assessing Black underachievement 35 years on, in B. Richardson (ed.) *Tell It Like It Is: How Our Schools Fail Black Children*. London: Bookmarks.

Montessori, M. ([1909] 2005) *The Montessori Method.* New York: Kessinger Publishing.

Moon, B. (1990) Patterns of control: school reform in Western Europe, in B. Moon (ed.) *New Curriculum – National Curriculum.* London: Hodder & Stoughton.

Moon, B. and Murphy, P. (eds) (1999) *Curriculum in Context.* London: Paul Chapman Publishing Ltd.

Morrison, K. and Ridley, K. (1989) Ideological contexts for curriculum planning, in M. Preedy (ed.) *Approaches to Curriculum Management.* Milton Keynes: Open University Press.

Mortimore, P. (2008) A league table to worry us all, *The Guardian,* 8 January.

Moss, P. and Penn, H. (1996) *Transforming Nursery Education.* London: Paul Chapman Publishing.

Mufti, E. (2006) New students: same old structures, in D. Kassem, E. Mufti and J. Robinson (eds) *Education Studies: Issues and Critical Perspectives.* Milton Keynes: Open University Press.

Murdoch, S. (2007) *IQ: The Brilliant Idea that Failed.* London: Duckworth & Co Ltd.

Murphy, L., Kassem, D. and Fenwick, G. (2006) The politics of the National Numeracy and Literacy Strategies, in D. Kassem, E. Mufti, and J. Robinson (eds) *Education Studies: Critical Issues and Perspectives.* Maidenhead: Open University Press.

National Curriculum Online (2007) www.nc.uk.net/nc_resources/html/inclusion.shtml (accessed 30 March 2008).

Neill, A. S. ([1960] 1968) *Summerhill.* Harmondsworth: Penguin Books.

Newman, M. (2006) When the evidence is not enough: freedom to choose versus prescribed choice: the case of Summerhill School, in D. Kassem, E. Mufti, and J. Robinson (eds) *Education Studies: Critical Issues and Perspectives.* Maidenhead: Open University Press.

Oakley, A. (1975) *Sex, Gender & Society.* London: Temple Smith.

O'Hagan, T. (2006) Jean-Jacques Rousseau, in J. A. Palmer (ed.) *Fifty Major Thinkers on Education: From Confucius to Dewey.* Abingdon: Routledge.

Organisation of Economic Cooperation and Development (2007) Education at a Glance 2007. OECD http://www.oecd.org/document/30/0,3343,de_2649_37455_39251550_1_1_1_37455,00.html (accessed 29 May 2008).

Ouvry, M. (2003) *Exercising Muscles and Minds: Outdoor Play and the Early Years Curriculum.* London: National Children's Bureau.

Paechter, C. (1998) *Educating the Other: Gender, Power and Schooling.* London: Falmer Press.

Parsons, T. (1964) *The Social System,* 2nd edn. New York: Macmillan.

Paterson, L. (2003) *Scottish Education in the Twentieth Century*. Edinburgh: University of Edinburgh Press.

Paton, G. (2005) School choice chaos, *Times Educational Supplement,* 18 November.

Penrose, R. (1989) *The Emperor's New Mind: Concerning Computers, Minds and the Laws of Physics*. New York: Oxford University Press.

Peters, R. S. (1966) *Ethics and Education*. London: Allen and Unwin.

Pinker, S. (2002) *The Blank Slate: The Modern Denial of Human Nature*. New York: Viking Penguin.

Plato ([360 BC] 2003) *The Republic,* 2nd edn. trans. H. D. P. Lee London: Penguin Books.

Pollock, L. A. (1983) *Forgotten Children: Parent–Child Relations from 1500–1900.* Cambridge: Cambridge University Press.

Pugh, G. and Duffy, B. (eds) (2001) *Contemporary Issues in the Early Years,* 3rd edn. London: Sage.

Pugh, G. and Duffy, B. (eds) (2006) *Contemporary Issues in the Early Years,* 4th edn. London: Sage.

QAA (2007) *Education Studies*, The Quality Assurance Agency for Higher Education. http://qaa.ac.uk/academicinfrastructure/benchmark/honours/Education07.pdf (accesses 17 March 2008).

Raynor, J. (1972) *The Curriculum in England*. Milton Keynes: Open University Press.

Reay, D. and Ball, S. (1997) Spoilt for choice, *Oxford Review of Education,* 23(1): 89–101.

Reay, D., David, M. and Ball, S. (2005) *Degrees of Choice: Social Class, Race and Gender in Higher Education.* Stoke on Trent: Trentham Books.

Rikowski, G. (2001) *The Battle in Seattle: Its Significance for Education*. London: Tufnell Press.

Robertson, S., Bonal, X. and Dale, R. (2006) GATS and the education service industry: The politics of scale and global reterritorialization, in H. Lauder, P. Brown, J-A. Dillabough and A.H. Halsey (eds) *Education, Globalization and Social Change*. Oxford: Oxford University Press.

Rogers, C. (1983) *Freedom to Learn in the Eighties,* 2nd edn. Colombus, OH: Merrill.

Rose, J. (2006) *Independent Review of the Teaching of Early Reading: Final Report*. London: DfES.

Rosenthal, R. and Jacobson, L. (1968) *Pygmalion in the Classroom*. Eastbourne: Holt, Rhinehart and Winston.

Ross, A. (2000) *Curriculum: Construction and Critique*. London: Falmer Press.

Rousseau, J. J. ([1762] 1979) *Emile or On Education.* trans. A. Bloom. New York: Basic Books Inc.

Rubenstein, D. and Simon, B. (1972) *The Evolution of the Comprehensive School 1926–1972.* London: Routledge & Kegan Paul.

Sacks, P. (2007) *Tearing Down the Gates Confronting the Class Divide in American Education.* Berkeley, CA: University of California Press.

Saltman, K. (2005) *The Edison Schools.* New York: Routledge.

Sarason, S. (1998) *Charter Schools: Another Flawed Educational Reform?* New York: Teachers College Press.

Schneider, J., Avis, M. and Leighton, P. (2007) *Supporting Children and Families: Lessons from Sure Start for Evidence-Based Practice in Health, Social Care and Education.* London: Jessica Kingsley Publishers.

Schunk, D. H. (1990) Goal setting and self-efficacy during self-regulated learning. *Educational Psychologist,* 25: 71–86.

Scottish Executive (SE) (2001) *For Scotland's Children.* Edinburgh: HMSO.

Sewell, T. (1997) *Black Masculinities and Schooling.* Stoke on Trent: Trentham Books.

Sharp (2002) *School Starting Age: European Policy and Recent Research.* www.nfer.ac.uk/publications/other-publications/conference-papers/pdf_docs/PaperSSF.pdf (accessed 27 March 2008).

Sharpe, S. (1976) *Just Like a Girl: How Girls Learn to be Women.* Harmondsworth: Penguin.

Simon, B. (1965) *Education and the Labour Movement, 1870–1920.* London: Lawrence & Wishart.

Simon, B. (1974) *The Politics of Educational Reform 1920–1940.* London: Lawrence & Wishart.

Simon, B. (1991) *Education and the Social Order, 1940–1990.* London: Lawrence and Wishart.

Skilbeck, M. (1976) *Curriculum Design and Development: Ideologies and Values.* Buckingham: Open University Press.

Smith, R. (2006) John Locke, in J. A. Palmer (ed.) *Fifty Major Thinkers on Education: From Confucius to Dewey.* Abingdon: Routledge.

Steedman, C. (1994) *Strange Dislocations: Childhood and the idea of human interiority, 1780–1930.* Cambridge, MA: Harvard University Press.

Steiner, R. [1907] (1996) *The Education of the Child.* London: Steiner Books.

Stepney, P. (2006) Mission Impossible? Critical practice in social work, *British Journal of Social Work,* 36(8): 1289–307.

Sternberg, R. J. (1985). *Beyond IQ: A Triarchic Theory of Human Intelligence*. New York: Cambridge University Press.

Sure Start (2005) Interview: Rt. Hon. Beverley Hughes, *Partners* 40, August/September, 2–3.

Sure Start (2008) *Spending Review 2004 Public Service Agreement*. www.surestart.gov.uk/improvingquality/targets/psatargets200508/fulldetails/ (accessed 18 March 2008).

Sylva, K. (2004) *The Effective Provision of Pre-School Education* (EPPE) *Project: Effective Pre-school Education: A Longitudinal Study, Funded by the DFES 1997–2004*. Nottingham: Department for Education and Skills.

Tawney, R. H. (1922) *Secondary Education for All*. London: Labour Party and George Allen & Unwin Ltd.

Taylor, W. (1963) *The Secondary Modern School*. London: Faber.

TDA (2008) *Training and Development Agency for Schools*. www.tda.gov.uk/ (accessed 27 March 2008).

Teachernet (2007) *Extended Schools*. www.teachernet.gov.uk/wholeschool/extendedschools (accessed 27 March 2007).

Thrupp, M. (1998) Exploring the politics of blame: school inspection and its contestation in New Zealand and England, *Comparative Education*, 34(2): 195–208.

Tomlinson, S. (1982) *A Sociology of Special Education*. London: Routledge & Kegan Paul.

Tomlinson, S. (2005) *Education in a Post-Welfare Society*, 2nd edn. Milton Keynes: Open University Press.

Topping, K. and Wolfendale, S. (1985) *Parental Involvement in Children's Reading*. New York: Nichol's Publishing.

Townsend, P. and Davidson, N. (eds) (1982) *Inequalities in Health: The Black Report*. Harmondsworth: Penguin.

Trowler, P. (2003) *Education Policy*. 2nd edn. London: Routledge.

Turing, A. M. (1950) Computing machinery and intelligence, *Mind*, 59: 433–60.

Tyler, R. (1949) *Basic Principles of Curriculum and Instruction*. Chicago: University of Chicago Press.

Tymms, P. (2004) Are standards rising in English primary schools? *British Educational Research Journal*, 30(4).

Tymms, P., Coe, R. and Merrell, C. (2005) *Standards in English Schools: Changes since 1997 and the Impact of Government Policies and Initiatives*. A report for the *Sunday Times*.

UNDESA (United Nations Department of Economic & Social Affairs.) (2007) *Millennium Development Goals* http://unstats.un.orglund/ndg/UNSD_MDG_Report_2007e.pdt (accessed 17th March 2008).

UNESCO (1994) *World Conference on Special Educational Needs: Access and Quality* (Salamanca Statement) Paris: UNESCO.

United Nations (UN) (1989) *Convention on the Rights of the Child.* New York: United Nations.

U.S. Department of Education (2006) Remarks by Secretary Spellings at No Child Left Behind Summit. http://www.ed.gov.new (accessed 30 May 2008).

Waller, T. (ed.) (2005) *An Introduction to Early Childhood: A Multi-Disciplinary Approach.* London: Sage.

Ward, L. (2005) Sure Start sets back the worst placed youngsters, study finds. education.guardian.co.uk/earlyyears/story/0,,1654720,00.html (accessed 4 July 2007).

Ward, L. (2007) 330,000 users to have access to database on England's children. www.guardian.co.uk/society/2007/jun/18/childrenservices.politics. (accessed 4 July 2007).

Warnock, M. (2005) *Special Educational Needs: A New Look.* London: Philosophy of Education Society of Great Britain.

Weber, M. (1994) *Sociological Writings 60.* New York: Continuum.

West, E. G. (1994) *Education and the State: A Study in Political Economy,* 3rd edn. Indianapolis, IN: Liberty Fund.

Wexler, P. (1976) *The Sociology of Education: Beyond Equality.* Indianapolis, IN: Bobbs-Merrill.

White, J. (1988) An unconstitutional National Curriculum, in D. Lawton and C. Chitty (eds) *The National Curriculum, Bedford Way Paper 33.* London: Institute of Education, University of London.

White, J. (ed.) (2004) *Rethinking the School Curriculum: Values, Aims and Purposes.* Abingdon: RoutledgeFalmer.

Whitebread, M. (1972) *The Evolution of the Nursery-Infant School.* London: Routledge and Kegan Paul.

Whitty, G. (1989) The New Right and the National Curriculum: state control or market forces? *Journal of Education Policy,* 4(4): 329–41.

Wilce, H. (2006) Visionary who gave us food for thought, *Times Educational Supplement,* 15 September.

Willis, P. (1977) *Learning to Labour.* Hants: Saxon House.

Wiseman, W. and Baker, P. (2005) The worldwide explosion of internationalized education policy, *International Perspectives on Education and Society,* 6: 1–21.

Wolf, A. (2002) *Does Education Matter? Myths about Education and Economic Growth.* London: Penguin.

Wood, E. and Attfield, J. (2005) *Play, Learning and the Early Childhood Curriculum*. 2nd edn. London: Paul Chapman Publishing.

Wyness, M. (2006) *Childhood and Society: An Introduction to the Sociology of Childhood*. Basingstoke: Palgrave. Macmillan.

Young, M. F. D. (1971) An approach to the study of curricula as socially organised knowledge, in M. F. D. Young (ed.) *Knowledge and Control: New Directions for the Sociology of Education*. London: Collier-Macmillan.

Young, M. F. D. (1973) Curricula and the social organization of knowledge, in R. Brown (ed.) *Knowledge, Education and Cultural Change*. London: Harper and Rowe.

Zelizer, V. (1985) *Pricing the Priceless Child: The Changing Social Value of Children*. New York: Basic Books.

Index

EDUCATION STUDIES

Issues & Critical Perspectives

Derek Kassem, Emmanuel Mufti and John Robinson (eds)

This major text for Education Studies students provides a critical account of key issues in education today. The text features:

- A critical analysis of key issues in Education Studies to encourage students' thinking about education in the broadest terms
- Themed sections with introductions to link the issues discussed in each chapter
- Use of specific examples of educational diversity to illustrate how concerns such as ethnicity, gender and class operate in educational institutions
- An examination of educational issues as they relate to other phases of educational provision, such as home schooling and universities

Education Studies: Issues and Critical Perspectives is an essential text for Education Studies students. It is also of value to students on QTS courses and students and professionals in areas such as sociology, childhood studies, community studies and education policy.

Contents: *Contributors – Acknowledgements – Foreword – Section 1: Inside the school – Section introduction – Early years education: mixed messages and conflicts – Evidenced-based education: finding out what works and what hurts – The politics of the National Numeracy and Literacy Strategies – Shaping pedagogy from psychological ideas – When evidence is not enough: freedom to choose versus prescribed choice: the case of Summerhill – Section 2: Policy, politics and education – Section introduction – New Labour's education policy – England: educating for the twenty-first century – What do we really know from school improvement and effectiveness research? – Away with all teachers: the cultural politics of home learning – New students: same old structures – Section 3: Education at the margins – Section introduction – Stephen and Anthony: the continuing implications of the Macpherson report for teacher education – Meeting the educational needs of forced migrants – Education of looked after children: who cares? – Women and state schools: Britain 1870 to present day – Lifelong learning, just a slogan? The reality for working-class women – Section 4: Global education: global issues – Section introduction – New Labour, globalisation and social justice: the role of teacher education – Pakistan: whither educational reforms? – Changing geographies of power in education: the politics of rescaling and its contradictions – Education for sustainable development – Index.*

2006 272pp

978-0-335-21972-8 (Paperback) 978-0-335-21973-5 (Hardback)

SUMMERHILL AND A.S. NEILL

Mark Vaughan (ed)

"Summerhill remains unique and different ... its underlying principles and its founding beliefs have informed and influenced generations of teachers in both sectors. It will continue to do so."

Professor Tim Brighouse, Commissioner for London Schools

Summerhill is a world-renowned school in England where pupils decide when and what they will learn. The school was established in 1921 by A. S. Neill, who was named by the Times Educational Supplement in 1999 as one of the twelve most influential educators of the 20th Century. Known as 'the oldest children's democracy in the world', Summerhill allows pupils to air their views, propose new school rules and construct future plans for life at the school at the regular school meeting.

This unique book contains key extracts from Neill's classic text *Summerhill*, a worldwide bestseller since its publication in 1962, and features contributions from A. S. Neill's daughter, Zoë Neill Readhead, who is the current Principal. She updates the story of the school – larger and more vibrant than ever before – from Neill's death in 1973 to the present day. In his contribution, Tim Brighouse discusses some of the ways in which the influence of Summerhill and A.S. Neill still extends throughout the world today. Ian Stronach, who acted as expert witness during the infamous court case, tells the story of the British Government's attempt to force untenable changes or close down the school in 2001, and the school's subsequent landmark victory in the Royal Courts of Justice.

The book offers a truly inspiring account of a remarkable school, which promotes progressive change in the way pupils are taught and shows how real experiences of democracy can be created for young people. It is essential reading for teachers and trainee teachers, headteachers and school leaders, local education authorities and parents.

Contents: *Preface – Introduction – Summerhill School – Summerhill today – Inspection and justice: HMI and Summerhill School – Questions and answers about Summerhill – Questions and answers about Summerhill – The A. S. Neill Summerhill Trust – Index.*

2006 208pp

978-0-335-21913-1 (Paperback) 978-0-335-21914-8 (Hardback)

APPROACHES TO LEARNING

A Guide for Teachers

Anne Jordan, Orison Carlile and Annetta Stack

"This book provides a really sound grounding in the theories that underpin successful teaching and learning. Without over-simplification it provides accessible introductions to the key learning theories with which teachers and students are likely to engage, and it has immense practical value."

Professor Sally Brown, Pro-Vice-Chancellor,

Leeds Metropolitan University, UK

This comprehensive guide for education students and practitioners provides an overview of the major theories of learning. It considers their implications for policy and practice and sets out practical guidelines for best pedagogical practice.

The book can be read as a series of stand-alone chapters or as an integrated overview of theoretical perspectives drawn from the philosophy, psychology, sociology and pedagogy that guide educational principles and practice. Each chapter contains:

- An accessible introduction to each theory
- A summary of key principles
- Critical insights drawn from the theories discussed
  vExamples and illustrations from contemporary research and practice
  vSummary boxes that highlight critical and key points made
- Practical implications for education professionals

Approaches to Learning is an invaluable resource for students and practitioners who wish to reflect on their educational constructs and explore and engage in the modern discourse of education.

Contents: *List of figures and tables – Acknowledgements – Introduction – Philosophy of education – Behaviourism – Cognitivism – Constructivism – Social learning – Cultural learning – Intelligence – Life course development – Adult learning – Values – Motivation – The learning body – Language and learning – Experiential and competency-based learning – Inclusivity – Blended learning – The future – Glossary.*

2008 304pp

978-0-335-22670-2 (Paperback) 978-0-335-22671-9 (Hardback)

Learning Resources